WHAT VIDEO GAMES HAVE TO TEACH US ABOUT LEARNING AND LITERACY

JAMES PAUL GEE

palgrave
macmillan

First published in hardcover in 2003 by Palgrave Macmillan
First PALGRAVE MACMILLAN™ paperback edition: May 2004
175 Fifth Avenue, New York, N.Y. 10010 and
Houndmills, Basingstoke, Hampshire, England RG21 6XS.
Companies and representatives throughout the world.

PALGRAVE MACMILLAN is the global academic imprint of the Palgrave
Macmillan division of St. Martin's Press, LLC and of Palgrave Macmillan Ltd.
Macmillan® is a registered trademark in the United States, United Kingdom
and other countries. Palgrave is a registered trademark in the European Union
and other countries.

ISBN 1-4039-6538-2

Library of Congress Cataloging-in-Publication Data
Gee, James Paul.
   What video games have to teach us about learning and literacy / James Paul
Gee.
      p.   cm.
   Includes bibliographical references and index.
   ISBN 1-4039-6538-2
   1. Video games—Psychological aspects.   2. Computer games—
Psychological aspects.   3. Learning, Psychology of.   4. Visual literacy.
5. Video games and children.   I. Title: What video games have to teach us
about learning and literacy.   II. Title.

GV1469.3 .G44   2003
794.8'01'9—dc21

                                                                          2002038153

A catalogue record for this book is available from the British Library.

Design by Letra Libre.

First PALGRAVE MACMILLAN paperback edition: May 2004

10 9 8 7 6 5 4 3 2 1

Printed in the United States of America.

I dedicate this book to my six-year-old son, Sam. I originally tried to play his computer games so I could teach him how to play them, but in the end, things worked out just the reverse and he taught me how to play. More, he taught me to take learning and playing games seriously, all the while having fun. I also dedicate the book to my twenty-two-year-old son, Justin. He didn't play computer or video games much as a kid, though he had no trouble thoroughly trouncing me when we last visited an arcade. Justin's early fascination with StarWars was my first guide, Sam's with Pokemon, my second guide, to the powerful and creative learning people can bring to the aspects of "popular culture" with which they choose to identify and which they often choose to transform for their own ends. The children, teenagers, and neotenic adults, including my identical twin brother, and now myself, who play computer and video games were my third.

CONTENTS

1

INTRODUCTION:
36 WAYS TO LEARN A VIDEO GAME

I WANT TO TALK ABOUT VIDEO GAMES—YES, EVEN VIOLENT VIDEO games—and say some positive things about them. By "video games" I mean both games played on game platforms (such as the Sony PlayStation 2, the Nintendo GameCube, or Microsoft's XBox) and games played on computers. So as not to keep saying "video and computer games" all the time, I will just say "video games." I am mainly concerned with the sorts of video games in which the player takes on the role of a fantasy character moving through an elaborate world, solving various problems (violently or not), or in which the player builds and maintains some complex entity, like an army, a city, or even a whole civilization. There are, of course, lots of other types of video games.

But, first, I need to say something about my previous work and how and why I arrived here to discuss video games. In two earlier books, *Social Linguistics and Literacies* and *The Social Mind*, I argued that two things that, at first sight, look to be "mental" achievements, namely literacy and thinking, are, in reality, also and primarily social achievements. (See the Bibliographic Note at the end of this chapter for references to the literature relevant to this chapter.) When you read, you are always reading something in some way. You are never just reading "in general" but not reading anything in particular. For example, you can read the Bible as history or literature or as a self-help guide or in many other ways. So, too, with any other text, whether legal tract, comic book, essay, or novel. Different people can interpret each type of text differently.

When you think, you must think about something in some way. You are never just thinking "in general" but not thinking anything in particular. The argument about thinking is, in fact, the same as the argument about reading. For example, you can think about people who kill themselves to set off a bomb, in pursuit of some cause they believe in, as suicide bombers, murderers, terrorists, freedom fighters, heroes, psychotics, or in many other different ways. Different people can read the world differently just as they can read different types of texts differently.

So, then, what determines how you read or think about some particular thing? Certainly not random chemicals or electrical events in your brain, although you do most certainly need a brain to read or think. Rather, what determines this is your own experiences in interacting with other people who are members of various sorts of social groups, whether these are biblical scholars, radical lawyers, peace activists, family members, fellow ethnic group or church members, or whatever. These groups work, through their various social practices, to encourage people to read and think in certain ways, and not others, about certain sorts of texts and things.

Does this mean you are not "free" to read and think as you like? No—you can always align yourself with new people and new groups—there is no shortage. But it does mean you cannot read or think outside of any group whatsoever. You cannot assign asocial and private meanings to texts and things, meanings that only you are privy to and that you cannot even be sure you remember correctly from occasion to occasion as you read or think about the same thing, since as a social isolate (at least in regard to meaning) you cannot, in fact, check your memory with anyone else. The philosopher Ludwig Wittgenstein made this case long ago in his famous argument against the possibility of "private languages." There are no "private minds" either.

Does all this mean that "anything goes" and "nothing is true"? Of course not. We humans have goals and purposes, and for some goals and purposes some groups' ways of reading and thinking work better than do others. But it does mean that things are not "true" apart from any purpose or goal whatsoever. In the world of physics, as an academic area, if you have pushed your stalled car until you are dripping with sweat but the car has not budged, you have done no "work" (given how physicists use this word), but in the world of "everyday" people, people not attempting at the moment to be physicists or do physics, you have worked very hard indeed. Neither meaning is right or wrong. Each belongs to a different social world. However, if you want to do physics—for good or ill—it's best to use the word "work" the way physicists do. In that case, they are "right."

These viewpoints seem obvious to me. They will seem so to some readers as well. Nonetheless, they occasion great controversy. Furthermore, they are not the views about reading and thinking on which most of our schools today operate. Take reading, for instance. We know a great deal about the psycholinguistics of reading—that is, about reading as a mental act taking part in an individual's head. These views strongly inform how reading is taught in school. And there is nothing wrong with this, save that psycholinguistics is only part—in my view the smaller part—of the reading picture. We know much less about reading as a social achievement and as part and parcel of a great many different social practices connected to a great many different social groups that contest how things should be read and thought about.

The same is true of thinking. Cognitive science has taught us a great deal about thinking as a mental act taking part in an individual's head. For various reasons, however, these views less strongly inform how teaching and learning work in today's schools than they used to. This is so, in part, because the views about thinking current in cognitive science stress the importance of active inquiry and deep conceptual understanding, things that are not politically popular any longer in schools, driven as they are today by standardized tests and skill-and-drill curricula devoted to "the basics."

Nonetheless, it is true that we know much less about thinking as a social achievement and as part and parcel of a great many different social practices connected to a great many different social groups that contest how things should be read and thought about. For example, it turns out that botanists and landscape architects classify and think about trees quite differently. Their different contexts, social practices, and purposes shape their thinking (and reading) in different ways. Neither way is "right" or "wrong" in general. We know little about how social groups, social practices, and institutions shape and norm thinking as a social achievement, that is, about how they shape human minds when those minds are being botanists or landscape architects, though not when these same people are being other things.

And this last point is crucial. Since reading and thinking are social achievements connected to social groups, we can all read and think in different ways when we read and think as members (or as if we are members) of different groups. I, for one, know well what it is like to read the Bible differently as theology, as literature, and as a religious skeptic, thanks to different experiences and affiliations in my life thus far. Any specific way of reading and thinking is, in fact, a way of being in the world, a way of being a certain "kind of person," a way of taking on a certain sort of identity. In that sense, each of us has multiple identities. Even a priest can read the Bible "as a priest," "as a literary critic," "as a historian," even "as a male" or " as an African American" (priest, literary critic, historian, or ethnic group member), even if he chooses to privilege one way of reading—one identity—over another.

This does not mean we all have multiple personality disorder. We each have a core identity that relates to all our other identities (as a woman, feminist, wife, ethnic of a certain sort, biologist, Catholic, etc.). We have this core identity thanks to being in one and the same body over time and thanks to being able to tell ourselves a reasonably (but only reasonably) coherent life story in which we are the "hero" (or, at least, central character). But as we take on new identities or transform old ones, this core identity changes and transforms as well. We are fluid creatures in the making, since we make ourselves socially through participation with others in various groups. Social practices and social groups are always changing, some slowly, some at a faster pace (and the pace of change, for many social practices and groups, gets faster and faster in our contemporary high-tech global world).

Although the viewpoints I have sketched above may (or may not) seem obvious, they have taken me a lot of time to work on and, in the act, I have become if not "old," then "older," what we might call a late-middle-age "baby boomer." I was born in 1948. So, for heaven's sake, what I am doing playing video games and, worse yet, writing about it? The short answer, but not really the whole answer, since I came to this desire after playing the games, was that I wanted to say about learning just what I have said above about reading and thinking.

The longer answer is this: When my six-year-old was four, I used to sit next to him as he played video games, starting with *Winnie the Pooh* and moving on to *Freddy Fish*, *Pajama Sam*, and *Spy Fox*. I was intrigued. One day I decided I wanted to help my child play *Pajama Sam in No Need to Hide When It's Dark Outside*. This is a game where the player (as the comic book superhero "Pajama Sam"—a character who is "just" the small boy Sam pretending to be a superhero in order to increase his courage) must solve problems in the "Land of Darkness" to meet "Darkness" and tame him, so that the player (Sam) need no longer be afraid of the dark. A typical problem in the game is deciding how to convince a talking wooden boat that wood floats, so that the boat, which is afraid of water, can feel free to go "boating" on the water and take Pajama Sam where he needs to go. I decided to play through the game by myself so I could "coach" my child as he played. (Now he charges me a dollar any time I attempt to "coach" him when he is playing a video game—he calls it "bossing him around" and "telling him what to do when he can figure it out for himself.")

When I played the game I was quite surprised to find out it was fairly long and pretty challenging, even for an adult. Yet a four-year-old was willing to put in this time and face this challenge—and enjoy it, to boot. I thought, as someone who has worked in the second half of his career in education (the first half was devoted to theoretical linguistics), "Wouldn't it be great if kids were willing to put in this much time on task on such challenging material in school and enjoy it so much?"

So I decided to buy and play an adult game ("adult" here means the game is played by teenagers on up; video-game players tend to be anywhere between 3 years old and 39). I somewhat arbitrarily picked the game *The New Adventures of the Time Machine*, a game involving adventure, problem solving, and shooting (based loosely on H. G. Wells), knowing nearly nothing about video games. Little did I know what I was getting myself into. This game, like nearly all such games, takes a great many hours to play. Many good video games can take 50 to 100 hours to win, even for good players. Furthermore, it was—for me—profoundly difficult.

In fact, this was my first revelation. This game—and this turned out to be true of video games more generally—requires the player to learn and think in ways in which I am not adept. Suddenly all my baby-boomer ways of learning and thinking, for which I had heretofore received ample rewards, did not work.

My second realization came soon after, when at the end of a day in which I had played *Time Machine* for eight straight hours, I found myself at a party, with a splitting headache from too much video motion, sitting next to a 300-pound plasma physicist. I heard myself telling the physicist that I found playing *Time Machine* a "life-enhancing experience," without even knowing what I meant by that. Fortunately, plasma physicists are extremely tolerant of human variation. (The plasma that physicists deal with is not, as he told me, a product from blood but a state of matter; when I asked him why he had not brought any to the party, he explained to me that plasma is so unstable and dangerous that if he had brought any, there would have been no party.)

Oddly enough, then, confronting what was, for me, a new form of learning and thinking was both frustrating and life enhancing. This was a state that I could remember from my days in graduate school and earlier in my career (and when I changed careers midstream). Having long routinized my ways of learning and thinking, however, I had forgotten this state. It brought back home to me, forcefully, that learning is or should be both frustrating and life enhancing. The key is finding ways to make hard things life enhancing so that people keep going and don't fall back on learning and thinking only what is simple and easy.

My third realization followed from these other two. I eventually finished *The New Adventures of the Time Machine* and moved onto *Deus Ex*, a game I chose because it had won Game of the Year on many Internet game sites. *Deus Ex* is yet longer and harder than *Time Machine*. I found myself asking the following question: "How, in heaven's name, do they sell many of these games when they are so long and hard?" I soon discovered, of course, that good video games (like *Deus Ex*) sell millions of copies. Indeed, the video-game industry makes as much or more money each year than the film industry.

So here we have something that is long, hard, and challenging. However, you cannot play a game if you cannot learn it. If no one plays a game, it does not sell, and the company that makes it goes broke. Of course, designers could keep making the games shorter and simpler to facilitate learning. That's often what schools do. But no, in this case, game designers keep making the games longer and more challenging (and introduce new things in new ones), and still manage to get them learned. How?

If you think about it, you see a Darwinian sort of thing going on here. If a game, for whatever reason, has good principles of learning built into its design—that is, if it facilitates learning in good ways—then it gets played and can sell a lot of copies, if it is otherwise good as well. Other games can build on these principles and, perhaps, do them one step better. If a game has poor learning principles built into its design, then it won't get learned or played and won't sell well. Its designers will seek work elsewhere. In the end, then, video games represent a process, thanks to what Marx called the "creativity of capitalism," that leads to better and better designs for good learning and, indeed, good learning of hard and challenging things.

It would seem intriguing, then, to investigate what these principles of learning are. How are good video games designed to enhance getting themselves learned—learned well and quickly so people can play and enjoy them even when they are long and hard? What we are really looking for here is this: the theory of human learning built into good video games.

Of course, there is an academic field devoted to studying how human beings learn best and well, namely the field of cognitive science. So we can, then, compare the theory of learning in good video games to theories of learning in cognitive science. Who's got the best theory? Well, it turns out that the theory of learning in good video games is close to what I believe are the best theories of learning in cognitive science. And this is not because game designers read academic texts on learning. Most of them don't. They spent too much of their time in high school and beyond playing with computers and playing games.

And, too, there is a key place—though hardly the only one—where learning takes place: school. So, we also can ask how the theory of learning in good video games compares to how teaching and learning work in school. Here we face a mixed bag, indeed. On one hand, the theory of learning in good video games fits well with what are I believe to be the best sorts of science instruction in school. On the other hand, this sort of science instruction is rare and getting yet rarer as testing and skill-and-drill retake our schools. In turn, the theories of learning one would infer from looking at schools today comport very poorly with the theory of learning in good video games.

If the principles of learning in good video games *are* good, then better theories of learning are embedded in the video games many children in elementary and particularly in high school play than in the schools they attend. Furthermore, the theory of learning in good video games fits better with the modern, high-tech, global world today's children and teenagers live in than do the theories (and practices) of learning that they see in school. Today's world is very different from the world baby boomers like me grew up in and on which we have based many of our theories. Is it a wonder, then, that by high school, very often both good students and bad ones, rich ones and poor ones, don't much like school?

This book discusses 36 principles of learning (individually in each chapter and listed together in the appendix) that I argue are built into good video games. From the way I opened this introduction, you already know that, while this book deals with learning, it will most certainly deal with learners (players) embedded in a material and social world. How could it be otherwise? After all, they are playing a game. Video games—like many other games—are inherently social, though, in video games, sometimes the other players are fantasy creatures endowed, by the computer, with artificial intelligence and sometimes they are real people playing out fantasy roles.

However, this book has another goal as well. It seeks to use the discussion of video games to introduce the reader to three important areas of current research and to relate these areas together. One of these areas is work on "situated cognition" (i.e., thinking as tied to a body that has experiences in the world). This work argues that human learning is not just a matter of what goes on inside people's heads but is fully embedded in (situated within) a material, social, and cultural world. Another one of these areas is the so-called New Literacy Studies, a body of work that argues that reading and writing should be viewed not only as mental achievements going on inside people's heads but also as social and cultural practices with economic, historical, and political implications.

Obviously, these two bodies of work have much in common, though their advocates often disagree with each other over details. People in New Literacy Studies often distrust psychology more than people working in the area of situated cognition. And, too, people working in New Literacy Studies tend to be more "political" than people working in the area of situated cognition.

The third area is work on so-called connectionism, a view that stresses the ways in which human beings are powerful pattern-recognizers. This body of work argues that humans don't often think best when they attempt to reason via logic and general abstract principles detached from experience. Rather, they think best when they reason on the basis of patterns they have picked up through their actual experiences in the world, patterns that, over time, can become generalized but that are still rooted in specific areas of experience.

This view of the mind is obviously one way to spell out what it means to say thinking and reasoning are "situated." I argue that it is one way to spell out how and why reading, writing, and thinking are inextricably linked to social and cultural practices. I don't actually use the term "connectionism" in the book; instead I simply talk about what it means to discover patterns in our experience and what it means to be "networked" with other people and with various tools and technologies (like computers and the Internet) so that one can behave "smarter" than one actually is.

None of these three areas—work on situated cognition, New Literacy Studies, and a pattern-recognition view of the mind—represents a viewpoint that is universally agreed on. Many disagree with each one and, indeed, all three. Furthermore, my "introduction" to these areas, via video games, is highly selective. People who know little about these areas will pick up only the big picture. People who know a lot about them will quickly realize that I am developing my own perspectives in each of these areas, while many other perspectives exist as well. Nonetheless, I believe that these three areas capture central truths about the human mind and human learning and that these truths are well represented in the ways in which good video games are learned and played.

These truths are often less well represented in today's schools. And this book is about schools as well. It is a plea to build schooling on better principles of learning. If we have to learn this from video games, and not from a field with as boring a name as cognitive science, then so be it. I know that many people, especially on the right wing of the political spectrum, will find this idea absurd. So be that as well. (My book *The New Work Order*, written with Glynda Hull and Colin Lankshear, is, in part, about why the old distinctions between "right" and "left" don't make much sense anymore in the modern global world of the so-called new capitalism.)

Let me end this introduction with a few short points. First, while I talk a good deal about actual video games, I really intend to discuss the *potential* of video games. The games get better and more sophisticated all the time and at a rapid pace. Much of what I have to say here will simply get "truer" as the games get even better. This is my consolation for the fact that any games I mention will be, for some players, "out of date," replaced by newer ones by the time anyone reads this book.

Second, I am aware that many readers will not have played—or will not currently be playing—video games, especially the type I discuss. I will try to be as clear and explicit as I can about the games, so that all readers can form a picture of what I am talking about.

Readers who want to explore the many types of video games, see pictures from them, even download demonstrations of various games, and otherwise find out more about them can log on to a wide array of Internet sites devoted to video games. Any game I mention in this book can be thoroughly investigated in this way. Here are some sites I can recommend, though there are many others: gamezone.com, gamedex.com, pcgamer.com, gamepro.com, gamespot.com, ign.com, MrFixitOnline.com, womengamers.com, and gamecritics.com. Joystick101.org offers up-to-the-minute articles and critical perspectives, beyond reviews, about games and controversial issues about games.

Third, I am not, in this book, meaning to imply that I think "old" baby boomers like me ought to run out and start playing video games. Many will find the games too hard and frustrating, without the personal payoff that makes for continued practice. Nonetheless, we can learn a lot from those young people who play games, if only we take them and their games seriously. And, indeed, I am always struck by how many people, even some of the liberal advocates of multiculturalism, readily decry and seek to override people's cultures when these cultures are popular peer-based ones centered around things like video games. Let it be said, too, having mentioned multiculturalism, that a great many African Americans love video games, just as do a great many Anglo Americans and everyone else in between. And, yes, poor children and teenagers do play video games, even if they have to find a computer or game console at school, in a library, or community center, or at a friend's house. There are important issues of equity here, though, and I discuss these at the end of the book.

Finally, there is this: Two issues have taken up the vast majority of writing about video games: violence (e.g., shooting and killing in games, depictions of crime) and gender (e.g., whether and how much girls play, whether and how video games depict women poorly). I have nothing whatsoever to say about these issues in this book. They are well discussed elsewhere. I do, however, discuss, in chapter 6, some very heated social and political issues that arise when considering video games at a time when, thanks to free powerful software, almost any group can design a sophisticated 3-D video game to represent its own values and interests.

Though they are not important for the basic argument of this book, my own views on the violence and gender issues are as follows: The issue of violence and video games is widely overblown (especially in a world where real people are regularly really killing real people in wars across the world that we watch on television). Debate over violence in video games is one more way in which we want to talk about technology (or drugs, for that matter) doing things to people rather than talking about the implications of people's overall social and economic contexts.

In any case, shooting is an easy form of social interaction (!) to program. As realistic forms of conversation become more computationally possible (a very hard task), I predict that shooting will be less important and talking more important in many games, even shooter games. Even now, many shooting games stress stealth, story, and social interaction more than they used to.

Furthermore, there are many categories of very sophisticated video games—simulations and some strategy games—that do not involve any violence at all. Nonetheless, I base my arguments in this book in part on shooter games, precisely because they are the "hardest" case. It's pretty clear that a simulation game (like *SimCity*) involves important learning principles, if only because many scientists themselves use such simulation techniques. However, it is easier to miss and dismiss the learning principles in other sorts of games. But they are very much there, nonetheless.

As to gender: I have no doubt that video games, like most other popular cultural forms, overstress young, buxom, and beautiful women in their content. Furthermore, with several major exceptions, these woman are often not the main characters in the games. However, as more girls and women play games, this will change. And, indeed, in role-playing games, you can design your own character. In a game I am playing at the present time (*Dungeon Siege*), I am an African American female, though I could only make my skin light black and my body fairly shapely; wider choices will, I am sure, be available as time goes on. (I personally don't want to play in a fantasy world as a balding, overweight, aging white male, since I get plenty of opportunity to do that in the real world, but, then, my identical twin was upset, when he was designing his character for the game that he could not design such a character as the hero.) Games, of course, reflect the culture we live in—a culture we can change.

As to the issue of girls and women playing games, they are quickly catching up with the boys and men, though they often play different games (e.g., *The Sims*). Nevertheless, there are Internet sites devoted to women who play the sorts of shooter games more commonly associated with males. When we academics feel our interests define the world, we should keep in mind the following fact: The largest category of video-game players are middle-age women playing video card games alone and together on the Internet. I have nothing here to say about card games. That just shows that we academics still have much to learn about the "real" world. I guess that's why we keep trying.

BIBLIOGRAPHICAL NOTE

In order not to clutter the text with references, I will not insert references directly into the text of each chapter but will instead give citations to the literature in a bibliographical note at the end of each chapter.

Poole 2000 and Herz 1996 are good analyses of the design of video games and their role in our culture. Poole 2000 discusses the statistics on who plays what video games, as well as the fact that the video game industry makes more money in a given year than does the movie industry. Kent 2001 is an entertaining history of video games. Greenfield 1984 and Loftus and Loftus 1983 are good early discussions of the role of learning and thinking in video games. King 2002, prepared for a museum exhibit on video games, contains a wide array of interesting articles on all aspects of the games.

Pinker 1999 is a good, basic introduction to cognitive science. For more on cognitive science, especially as it applies to schools and learning, see Bransford, Brown, & Cocking 1999; Bruer 1993; Gardner 1991; and Pelligrino, Chudowksy, & Glaser 2001. These sources discuss work on situated cognition, as well as a number of other areas. For additional work on situated cognition, see Brooks 2002; Brown, Collins, & Dugid 1989; Clark 1997; Gee 1996; Lave 1988; Lave and Wenger 1991; Rogoff 1990; and Tomasello 1999. The fact that botanists and landscape architects classify and think about trees differently is taken from Medlin, Lynch, & Coley 1997.

For a discussion of good, conceptually based science instruction in schools, see Bruer 1993; Cognition and Technology Group at Vanderbilt 1997; and diSessa 2000. For introductions to the New Literacy Studies, see Barton 1994; Gee 1996; and Street 1995. For work on connectionism and the human mind as a pattern recognizer, see Clark 1989, 1993; Gee 1996; Margolis 1987, 1993; and Rumelhart, McClelland, & the PDP Research Group 1986.

2

SEMIOTIC DOMAINS:
IS PLAYING VIDEO GAMES
A "WASTE OF TIME"?

LITERACY AND SEMIOTIC DOMAINS

WHEN PEOPLE LEARN TO PLAY VIDEO GAMES, THEY ARE LEARNING a new *literacy*. Of course, this is not the way the word "literacy" is normally used. Traditionally, people think of literacy as the ability to read and write. Why, then, should we think of literacy more broadly, in regard to video games or anything else, for that matter? There are two reasons.

First, in the modern world, language is not the only important communicational system. Today images, symbols, graphs, diagrams, artifacts, and many other visual symbols are particularly significant. Thus, the idea of different types of "visual literacy" would seem to be an important one. For example, being able to "read" the images in advertising is one type of visual literacy. And, of course, there are different ways to read such images, ways that are more or less aligned with the intentions and interests of the advertisers. Knowing how to read interior designs in homes, modernist art in museums, and videos on MTV are other forms of visual literacy.

Furthermore, very often today words and images of various sorts are juxtaposed and integrated in a variety of ways. In newspaper and magazines as well as in textbooks, images take up more and more of the space alongside words. In fact, in many modern high school and college textbooks in the sciences images not only take up more space, they now carry meanings that are independent of the words in the text. If you can't read these images, you will not be able to recover their meanings from the words in the text as was more usual in the past.

In such *multimodal* texts (texts that mix words and images), the images often communicate different things from the words. And the combination of the two modes communicates things that neither of the modes does separately. Thus, the idea of different sorts of multimodal literacy seems an important one. Both modes and multimodality go far beyond images and words to include sounds, music, movement, bodily sensations, and smells.

None of this news today, of course. We very obviously live in a world awash with images. It is our first answer to the question why we should think of literacy more broadly. The second answer is this: Even though reading and writing seem so central to what literacy means traditionally, reading and writing are not such general and obvious matters as they might at first seem. After all, we never just read or write; rather, we always read or write *something in some way*.

There are many different ways of reading and writing. We don't read or write newspapers, legal tracts, essays in literary criticism, poetry, rap songs, and on through a nearly endless list in the same way. Each of these domains has its own rules and requirements. Each is a culturally and historically separate way of reading and writing, and, in that sense, a different literacy. Furthermore, in each case, if we want to "break the rules" and read against the grain of the text—for the purposes of critique, for instance—we have to do so in different ways, usually with some relatively deep knowledge of how to read such texts "according to the rules."

So there are different ways to read different types of texts. Literacy is multiple, then, in the sense that the legal literacy needed for reading law books is not the same as the literacy needed for reading physics texts or superhero comic books. And we should not be too quick to dismiss the latter form of literacy. Many a superhero comic is replete with post-Freudian irony of a sort that would make a modern literary critic's heart beat fast and confuse any otherwise normal adult. Literacy, then, even as traditionally conceived to involve only print, is not a unitary thing but a multiple matter. There are, even in regard to printed texts and even leaving aside images and multimodal texts, different "literacies."

Once we see this multiplicity of literacy (literacies), we realize that when we think about reading and writing, we have to think beyond print. Reading and writing in any domain, whether it is law, rap songs, academic essays, superhero comics, or whatever, are not just ways of decoding print, they are also caught up with and in social practices. Literacy in any domain is actually not worth much if one knows nothing about the social practices of which that literacy is but a part. And, of course, these social practices involve much more than just an engagement with print.

One can know a good deal about a social practice—such as arguing before the Supreme Court, carrying out an experiment in nuclear physics, or memorializing an event in gang history through graffiti—without actually being able to participate in the social practice. But knowing about a social practice always involves recognizing various distinctive ways of acting, interacting, valuing, feeling, knowing, and using various objects and technologies that constitute the social practice.

Take something so simple as the following sentence about basketball: "The guard dribbled down court, held up two fingers, and passed to the open man." You may very well know what every word in this sentence means in terms of dictionary definitions, but you cannot read the sentence with any real worthwhile understanding unless you can recognize, in some sense (perhaps only in simulations in your mind), guards, dribbling, basketballs, open men, and basketball courts. But to be able to recognize these things is already to know a good deal about basketball as a game, that is, as a particular sort of social practice. The same thing is equally true about any sentence or text about the law, comic books, a branch of science, or anything else for that matter.

We can go further. One's understanding of the sentence "The guard dribbled down court, held up two fingers, and passed to the open man" is different—in some sense, deeper and better—the more one knows and can recognize about the social practice (game) of basketball. For example, if you know a good bit about basketball, you may see that one possible meaning of this sentence is that the guard signaled a particular play by holding up two fingers and then passed to the player the play left momentarily unguarded.

But then this brings us to another important point. While you don't need to be able to enact a particular social practice (e.g., play basketball or argue before a court) to be able to understand texts from or about that social practice, you can *potentially* give deeper meanings to those texts if you can. This claim amounts to arguing that producers (people who can actually engage in a social practice) *potentially* make better consumers (people who can read or understand texts from or about the social practice).

A corollary of this claim is this: Writers (in the sense of people who can write texts that are recognizably part of a particular social practice) *potentially* make better readers (people who can understand texts from or about a given social practice). Note that by "writers" here I do not mean people who can just write down words appropriate to a particular practice such as field biology. I mean people who can write a text that field biologists would recognize as an acceptable text within their family of social practices.

Why do I say "potentially" here? Because there is a paradox about producers. On one hand, producers are deeply enough embedded in their social practices that they can understand the texts associated with those practices quite well. On the other hand, producers are often so deeply embedded in their social practices that they take the meanings and values of the texts associated with those practices for granted in an unquestioning way. One key question for deep learning and good education, then, is how to get producer-like learning and knowledge, but in a reflective and critical way.

All these claims are pretty obvious. It is, thus, fascinating that they are so often ignored in schools. In school, many times children are expected to read texts with little or no knowledge about any social practices within which those texts are used. They are rarely allowed to engage in an actual social practice in ways that are recognizable to "insiders" (e.g., field biologists) as meaningful and acceptable, before and as they read texts relevant to the practice.

Indeed, children are regularly given reading tests that ask general, factual, and dictionarylike questions about various texts with no regard for the fact that these texts fall into different genres (i.e., they are different kinds of texts) connected to different sorts of social practices. Children often can answer such questions, but they learn and know nothing about the genres and social practices that are, in the end, the heart and soul of literacy.

Schools will continue to operate this way until they (and reading tests) move beyond fixating on reading as silently saying the sounds of letters and words and being able to answer general, factual, and dictionarylike questions about written texts. You do have to silently say the sounds of letters and words when you read (or, at least, this greatly speeds up reading). You do have do be able to answer general, factual, and dictionarylike questions about what you read: This means you know the "literal" meaning of the text. But what so many people—unfortunately so many educators and policymakers—fail to see is that if this is all you can do, then you *can't really read*. You will fail to be able to read well and appropriately in contexts associated with specific types of texts and specific types of social practices.

For example, consider once again our sentence about basketball: "The guard dribbled down court, held up two fingers, and passed to the open man." A typical reading test would ask a question like this: "What did the guard do to the ball?" and give "bounce it" as one of the choices. Unfortunately, you can answer such general, factual, dictionarylike questions and really have no idea what the sentence means in the domain of basketball. When we see that the same thing applies to sentences from science or any other school subject, we immediately see why so many children pass early reading tests but cannot learn later on in the subject areas.

This phenomenon is so pervasive that it has been given a name by researchers: "the fourth-grade slump." It is called this because, in the past, the first three years of school were largely devoted to learning to read (in the sense of being able to decode print and get the literal meanings of texts), and fourth grade was where children began to read to learn (in the subject areas). However, very often today children are being asked to read to learn things like science and math from first or second grade on, at least in affluent schools.

However, let's leave school aside, and return to our main question as to why we should be willing to broaden how we talk about literacy. I can now note that talking about literacy and literacies in this expanded, nontraditional way (as multiple and connected to social practices) leads us at once to an interesting dilemma: What do we want to say of someone, for instance, who can understand and even compose rap songs (words and music), but cannot read or write language or musical notation?

Of course, in traditional terms, this person is illiterate in terms of both language and musical notation. But yet he or she is able to understand and compose in a language style that is distinctively different from everyday language and in a musical form that is distinctively different from other forms of music. We might want to say that the person is literate in the domain of rap songs (as a distinctive domain combining language and music in certain characteristic ways), though the person is not print literate or musical-notation literate.

Cases like this display the limitations of thinking about literacy first and foremost in terms of print. We need, rather, to think first in terms of what I call *semiotic domains* and only then get to literacy in the more traditional terms of print literacy. "Semiotic" here is just a fancy way of saying we want to talk about all sorts of different things that can take on meaning, such as images, sounds, gestures, movements, graphs, diagrams, equations, objects, even people like babies, midwives, and mothers, and not just words. All of these things are signs (symbols, representations, whatever term you want to use) that "stand for" (take on) different meanings in different situations, contexts, practices, cultures, and historical periods. For example, the image of a cross means Christ (or Christ's death) in the context of Christian social practices, and it means the four points of the compass (north, south, west, and east) in the context of other social practices (e.g., in some African religions).

By a semiotic domain I mean any set of practices that recruits one or more modalities (e.g., oral or written language, images, equations, symbols, sounds, gestures, graphs, artifacts, etc.) to communicate distinctive types of meanings. Here are some examples of semiotic domains: cellular biology, postmodern literary criticism, first-person-shooter video games, high-fashion advertisements, Roman Catholic theology, modernist painting, midwifery, rap music, wine connoisseurship—through a nearly endless, motley, and ever-changing list.

Our sentence about basketball—"The guard dribbled down court, held up two fingers, and passed to the open man"—is a sentence from the semiotic domain of basketball. It might seen odd to call basketball a semiotic domain. However, in basketball, particular words, actions, objects, and images take on distinctive meanings. In basketball, "dribble" does not mean drool; a pick (an action where an offensive player positions him or herself so as to block a defensive player guarding one of his or her teammates) means that some defensive player must quickly switch to guard the now-unguarded offensive player; and the wide circle on each end of the court means that players who shoot from beyond it get three points instead of two if they score a basket.

If you don't know these meanings—cannot read these signs—then you can't "read" (understand) basketball. The matter seems fairly inconsequential when we are talking about basketball. However, it quickly seems more consequential when we are talking about the semiotic domain of some type of science being studied in school. Equally here, if you don't know how to read the distinctive signs (words, actions, objects, and images), you can't read (understand) that sort of science.

If we think first in terms of semiotic domains and not in terms of reading and writing as traditionally conceived, we can say that people are (or are not) literate (partially or fully) in a domain if they can recognize (the equivalent of "reading") and/or produce (the equivalent of "writing") meanings in the domain. We can reserve the term "print literate" for talking about people who can read and/or write a language like English or Russian, though here, still, we will want to insist that there are different ways to read and write different things connected to different social practices so, in that sense, there are multiple print literacies. Thus, the rap artist who could understand and compose rap songs but not read print or musical notation is literate in the semiotic domain of rap music but not print literate.

In the modern world, print literacy is not enough. People need to be literate in a great variety of different semiotic domains. If these domains involve print, people often need the print bits, of course. However, the vast majority of domains involve semiotic (symbolic, representational) resources besides print and some don't involve print as a resource at all. Furthermore, and more important, people need to be able to learn to be literate in new semiotic domains throughout their lives. If our modern, global, high-tech, and science-driven world does anything, it certainly gives rise to new semiotic domains and transforms old ones at an ever faster rate.

This book deals with video games as a semiotic domain, actually as a family of related, but different domains, since there are different types or genres of video games (e.g., first-person shooter games, fantasy role-playing games, real-time strategy games, simulation games, etc.). People can be literate, or not, in one or more of these video-game semiotic domains. However, in talking about learning and literacy in regard to video games, I hope to develop, as well, a perspective on learning, literacy, and semiotic domains that applies more generally to domains beyond video games.

However, if we want to take video games seriously as a family of semiotic domains in which one can learn to be literate, we face an immediate problem. Many people who don't play video games, especially older people, are sure to say that playing video games is "a waste of time." In the next section, I sketch out one version of what I think this claim often amounts to, using a specific example involving a six year old child.

LEARNING AND THE PROBLEM OF CONTENT

To spell out what I think the claim that playing video games is a waste of time often means, I need first to tell you about the game the six-year-old boy was playing, a game called "*Pikmin.*" *Pikmin* is a game for the Nintendo Game-Cube, rated "E," a game acceptable for all ages.

In *Pikmin*, the player takes on the role of Captain Olimar, a small (he's about the size of an American quarter), bald, big-eared, bulbous-nosed spaceman who crashes into an unfamiliar planet when a comet hits his spaceship.

Captain Olimar (i.e., the player) must collect the spaceship's lost parts, scattered throughout the planet, while relying on his spacesuit to protect him from the planet's poisonous atmosphere. Thus, the player must carefully monitor the damage done to Captain Olimar's suit and repair it when needed. To make matters more complicated, the spacesuit's life support will fail after 30 days, so the captain (the player) must find all the missing parts in 30 days (each day is 15 minutes of game-time play). So the game is a race against time and represents the rare case of a game that one can play to the end and still "lose."

However, Captain Olimar gets help. Soon after arriving on the strange planet, he comes upon native life that is willing to aid him. Sprouts dispensed from a large onionlike creature yield tiny (they're even smaller than Captain Olimar) cute creatures that Olimar names "Pikmin" after a carrot from his home planet. These little creatures appear to be quite taken with Olimar and follow his directions without question. Captain Olimar learns to raise Pikmin of three different colors (red, yellow, and blue), each of which has different skills. He learns, as well, to train them so that each Pikmin, regardless of color, can grow through three different ever stronger forms: Pikmin sprouting a leaf, a bud, or a flower from their heads.

His colorful Pikmin following him as his army, Captain Olimar uses them to attack dangerous creatures, tear down stone walls, build bridges, and explore a great many areas of the strange planet in search of the missing parts to his spaceship. While Captain Olimar can replace killed Pikmin from remaining Pikmin, he must, however, ensure that at no point do all his Pikmin perish—an event called, by the game and by the child player, "an extinction event."

It is quite a sight to watch a six-year-old, as Captain Olimar, lead a multicolored army of little Pikmin to fight, build, grow more Pikmin, and explore a strange landscape, all the while solving multiple problems to discover and get to the locations of the spaceship's missing parts. The child then orders his Pikmin to carry the heavy parts back to the ship. When this child's grandfather watched him play the game for several hours, the grandfather made the following remark, which I think captures at least one of the common meanings of the playing video games is a waste of time theme: "While it may be good for his hand-eye coordination, it's a waste of time, because there isn't any content he's learning." I call this *the problem of content*.

The problem of content is, I believe, based on common attitudes toward school, schooling, learning, and knowledge. These attitudes are compelling, in part because they are so deeply rooted in the history of western thought, but, nonetheless, I think they are wrong. The idea is this: Important knowledge (now usually gained in school) is content in the sense of information rooted in, or, at least, related to, intellectual domains or academic disciplines like physics, history, art, or literature. Work that does not involve such learning is "meaningless." Activities that are entertaining but that themselves do not involve such learning are just "meaningless play." Of course, video games fall into this category.

A form of this viewpoint has long existed in western culture. It is akin to the viewpoint, held by Plato and Aristotle, for example, that knowledge, in something like the sense of content above, is good in and of itself. Other pursuits, including making practical use of such knowledge—pursuits that do not involve learning and reflecting on such content in and of itself outside the realm of practical applications—are lesser; in some sense, mundane and trivial. Such a view, of course, makes the grandfather's remark about the child playing *Pikmin* seem obvious.

The problem with the content view is that an academic discipline, or any other semiotic domain, for that matter, is not primarily content, in the sense of facts and principles. It is rather primarily a lived and historically changing set of distinctive social practices. It is in these social practices that "content" is generated, debated, and transformed via certain distinctive ways of thinking, talking, valuing, acting, and, often, writing and reading.

No one would want to treat basketball as "content" apart from the game itself. Imagine a textbook that contained all the facts and rules about basketball read by students who never played or watched the game. How well do you think they would understand this textbook? How motivated to understand it do you think they would be? But we do this sort of thing all the time in school with areas like math and science. We even have politicians and educators who condemn *doing* math and science in the classroom instead of drilling-and-skilling on math and science facts ("content") as "permissive."

There is, however, an alternative way to think about learning and knowing that makes the content view seem less obvious and natural. I turn to developing this viewpoint in the following sections. Under this alternative perspective it will become less clear that playing video games is necessarily a "a waste of time," though it will be a while until I can return to that claim and answer it directly.

AN ALTERNATIVE PERSPECTIVE
ON LEARNING AND KNOWING

The alternative perspective starts with the claim that there really is no such thing as learning "in general." We always learn *something*. And that something is always connected, in some way, to some semiotic domain or other.

Therefore, if we are concerned with whether something is worth learning or not, whether it is a waste of time or not—video games or anything else—we should start with questions like the following: What semiotic domain is being entered through this learning? Is it a valuable domain or not? In what sense? Is the learner learning simply to understand ("read") parts of the domain or also to participate more fully in the domain by learning to produce ("write") meanings in the domain? And we need to keep in mind that in the modern world, there are a great many more potentially important semiotic domains than just those that show up in typical schools. I return to these questions later in regard to the child playing *Pikmin*.

Once we learn to start with such questions, we find that it is often a tricky question as to what semiotic domain is being entered when someone is learning or has learned something. For example, consider college freshmen who have taken their first college-level physics class, passed it with good grades, and can write down Newton's laws of motion. What domain have they entered? It will not do to say "physics" and leave the matter at that, though the content view would take this position.

Lots of studies have shown that many such students, students who can write down Newton's laws of motion, if asked so simple a question as "How many forces are acting on a coin when it has been thrown up into the air?" (the answer to which can actually be deduced from Newton's laws) get the answer wrong. Leaving aside friction, they claim that two forces are operating on the coin, gravity and "impetus," the force the hand has transferred to the coin. Gravity exists as a force and, according to Newton's laws, is the sole force acting on the coin when it is in the air (aside from air friction). Impetus, in the sense above, however, does not exist, though Aristotle thought it did and people in their everyday lives tend to view force and motion in such terms quite naturally.

So these students have entered the semiotic domain of physics as passive *content* but not as something in terms of which they can actually see and operate on their world in new ways. There may be nothing essentially wrong with this, since their knowledge of such passive content might help them know, at some level, what physics, an important enterprise in modern life, is "about." I tend to doubt this, however. Be that as it may, these students cannot produce meanings in physics or understand them in producerlike ways.

They have not learned to experience the world in a new way. They have not learned to experience the world in a way in which the natural inclination to think in terms of the hand transmitting a force to the coin, a force that the coin stores up and uses up ("impetus"), is not part of one's way of seeing and operating on the world (for a time and place, i.e., when doing modern physics).

When we learn a new semiotic domain in a more active way, not as passive content, three things are at stake:

1. We learn to experience (see, feel, and operate on) the world in new ways.
2. Since semiotic domains usually are shared by groups of people who carry them on as distinctive social practices, we gain the potential to join this social group, to become affiliated with such kinds of people (even though we may never see all of them, or any of them, face to face).
3. We gain resources that prepare us for future learning and problem solving in the domain and, perhaps, more important, in related domains.

Three things, then, are involved in active learning: *experiencing* the world in new ways, forming new *affiliations*, and *preparation* for future learning.

This is "active learning." However, such learning is not yet what I call "critical learning." For learning to be critical as well as active, one additional feature is needed. The learner needs to learn not only how to understand and produce meanings in a particular semiotic domain that are recognizable to those affiliated with the domain, but, in addition, how to think about the domain at a "meta" level as a complex system of interrelated parts. The learner also needs to learn how to innovate in the domain—how to produce meanings that, while recognizable, are seen as somehow novel or unpredictable.

To get at what all this really means, though, I need to discuss semiotic domains a bit more. This will allow me to clarify what I mean by critical learning and to explicate the notions of experiencing the world in new ways, forming new affiliations, and preparation for future learning a bit more.

MORE ON SEMIOTIC DOMAINS:
SITUATED MEANINGS

Words, symbols, images, and artifacts have meanings that are specific to particular semiotic domains and particular situations (contexts). They do not just have general meanings.

I was once a cannery worker; later I became an academic. I used the word "work" in both cases, but the word meant different things in each case. In my cannery life, it meant something like laboring for eight straight hours in order to survive and get home to lead my "real" life. In my academic life, it means something like chosen efforts I put into thinking, reading, writing, and teaching as part and parcel of my vocation, efforts not clocked by an eight-hour workday. In the domain of human romantic relationships, the word means something else altogether; for example, in a sentence like "Relationships take work." Later I will point out that a word like "work," in fact, has different meanings even within a single domain, like the cannery, academics, or romantic relationships, meanings that vary according to different situations in the domain.

But here we face one of the most widespread confusions that exists in regard to language and semiotic domains. People tend to think that the meaning of a word or other sort of symbol is a general thing—the sort of thing that, for a word, at least, can be listed in a dictionary. But meaning for words and symbols is specific to particular situations and particular semiotic domains. You don't really know what a word means if you don't carefully consider both the specific semiotic domain and the specific situation you are in.

We build meanings for words or symbols "on the spot," so to speak, so as to make them appropriate for the actual situations we are in, though we do so with due respect for the specific semiotic domain in which we are operating. What general meaning a word or other symbol has is just a theme around which, in actual situations of use, we must build more specific instantiations (meanings).

To understand or produce any word, symbol, image, or artifact in a given semiotic domain, a person must be able to situate the meaning of that word, symbol, image, or artifact within embodied experiences of action, interaction, or dialogue in or about the domain. These experiences can be ones the person has actually had or ones he or she can imagine, thanks to reading, dialogue with others, or engagement with various media. This is what our college physics students could not do: They could not situate the components of Newton's laws in terms of specific situations and embodied ways of seeing and acting on and within the world from the perspective of the semiotic domain of mechanical physics.

Meaning, then, is both situation and domain specific. Thus, even in a single domain, the meaning of a word varies across different situations. Let me give an example of what I am talking about by taking up again the example of the word "work." In semiotic domains connected to academics, the word "work" takes on a range of possible situated meanings different from the range possible in other semiotic domains (e.g., law, medicine, manual work, etc.).

In one situation I might say of a fellow academic, "Her work has been very influential" and by "work" mean her research. In another situation I might say the same thing, but now in regard to a particular committee she has chaired, and by "work" mean her political efforts within her discipline or institution. To understand the word "work" in these cases, you need to ask yourself what you take the situation to be (e.g., talk about contributions to knowledge or about disciplinary or institutional political affairs) and what semiotic domain is at stake (here academics, not law offices).

The same thing is true in all domains. Even in the rigorous semiotic domain of physics, one must situate (build) different specific meanings for the word "light" in different situations. In different situations, one has to build meanings for the word that involve thinking, talking about, or acting on different things like waves, particles, straight lines, reflection and refraction, lasers, colors, and yet other things in other situations. Even in physics, when someone uses the word "light," we need to know whether they are talking about waves or particles, colors or lasers, or something else (perhaps they are talking about the general theory of electromagnetism)?

In a different domain altogether, the same word takes on yet different meanings in different situations. For example, in religion, one has to build meanings for the word "light" that involve thinking, talking about, or acting on and with different themes like illumination, insight, life, grace, peace, birth, and yet other things in other situations.

If you cannot even imagine the experiences and conditions of an academic life, you really can't know what "work" means, either specifically or in terms of its possible range of meanings, in a sentence like "Her work was very influential." Of course, you don't have to be an academic to imagine academic life. But you do have to be able to build simulated worlds of experience in your mind (in this case, the sorts of experiences, attitudes, values, and feelings an academic might have), however unconsciously you do this. And, perhaps, you can do this because of your reading or other vicarious experiences. Perhaps you can do it through analogies to other domains with which you are more familiar (e.g., you might equate your hobby as an artist with the academic's research and understand how "work" can mean, in a certain sort of situation, efforts connected to a vocation).

Why I am belaboring this point? For two reasons: first, to make clear that understanding meanings is an active affair in which we have to reflect (however unconsciously) on the situation and the domain we are in. And, second, because I want to argue that learning in any semiotic domain crucially involves learning how to situate (build) meanings for that domain in the sorts of situations the domain involves. That is precisely why real learning is active and always a new way of experiencing the world.

Furthermore, I want to argue later that video games are potentially particularly good places where people can learn to situate meanings through embodied experiences in a complex semiotic domain and meditate on the process. Our bad theories about general meanings; about reading but not reading something; and about general learning untied to specific semiotic domains just don't make sense when you play video games. The games exemplify, in a particularly clear way, better and more specific and embodied theories of meaning, reading, and learning.

MORE ON SEMIOTIC DOMAINS: INTERNAL AND EXTERNAL VIEWS

There are two different ways to look at semiotic domains: internally and externally. Any domain can be viewed internally as a type of content or externally in terms of people engaged in a set of social practices. For example, first-person shooter games are a semiotic domain, and they contain a particular type of content. For instance, as part of their typical content, such games involve moving through a virtual world in a first-person perspective (you see only what you are holding and move and feel as if you yourself are holding it) using weapons to battle enemies. Of course, such games involve a good deal more content as well. Thus we can talk about the typical sorts of content we find in first-person shooter games. This is to view the semiotic domain internally.

On the other hand, people actually play first-person shooter games as a practice in the world, sometimes alone and sometimes with other people on the Internet or when they connect several game platforms or computers together. They may also talk to other players about such games and read magazines and Internet sites devoted to them. They are aware that certain people are more adept at playing such games than are others. They are also aware that people who are "into" such games take on a certain identity, at least when they are involved with those games. For example, it is unlikely that people "into" first-person shooter games are going to object to violence in video games, though they may have strong views about how that violence ought to function in games.

I call the group of people associated with a given semiotic domain—in this case, first-person shooter games—an *affinity group*. People in an affinity group can recognize others as more or less "insiders" to the group. They may not see many people in the group face-to-face, but when they interact with someone on the Internet or read something about the domain, they can recognize certain ways of thinking, acting, interacting, valuing, and believing as more or less typical of people who are "into" the semiotic domain. Thus we can talk about the typical ways of thinking, acting, interacting, valuing, and believing as well as the typical sorts of social practices associated with a given semiotic domain. This is to view the domain externally.

What I have said about viewing first-person shooter games internally or externally applies to any semiotic domain. Take, for instance, my own academic field of linguistics, viewed as a semiotic domain. Within linguistics there is a well-defined subdomain often referred to as theoretical linguistics or the theory of grammar, a field largely defined by the work of the noted linguist Noam Chomsky and his followers. (Even alternative views in the field have to be defined in reference to Chomsky's work.) If we view this semiotic domain internally, in terms of content, we can point out that a claim like "All human languages are equal" is a recognizable one—is recognizably a possible piece of content—in this semiotic domain, though Chomskian linguists give very specific meanings to words like "language" and "equal," meanings that are not the same as these words have in "everyday" life.

On the other hand, a claim like "God breathed life into the word" is not a recognizable claim—is not recognizably a possible piece of content in—the semiotic domain of theoretical linguistics. If history had been different, perhaps there would have been a field called linguistics in which this was a possible piece of content. But given how history did happen, and how we therefore now define the nature of science and academic fields, this is not a possible piece of content in the semiotic domain of theoretical linguistics.

So far, then, we have been talking about and viewing the semiotic domain of theoretical linguistics internally in terms of its content. But we can also talk about and view the domain externally in terms of the ways in which such linguists tend to think, act, interact, value, and believe when they are being linguists. This is to ask about the sorts of identities they take on when they are engaged with, or acting out of their connections to, the semiotic domain of theoretical linguistics. This is to view the domain externally.

Theoretical linguists tend to look down on people who study the social and cultural aspects of language (people like me now). They tend to believe that only the structural aspects of language (e.g., syntax or phonology) can be studied rigorously and scientifically in terms of deducing conclusions from quite abstract and mathematically based theories. In turn, they tend to see affiliations between themselves and "hard scientists" like physicists. Since physics has high prestige in our society, theoretical linguistics tends to have higher prestige within the overall field of linguistics than does, say, sociolinguistics.

The claim here is not that each and every theoretical linguist looks down on linguists who study social and cultural affairs (though when I was a theoretical linguist earlier in my career I did!). Rather, the claim is that each and every such linguist would recognize these ways of thinking and valuing as part of the social environment in and around the field of theoretical linguistics. This is to view the domain externally.

The external view of theoretical linguistics, and not the internal one, explains why this subbranch of linguistics is regularly called theoretical linguistics when, in fact, people who study language socially and culturally also engage in building and arguing over "theories" (though less abstract and mathematically based ones). Given its assumptions about being rigorous science in a wider culture that values physics more than literature or sociology, for instance, this branch of linguistics has easily been able to co-opt the term for itself. People who study language socially and culturally often use the term "theoretical linguistics" just for Chomskian (and related) work, thereby enacting their own "subordination." This last comment, of course, is an external view on the larger semiotic domain of linguistics as a whole.

Do the internal and external aspects of a semiotic domain have anything to do with each other? Of course, if we are talking about academic disciplines as semiotic domains, most academics would like to think that the answer to this question is no. But the answer is, in fact, yes. Content, the internal part of a semiotic domain, gets made in history by real people and their social interactions. They build that content—in part, not wholly—in certain ways because of the people they are (socially, historically, culturally). That content comes to define one of their important identities in the world. As those identities develop through further social interactions, they come to affect the ongoing development and transformation of the content of the semiotic domain in yet new ways. In turn, that new content helps further develop and transform those identities. The relationship between the internal and external is reciprocal.

I am not trying to make some postmodern relativistic point that nothing is true or better than anything else. The potential content of a semiotic domain can take a great many shapes. Some of them are better than others for certain purposes (e.g., as truth claims about grammar or language), but there is always more than one good (and bad) shape that content can take, since there are so many fruitful and correct facts, principles, and patterns one can discover in the world.

For example, Noam Chomsky and his early students spoke English as their native language and, thus, tended to use this language as their initial database for forming their theories. These were, in fact, theories not about English but about what is universal in language or common to the design of all languages. This early emphasis on English (treating English as the "typical" language) gave the theory a certain sort of initial shape that helped lead to certain developments and not others. Later the theory changed as more languages—ones quite different from English—received more careful consideration. Nonetheless, no matter how good the theory is now (assuming for the moment the theory is good), if Chomsky and others had been speakers of Navajo, it might be equally good now but somewhat different.

There are a myriad of things to get right and wrong, and theoretical linguistics as it is now undoubtedly has some things right and some things wrong. Theoretical linguistics as it might have been had Chomsky spoken Navajo would have had other things right and wrong, though it may well have had some of the same things right and wrong as well. The American philosopher Charles Sanders Pierce argued that "in the end," after all the efforts of scientists over time, all possible theories in an area like theoretical linguistics would converge on the "true" one. But you and I won't be here for "the end" of time, so we are stuck with the fact that the internal and external aspects of semiotic domains—even academic fields and areas of science— influence each other.

MORE ON SEMIOTIC DOMAINS: DESIGN GRAMMARS

Semiotic domains have what I call *design grammars*. Each domain has an internal and an external design grammar. By an internal design grammar, I mean the principles and patterns in terms of which one can recognize what is and what is not acceptable or typical content in a semiotic domain. By an external design grammar, I mean the principles and patterns in terms of which one can recognize what is and what is not an acceptable or typical social practice and identity in regard to the affinity group associated with a semiotic domain.

Do you know what counts as a modernist piece of architecture? What sort of building counts as typical or untypical of modernist architecture ? If you do, then you know, consciously or unconsciously, the internal design grammar of the semiotic domain of modernist architecture (as a field of interest).

If all you know is a list of all the modernist buildings ever built, then you don't know the internal design grammar of the domain. Why? Because if you know the design grammar—that is, the underlying principles and patterns that determine what counts and what doesn't count as a piece of modernist architecture—you can make judgments about buildings you have never seen before or even ones never actually built, but only modeled in cardboard. If all you have is a list, you can't make any judgments about anything that isn't on your list.

Do you know what counts as thinking, acting, interacting, and valuing like someone who is "into" modernist architecture? Can you recognize the sorts of identities such people take on when they are in their domain? Can you recognize what count as valued social practices to the members of the affinity group associated with the semiotic domain of modernist architecture and what counts as behaving appropriately in these social practices? If the answer to these questions is "yes," then you know, consciously or unconsciously, the external design grammar of the semiotic domain.

Do you understand what counts and what doesn't count as a possible piece of content in theoretical linguistics? Do you know that claims like "All languages are equal" (in one specific meaning) and "The basic syntactic rules in the core grammar of any language are optimal" count as possible claims in theoretical linguistics and that claims like "God breathed life into the word" and "Nominalizations are very effective communicative devices in science" don't? Do you know why this is so, how it follows from the ways in which the elements of the content of theoretical linguistics relate to each other as a complex system? If you do, you know the internal design grammar of theoretical linguistics. If all you know is a list of facts from the domain, you will never know whether a claim not on your list should or shouldn't count or even whether the matter is open to debate or not. You can't "go on" in the domain.

Are you aware that theoretical linguists don't value work on the social aspects of language as much as they do work on the structural aspects of grammar? Do you know that even when they are assessing work in the social sciences and humanities, they tend to value logical deductive structure and abstract theories in these domains over richly descriptive but less abstract and less theoretical studies? Are you aware that the term "descriptive" is (or, at least, used to be) a term of insult and "explanatory" a term of praise when such people are talking about academic work inside and outside their field? Do you know why? If you know things like this, you know the external design grammar of the semiotic domain of theoretical linguistics. You find certain ways of thinking, acting, and valuing expectable in the affinity group associated with the domain, others not.

Of course, the internal and external grammars of a domain change through time. For example, it was once common to find linguists who saw studying issues germane to the translation of the Bible, for example into Native American languages, as a core part of their academic work and identity as linguists. They hoped to facilitate the work of missionaries to the speakers of these languages. They saw no conflict between doing linguistics and serving their religious purposes at the same time. Other linguists, not involved in Bible translation, did not necessarily dispute this at the time and often did not withhold professional respect from such religious linguists. The external grammar of the domain (and this was certainly influenced by the wider culture at the time) allowed a connection between linguistic work as science and religious commitments as an overt part of that work.

Today most linguists, theoretical and otherwise, would be skeptical of any connection between linguistic work and religion. They would not see translating the Bible into languages connected to cultures without the Bible, to facilitate the work of missionaries, as a central part of any branch of linguistics.

Today the external design grammar of the field does not readily allow for a connection between work as a linguist and religion, for identities as a linguist that are formed around this connection or for social practices germane to it.

So why I am being so perverse as to use the term "design grammar" for these matters? Because I want us to think about the fact that for any semiotic domain, whether it is first-person shooter games or theoretical linguistics, that domain, internally and externally, was and is designed by someone. But who was/is this someone who designed the semiotic domains of first-person shooter games and theoretical linguistics?

Obviously real game designers and producers determine what counts as recognizable content for first-person shooter games by actually making such games. Over time, as they apply certain principles, patterns, and procedures to the construction of such games, the content of first-person shooter games comes to have a recognizable shape such that people not only say things like "Oh, yeah, that's a first-person shooter game" or "No, that's not a first-person shooter" but also "Oh, yeah, that a typical first-person shooter game" or "Oh, no, that's a groundbreaking first-person shooter game."

Yet these designers and producers are only part of the people who produce the external grammar of first-person shooter games. People who play, review, and discuss such games, as well as those who design and produce them, shape the external design grammar of the semiotic domain of first-person shooter games through their ongoing social interactions. It is their ongoing social interactions that determine the principles and patterns through which people in the domain can recognize and judge thinking, talking, reading, writing, acting, interacting, valuing, and believing characteristic of people who are in the affinity group associated with first-person shooter games.

And, of course, the acts of people helping to design the domain externally as a set of social practices and typical identities rebound on the acts of those helping to design the domain internally as content, since that content must "please" the members of the affinity group associated with the domain as well as recruit newcomers to the domain. At the same time, the acts of those helping to design the domain internally in terms of content rebound on the acts of those helping to design the domain externally as a set of social practices and identities, since that content shapes and transforms those practices and identities.

Just the same things can be said about those who design the semiotic domain of theoretical linguistics, internally and externally. Linguists who write and publish and give talks at conferences shape the internal design grammar of the domain through their research. They shape and transform the principles and patterns that determine what counts as the content of theoretical linguistics.

All linguists shape the external grammar of the domain through their social interactions and the identities they take on in those interactions. It is their ongoing social interactions and related identity work that determine the principles and patterns through which people in the domain can recognize and judge thinking, talking, reading, writing, acting, interacting, valuing, and believing characteristic of people who are in the affinity group associated with theoretical linguistics.

It is crucial, as I have pointed out, to see that the internal and external grammars and designs of semiotic domains interrelate with each other, mutually supporting and transforming each other. Let me exemplify this point, and further clarify the notion of design grammars, by returning to video games.

Some people play video games on game platforms like the Playstation (X or 2), the Nintendo GameCube, or the Xbox. Some people play them on computers like the one on which I am typing this book. When people play video games on game platforms, they use a handheld controller with various buttons and often a little built-in joystick or two. They never use the sort of keyboard associated with a computer.

It is part of the external design of the semiotic domain of video games for game platforms that games and handheld controllers go together and part of the design of the semiotic domain of video games on computers that games and keyboards or handheld controllers go together, since some players do, in fact, plug handheld controllers into their computers to replace the keyboard.

So far this just seems to be a matter of brute technological facts. But things work in the world in certain ways because people make them do so or, at the very least, are willing to accept them as such. Then, when they work that way, people come to expect them to do so and build values and norms around them working that way.

One could conceivably get a keyboard to work with a game platform. At the very least, it would be easy for designers to modify a platform so that it would work with a keyboard. However, you don't understand the external design grammar of the domain of platform-based video-game playing if you don't realize that doing this would "break the rules." It would be a serious departure from what the affinity group associated with this domain expects, wants, and values. Many platform-game players think keyboards are a bad way to play video games, while some computer-game players think they are a good way. In turn, these matters are connected to their identities as game players (e.g., the editors of *PC Gamer* magazine regularly "apologize" when they have spent time playing games on a game platform and not on a computer, and look down on the enterprise).

When Microsoft's Xbox came out in 2002, it was the first game platform to contain a computerlike hard drive. Hard drives allow games to be saved at any point. Heretofore, games played on game platforms, thanks to the technological limitations of the platforms, could be saved much less regularly than computer games. Players on typical game platforms, for example, can save only at the end of a level or when they have found a special save symbol in the game. This means that in an action game, they have to stay alive long enough to get to the end of the level or find the save symbol, no matter how long they already have been playing.

In a computer game, thanks to the computer's hard drive, players can save their progress at any time they wish. (There are some games made for computers in which this is not true). This can make a difference in the strategies one uses. When playing on a computer, the player can save after a particularly hard battle and not ever have to repeat that battle. If the player dies a bit later, he or she starts again from the game that was saved after the big battle was already won.

On a game platform, if there was no save symbol after the big battle or if the battle was not the end of a level, the player could not save and must move on. If he or she dies, the big battle will have to be fought again, since the game will reload from an earlier saved game that did not contain that battle. Indeed, the last save could have been quite far in the past, and the player may be required to repeat a good deal of the game.

However, again, these are not just technological matters. Platform users do not necessarily see being unable to save whenever they want as a limitation. Many of them see it as a virtue; they say it adds more excitement and challenge to a game. Computer-game players who save after each big battle or dangerous jump might be thought of as "wimps" who can't last any length of time against rigorous challenges. Furthermore, in my experience, many platform users do not see playing large parts of a game over and over again as repetition in the way in which I do. They see it an opportunity to perfect their skills and get more play out of a game they enjoy.

So we see here the ways in which external technological and material facts become social facts and values. The Xbox's coming out with a hard drive led to a debate that anyone who understands the external design grammar of the platform domain could have predicted. Was the Xbox really a game platform? Could a real game platform have a hard drive? Perhaps the Xbox is really a computer in disguise. This is a debate over the very external design grammar of the domain: Is the pattern "video game, game platform, hard drive" acceptable within the external design grammar of the domain? Does it count as an acceptable part of valued social practices and identities in the domain? Should it?

It is not surprising, either, that of the games Microsoft initially brought out for the Xbox some used the hard drive to allow players to save whenever and wherever they wanted (e.g., *Max Payne*) and others did not and functioned like a "proper" platform game (e.g., *Nightcaster*). The company obviously wanted to entice both platform players and computer-game players onto its system, though this can, in some cases, be a bit like enticing cats and dogs to play ball together.

A good number of people play both platform games and computer games, of course. Nonetheless, somewhat different affinity groups, with different attitudes and values, have arisen around each domain, with lots of overlap in between. There are people who play in both domains but have strong opinions about what sorts of games are best played on platforms and what sorts are best played on computers. All this is typical: Semiotic domains and affinity groups often don't have sharp boundaries (though some do), and in any case the boundaries are often fluid and changing.

Since the Xbox has the capacity to break the pattern that associates game platforms and limited saves while still retaining some of the other patterns typical of game platforms, it has the potential to create a new affinity group and/or to transform old ones. In the act, it and the social interactions of people around it might eventually create a new semiotic domain within the bigger domain of video-game playing, a new domain with a new external design grammar determining new social practices and identities. Indeed, the matter is already in progress, as the Xbox has already generated (with the help of Microsoft, of course) its own magazines, Internet sites, and aficionados.

But all this transformation and change in the external design grammar will rebound on and change the internal design grammar. Designers and producers will use the hard drive on the Xbox together with its more typical platform features to design new games. Hybrids between typical platform games and typical computer games will arise. The distinction in content between platform games (which tended to stress fast action) and computer games (which can store more information and stress deeper stories) may blur. As new content arises and new principles and patterns regarding the acceptable content of various different types of games also arise, the affinity groups associated with those different types of games will change their social interactions, values, and identities, and so, too, the external design grammar of their respective domains.

Some of these changes will be small, some large. But that is the way of all semiotic domains in the world. They are made, internally and externally, by humans and changed by them as these humans take up technological and material circumstances in certain ways and not others and as they shape and reshape their social interactions with each other.

LIFEWORLDS

Our talk about semiotic domains may lead some to think that everything said thus far only applies to "specialist" areas like video games, theoretical linguistics, law, or the workings of urban gangs, not "everyday," "ordinary" life. However, "everyday," "ordinary" life is itself a semiotic domain. In fact, it is a domain in which all of us have lots and lots of experience. It is what I call the *lifeworld domain*.

By the lifeworld domain I mean those occasions when we are operating (making sense to each other and to ourselves) as "everyday" people, not as members of more specialist or technical semiotic domains. Not everyone does physics or plays video games, but everyone spends lots of time in his or her lifeworld domain. And, of course, people move quite readily between specialist domains and their lifeworld domain. For example, a group of physicists at a dinner meeting might, at one moment, be discussing physics as specialists in physics and, at the next moment, be discussing the weather or movies as "everyday" nonspecialists. (Of course, there are people who can and do discuss the weather or movies as specialists in a specialist semiotic domain devoted to the weather or movies.)

Lifeworld domains are culturally variable; that is, different cultural groups have, more or less, different ways of being, doing, feeling, valuing, and talking as "everyday people." Thus there are many lifeworld domains, though they overlap enough to allow for, better or worse, communication across cultures,

If we look at lifeworld domains internally, we can say that their content is just the wide range of nonspecialist experiences of the world that people share with other people with whom they share various group memberships, up to and including the human race. Once a group has carved out an area of this experience (whether this is playing in the guise of video games or dealing with the weather as a science) and created "specialist" ways of talking and thinking about it ("policed" by themselves as "insiders," who determine what is acceptable and what not, who is adept and who is not), then they have left the lifeworld (and the rest of us behind) and created a specialist semiotic domain.

If we look at lifeworld domains externally, we can ask about the ways of thinking, talking, acting, interacting, valuing, and, in some cases, writing and reading that allow a particular culturally distinctive group of people to recognize each other as being, at a time and place, "everyday" or "ordinary" nonspecialist people. For example, how do you know when a friend of yours who is a theoretical linguist (and you are not) is talking to you and engaging with you not as a specialist linguist but just as an "everyday" nonspecialist person? How do you know this even when, in fact, you happen to be talking about language?

And, of course, these matters will differ if you and the linguist are from quite different cultures—say you are an African American and the linguist is a Russian. But, again, I caution against assuming too much variation across human beings. People can and very often do recognize "normal" human behavior across cultural groups, however problematic this sometimes may be (even to the point of leading to violence).

It is important to realize that meanings are no more general—they are just as situated—in lifeworld domains as they are in any other semiotic domain. For example, in different situations, even such a mundane word as "coffee" has different situated meanings. Consider, for instance, what happens in your head when I say "The coffee spilled, get a mop" versus "The coffee spilled, get a broom." In different situations, the word "coffee" can mean a liquid, grains, beans, tins, or a flavor. It can mean yet other things in other situations, and sometimes we have to come up with novel meanings for the word; for example in a sentence like "Her coffee skin glistened in the bright sunshine," "coffee" names a skin color.

For another example, think of the different situated meanings of the word "light" in everyday interactions in these sentences: Turn the light on.

This light isn't giving much light. I can see a far off light. I am just bathing in this light. The effects of light in this part of the county are wonderful. The last thing I saw was a bright light. Of course, when we consider, in the context of lifeworld domains, words like "truth," "good," "democracy," "fairness," "honesty," and so forth, things get yet more variable, more deeply rooted in specific situations in specific culturally relative lifeworld domains.

There are a number of important points to make about lifeworld domains. First, we are all used to making claims to know things based not on any specialist knowledge we have but just as "everyday" human beings. However, in the modern world, specialist domains are taking more and more space away from lifeworld domains wherein people can make nonspecialist claims to know things and not face a challenge from a specialist.

For example, I once lived in Los Angeles. Every nonspecialist in Los Angeles "knows" the air is polluted and dangerous, and they are usually willing to say so. Nonetheless, it was not at all uncommon to read in the newspaper, say, that "lay people" didn't really know what they were talking about (and choking on). Specialists in the matter claimed that there was no technical "evidence" that the air was particularly unsafe. Tobacco companies tried the same thing for years in regard to the dangers of smoking. Companies that pollute ground and water often engage in the same tactic when people in their areas of operation claim to feel sick (or drop dead) from their pollution.

Helping students learn how to think about the contrasting claims of various specialists against each other and against lifeworld claims to know certainly ought to be a key job for schools. To do this, students would have to investigate specialist domains and different culturally distinctive lifeworlds, internally in terms of content and externally in terms of social practices and identities.

A second point to be made about lifeworld domains is this: In the modern world, we are used to having to face the fact that children, including our own, are specialists when and where we are not. Many children are adept at the semiotic domain of computers—sometimes because they play video games and that interest has led them to learn more about computers—when the adults in the house are intimidated by computers.

Kids have turned video games, roller-blading, skateboarding, and snowboarding into specialist domains that internally in terms of content and externally in terms of social practices bewilder adults. Many children have learned through the Internet and television more about stock trading or even law than many of the adults around them could ever imagine knowing. (One teenager had the top rating for legal advice on a legal Internet site in which many of the others on the highly ranked list were professional lawyers.)

Adults are getting used to the fact that they are "immigrants" in many a domain where their own children are "natives" (specialists). The lifeworld— the domain in which people can claim to know and understand things as "everyday" people and not as specialists—is shrinking, not just under the attack of specialist domains like science but because our children are creating and mastering so many specialist domains themselves.

A third point I want to make is this: I firmly believe we need to protect lifeworld domains from the assaults of specialists (yes, even our own children). We need to understand and value people's "everyday" knowledge and understandings. At the same time, I believe it is crucial, particularly in the contemporary world, that all of us, regardless of our cultural affiliations, be able to operate in a wide variety of semiotic domains outside our lifeworld domains.

It is very often in these non-lifeworld domains that people form affiliations with others outside their own cultural groups and transcend the limitations of any one person's culture and lifeworld domain. Of course, it is important not to insult anyone's culture or lifeworld domain; it is important, as well, to build bridges to these when introducing people to new semiotic domains. But in my view, it is a poor form of respect for anyone to leave people trapped in their own culture and lifeworld as the whole and sole space within which they can move in the modern world. If this view comports poorly with some versions of multiculturalism, so be it.

BACK TO *PIKMIN:* CRITICAL LEARNING

If learning is to be active, it must involve experiencing the world in new ways. I have spelled this out in terms of learning new ways to situate the meanings of words, images, symbols, artifacts, and so forth when operating within specific situations in new semiotic domains. Active learning must also involve forming new affiliations. I have explained this in terms of learners joining new affinity groups associated with new semiotic domains.

Active learning in a domain also involves preparation for future learning within the domain and within related domains. I will deal with this issue below, when I draw a comparison between the sorts of learning that take place when playing good video games and the sorts of learning that take place in good science classrooms and when I discuss the notion of precursor domains.

However, as I said earlier, critical learning involves yet another step. For active learning, the learner must, at least unconsciously, understand and operate within the internal and external design grammars of the semiotic domain he or she is learning. But for critical learning, the learner must be able consciously to attend to, reflect on, critique, and manipulate those design grammars at a metalevel. That is, the learner must see and appreciate the semiotic domain as a *design space*, internally as a system of interrelated elements making up the possible content of the domain and externally as ways of thinking, acting, interacting, and valuing that constitute the identities of those people who are members of the affinity group associated with the domain.

Let me return to the child playing *Pikmin* for a specific example of what I mean. What does it take just to play a game as an active learner? To do this the player must understand and produce situated meanings in the semiotic domain that this game, and games like it, constitutes. Elements in the content of *Pikmin*—for example, a yellow Pikmin—do not have just one general meaning or significance in the game world. Learners must learn to situate different meanings for such elements within different specific situations within the domain.

For example, when a player is faced with a rock wall, his yellow Pikmin (who can throw bomb rocks) take on the situated meaning *the type of Pikmin who can use bombs* (unlike red and blue Pikmin), since a good strategy for destroying walls in the game is to have yellow Pikmin throw bombs at them. However, when attacking a fat, sleeping, dangerous spotted creature (a Spotty Bulborb) found throughout the first levels of the game, the yellow Pikmin take on the situated meaning *the sorts of Pikmin who can be thrown farther than other sorts of Pikmin*, since a good strategy when fighting big creatures like these is to have Captain Olimar tell the red Pikmin to run up and attack from the rear, while he throws the yellow Pikmin onto their backs to attack from up top.

Additionally, players need to know what patterns or combinations of elements the game's internal design grammar allows. They need to know, given the situated meanings they have given to each element in the pattern or combination, what the whole pattern or combination means in a situated way useful for action.

For example, the internal design grammar of *Pikmin* allows the player to bring together (by moving Captain Olimar and his Pikmin) the combination of Pikmin, a rock wall, and a small tin can laying near the wall, containing little rock bombs. Of course, the game did not need to allow this pattern or combination to be able to occur; its design grammar could have been built differently. Even given that the design grammar does allow this combination, players still have to build a situated meaning for this combination out of the situated meanings they have given to each element in the game based on the situation they take themselves to be in and their own goals.

If this is a point in the game where the player needs to get past the wall, and given the fact that he or she can build a situated meaning for yellow Pikmin like *the type of Pikmin that can throw bombs*, the player can build a situated meaning for this combination something like: *Equip the yellow Pikmin with the rock bombs and have them use the bombs to blow up the wall.*

Here is another example from *Pikmin* of a combination of elements allowable by the internal design grammar of the game. The player often finds a Spotty Bulborb—a creature with big teeth and jaws suitable for swallowing Pikmin whole—sleeping peacefully in a fairly exposed space. So the design grammar of the domain allows the combination: Spotty Bulborb, sleeping, in exposed area. Depending on what situation the player takes him- or herself to be in, this combination can be assigned several different situated meanings. For instance, it could be taken to mean: *Attack the Spotty Bulborb carefully from the rear before it wakes up;* or it could be taken to mean: *Sneak quietly by the Spotty Bulborb to get where you want to go without trouble.* Nothing stops the player from assigning the combination a more unexpected situated meaning, perhaps something like: *Wake the Spotty Bulborb up so you can get a more exciting (and fair?) fight.*

Since the child can successfully break down rock walls and attack Spotty Bulborbs, he can understand ("read") and produce ("write") appropriate situated meanings for elements and combinations of elements in the domain (game). But all of this is "just" playing the game in a proactive way—that is, using situated meanings and the design grammar of the game to understand and produce meanings and actions (which are a type of meaning in the domain). Of course, one could just ritualize one's response to the game and try pretty much the same strategy in every situation, but this would not be a proactive way to play and learn.

All these meanings and actions are a product of what I have called active learning, but they are not yet critical learning that leverages the design grammar at a metalevel in a reflective way that can lead to critique, novel meanings, or transformation of the domain. However, the child is learning to do this as well—that is, his process of learning the game is not only active, it is increasingly critical.

When the child had recovered 5 of the spaceship's 30 missing parts, he was able to search in a new area called The Forest's Navel. This area had a much harsher and more dangerous-looking landscape than the previous areas the child had been in. It had different dangerous creatures, including a number of closely grouped creatures that breathed fire. And the background music had changed considerably. Since the player has already found five parts, the game assumes that he is now more adept than when he began the game; thus, the landscape and creatures are getting harder to deal with, offering a bigger challenge. At the same time, these changes in features communicate a new mood, changing the tone of the game from a cute fairy tale to a somewhat darker struggle for survival.

The child was able to think about and comment on these changes. He said that the music was now "scary" and the landscape much harsher-looking than the ones he had previously been in. He knew that this signaled that things were going to get harder. Furthermore, he was aware that the changes signaled that he needed to rethink some of his strategies as well his relationship to the game. He was even able to comment on the fact that the earlier parts of the game made it appear more appropriate for a child his age than did the Forest Navel area and considered whether the game was now "too scary" or not. He decided on a strategy of exploring the new area only a little bit at a time, avoiding the fire-breathing creatures, and returning to old areas with the new resources (e.g., blue Pikmin) he got in the Forest Navel area to find more parts there more quickly and easily (remember, the player has only 30 game days to get all the parts and so wants to get some of them quickly and easily.)

What we are dealing with here is talk and thinking about the (internal) design of the game, about the game as a complex system of interrelated parts meant to engage and even manipulate the player in certain ways. This is met-alevel thinking, thinking about the game as a system and a designed space, and not just playing within the game moment by moment. Such thinking can open up critique of the game. It can also lead to novel moves and strategies, sometimes ones that the game makers never anticipated. This is what I mean by critical learning and thinking. Of course, the six-year-old is only beginning the process of critical learning in regard to *Pikmin* and other video games, but he is well begun.

The child is learning to think reflectively about the internal design grammar (the grammar of content) of *Pikmin* and games like it. As he interacts with others, he will have opportunities to reflect on the external design grammar (the grammar of social practices and identities) too. For example, he has already learned that he can search the Internet for helpful tips about playing the game, including what are called Easter Eggs (little surprises players can find in a game if they know where and how to look for them). He considers these tips part of playing the game. On the other hand, he characterizes advice about how to play as "bossing him around" and claims he can "do his own thinking."

These are early moments in the child's induction into the affinity groups associated with video-game playing, their characteristic social practices, and the sorts of identities people take on within these groups and practices. If he is to engage with these external aspects of game playing critically, he will need to reflect in an overt way on the patterns and possibilities he does and does not find in these social practices and identities. Doing this is to reflect on the external design grammar of the domain.

Critical learning, as I am defining it here, involves learning to think of semiotic domains as design spaces that manipulate us (if I can use this term without necessary negative connotations) in certain ways and that we can manipulate in certain ways. The child has much more to learn about *Pikmin* as a design space (internally and externally). He also has much more to learn about not just the single game *Pikmin* but the genre (family) of games into which *Pikmin* falls (adventure strategy games) as a design space. And he has much more to learn about not just this genre but about video games in general (a larger and more loosely connected family) as a design space.

Then there is the crucial matter of learning how these design spaces relate to each other and to other sorts of semiotic domains, some more closely related to video games as semiotic domains, some less closely related. That is, the child can learn how to think about, and act on, semiotic domains as a larger design space composed of clusters (families) of more or less closely related semiotic domains.

So, then, why do I call learning and thinking at a metalevel about semiotic domains (alone and in relation to each other) as design spaces *critical* learning and thinking? For this reason: Semiotic systems are human cultural and historical creations that are designed to engage and manipulate people in certain ways. They attempt through their content and social practices to recruit people to think, act, interact, value, and feel in certain specific ways. In this sense, they attempt to get people to learn and take on certain sorts of new identities, to become, for a time and place, certain types of people. In fact, society as a whole is simply the web of these many different sorts of identities and their characteristic associated activities and practices.

Some of these identities constitute, within certain institutions or for certain social groups in the society, social goods. By a "social good" I mean anything that a group in society, or society as a whole, sees as bringing one status, respect, power, freedom, or other such socially valued things. Some people have more or less access to valued or desired semiotic domains and their concomitant identities. Furthermore, some identities connected to some semiotic domains may come, as one understands the domain more reflectively, to seem less (or more) good or valuable than one had previously thought.

Finally, one might come to see that a given identity associated with a given semiotic domain relates poorly (or well)—in terms of one's vision of ethics, morality, or a valued life—with one's other identities associated with other semiotic domains. For example, a person might come to see that a given semiotic domain is designed so as to invite one to take on an identity that revels in a disdain for life or in a way of thinking about race, class, or gender that the person, in terms of other identities he or she takes on in other semiotic domains, does not, on reflection, wish to continue. In this sense, then, semiotic domains are inherently political (and here I am using the term "political" in the sense of any practices where the distribution of social goods in a society is at stake).

Let me make this discussion more concrete. A game like *Pikmin* recruits from the our six-year-old a complex identity composed of various related traits. The game encourages him to think of himself an active problem solver, one who persists in trying to solve problems even after making mistakes; one who, in fact, does not see mistakes as errors but as opportunities for reflection and learning. It encourages him to be the sort of problem solver who, rather than ritualizing the solutions to problems, leaves himself open to undoing former mastery and finding new ways to solve new problems in new situations.

At the same time, the boy is encouraged to see himself as solving problems from the perspective of a particular fantasy creature (Captain Olimar) and his faithful helpers (the Pikmin) and, thus, to get outside his "real" identity and play with the notions of perspectives and identities themselves. He is also encouraged to focus on the problem-solving and fantasy aspects of his new identity and not, say, his worries about killing (virtual) "living" creatures, however odd they may be, though he can choose to avoid killing some of the creatures by running from them or sneaking around them. The learner, in this case, gets to customize the identity the game offers him to a certain extent—this, in fact, is an important feature of good video games.

The identity that *Pikmin* invites the player to take on relates in a variety of ways to other identities he takes on in other domains. I believe, for example, that the identity *Pikmin* recruits relates rather well to the sort of identity a learner is called on to assume in the best active science learning in schools and other sites.

If this is true, then our six-year-old is privileged in this respect over children who do not have the opportunity to play such games (in an active and critical way). An issue of social justice is at stake here in regard to the distribution of, and access to, this identity, whether through video games or science. We can note, as well, that the boy is using the video game to practice this identity, for many hours, at an early age, outside of science instruction in school, which may very well take up very little of the school day. Other children may get to practice this identity only during the limited amount of time their school devotes to active and critical learning in science of the sort that lets children take on the virtual identity of being and doing science rather than memorizing lists of facts—which often is no time at all.

VIDEO GAMES: A WASTE OF TIME?

I have now discussed a perspective on learning that stresses active and critical learning within specific semiotic domains. So, let me now return to the grandfather's remark that playing video games is a waste of time because the child is learning no "content."

If children (or adults) are playing video games in such a way as to learn actively and critically then they are:

1. Learning to experience (see and act on) the world in a new way
2. Gaining the potential to join and collaborate with a new affinity group
3. Developing resources for future learning and problem solving in the semiotic domains to which the game is related

4. Learning how to think about semiotic domains as design spaces that engage and manipulate people in certain ways and, in turn, help create certain relationships in society among people and groups of people, some of which have important implications for social justice

These, of course, are just the four things one learns when engaging actively and critically with any new semiotic domain. So the questions in regard to any specific semiotic domain become: Are these good or valuable ways to experience the world? Is this a good or valuable affinity group to join? Are these resources for future learning applicable to other good and valued semiotic domains? Is this domain leading the learner to reflect on design spaces (and the concomitant identities they help create), and their intricate relationships to each other, in ways that potentially can lead to critique, innovation, and good or valued thinking and acting in society?

The answers to these questions will vary along a variety of parameters. But they show that a great deal more is at stake than "content" in the grandfather's sense. This book offers a positive answer to these questions in regard to a good many (certainly not all) video games, as long as people are playing them in ways that involve active and critical learning. Video games have the potential to lead to active and critical learning. In fact, I believe that they often have a greater potential than much learning in school (even though school learning may involve learning "content"). Indeed, I hope my discussion of the child playing *Pikmin* already suggests some of the lines of my argument.

What ensures that a person plays video games in a way that involves active and critical learning and thinking? Nothing, of course, can ensure such a thing. Obviously, people differ in a variety of ways, including how much they are willing to challenge themselves, and they play video games for a great variety of different purposes. But two things help to lead to active and critical learning in playing video games.

One is the internal design of the game itself. Good games—and the games get better in this respect all the time—are crafted in ways that encourage and facilitate active and critical learning and thinking (which is not to say that every player will take up this offer). The other is the people around the learner, other players and nonplayers. If these people encourage reflective metatalk, thinking, and actions in regard to the design of the game, of video games more generally, and of other semiotic domains and their complex interrelationships, then this, too, can encourage and facilitate active and critical learning and thinking (though, again, the offer may not be taken up). And, indeed, the affinity groups connected to video games do often encourage metareflective thinking about design, as a look at Internet game sites will readily attest.

This last point—that other people can encourage in the learner metareflective talk, thinking, and actions in regard to a semiotic domain as a design space—leads to another point: Often it is critical learning—focusing on the semiotic domain one is learning as a design space in a reflective way—that actually encourages and pushes active learning. One can learn actively without much critical learning, but one cannot really learn much critically without a good deal of active learning in a semiotic domain. The critical is not a later add-on. It should be central to the process of active learning from the beginning.

There is another important issue here that bears on deciding whether a given semiotic domain—like video games—is valuable or not: Semiotic domains in society are connected to other semiotic domains in a myriad of complex ways. One of these is that a given domain can be a good precursor for learning another one. Because mastering the meaning-making skills in, and taking on the identity associated with, the precursor domain facilitates learning in the other domain. Facilitation can also happen because being (or having been) a member of the affinity group associated with the precursor domain facilitates becoming a member of the affinity group associated with the other domain, because the values, norms, goals, or practices of the precursor group resemble in some ways the other group's values, norms, goals, or practices.

Let me give a concrete example of such connections. In the larger semiotic domain of video games, first- and third-person shooter games are a well-defined subdomain. However, such games often have elements that are similar to features found in arcade games, games (like *Space Invaders, Pacman,* and *Frogger*) that involve a good deal of fast hand-eye coordination to move and respond quickly. (In fact, one of the original first-person shooter games, a game that helped start the genre—*Wolfenstein 3D*—operates very much like an arcade game.) Thus, someone who has mastered the domain of arcade games has mastered a precursor domain for shooter games, though such games now contain many other elements, as well.

On the other hand, fantasy role-playing games are another well-defined subdomain of the video-game domain. People who have earlier played and mastered the *Dungeons and Dragons* semiotic domain (as make-believe play or with books and cards) are advantaged when they play fantasy role-playing games, since such games developed out of *Dungeons and Dragons*, though they now contain a good many additional elements.

Both the shooter domain and the fantasy role-playing domain have other precursor domains, and they share some precursor domains (e.g., make-believe play wherein one is willing to take on different identities—a domain that some cultures and social groups do not encourage in children or adults). Some of these video-game (sub-) domains may well serve as precursor domains for other semiotic domains. For example, it may well be that the popular (sub-) domain of simulation games (so-called god games, like *SimCity*, *The Sims*, *Railroad Tycoon*, and *Tropico*) could be, for some children, a precursor domain for those sciences that heavily trade in computer-based simulations as a method of inquiry (e.g., some types of biology and cognitive science).

In interviews my research team and I have conducted with video-game players, we have found a number of young people who have used the domain of video games as a fruitful precursor domain for mastering other semiotic domains tied to computers and related technologies. Indeed, several of these young people plan to go to college and major in computer science or related areas.

So we can ask: Can various subdomains in the larger domain of video-game playing serve as precursor domains facilitating later learning in and out of school?. I believe that the sorts of active and critical learning about design—and the type of problem-solving identity—that a game like *Pikmin* can involve may well relate to later learning in domains like science, at least when we are talking about teaching and learning science as an active process of inquiry and not the memorization of passive facts.

I am convinced that playing video games actively and critically is not "a waste of time." And people playing video games are indeed (*pace* the six-year-old's grandfather), learning "content," albeit usually not the passive content of school-based facts. (Many games, such as the *Civilization* games, do contain a good number of facts.) The content of video games, when they are played actively and critically, is something like this: *They situate meaning in a multimodal space through embodied experiences to solve problems and reflect on the intricacies of the design of imagined worlds and the design of both real and imagined social relationships and identities in the modern world.* That's not at all that bad—and people get wildly entertained to boot. No wonder it is hard for today's schools to compete.

LEARNING PRINCIPLES

The discussion in this chapter suggests a variety of learning principles that are built into good video games, games like *Pikmin*, as will the discussion in each of the following chapters. Some of the learning principles suggested in this chapter are a bit more general than are those in later chapters. Here I bring together these principles to start a list that will continue in subsequent chapters.

I state only five very basic principles, since quite a number of other principles that are implicated in the earlier discussion will be discussed in greater detail later. The order of the principles is not important. All the principles are equally important, or nearly so. Some of the principles overlap and, in actuality, reflect different aspects of much the same general theme. Furthermore, these principles are not claims about all and any video games played in any old fashion. Rather, they are claims about the potential of good video games played in environments that encourage overt reflection. (While good video games do indeed encourage overt reflection, this feature can be greatly enhanced by the presence of others, both players and viewers.)

I state each principle in a way that is intended to be equally relevant to learning in video games and learning in content areas in classrooms.

1. **Active, Critical Learning Principle**
   All aspects of the learning environment (including the ways in which the semiotic domain is designed and presented) are set up to encourage active and critical, not passive, learning.

2. **Design Principle**
   Learning about and coming to appreciate design and design principles is core to the learning experience.

3. **Semiotic Principle**
   Learning about and coming to appreciate interrelations within and across multiple sign systems (images, words, actions, symbols, artifacts, etc.) as a complex system is core to the learning experience.

4. **Semiotic Domains Principle**
   Learning involves mastering, at some level, semiotic domains, and being able to participate, at some level, in the affinity group or groups connected to them.

5. **Metalevel Thinking about Semiotic Domains Principle**
   Learning involves active and critical thinking about the relationships
   of the semiotic domain being learned to other semiotic domains.

BIBLIOGRAPHICAL NOTE

See Kress 1985, 1996, and Kress & van Leeuwen 1996, 2001 for insightful discussions on reading images and multimodal texts, that is, texts that mix words and images. For work on literacy as involving multiple literacies, see the citations to the New Literacy Studies at the end of chapter 1 as well as Cope & Kalantzis 2000; Heath 1983; Scollon & Scollon 1981; and Street 1984.

The discussion of physics students who know Newton's laws of motion but cannot apply them to a specific situation is taken from Chi, Feltovich, & Glaser 1981. For further discussion, see Gardner 1991 and Mayer 1992.

On the nature of reading tests, see Hill & Larsen's 2000 superb analyses of actual test items in relationship to different ways of reading. On reading more generally, see Adams 1990; Coles 1998; Gee 1991; Snow, Burns, & Griffin 1998; see Pearson 1999 for discussion of the range of controversy in the area. The "fourth-grade slump" is discussed in Gee 1999a; see Chall 1967 for an early and influential discussion.

On Noam Chomsky's work, see McGilvray 1999. For C. S. Peirce's work, see Kloesel & Houser 1992.

On semiotics and content learning, especially in regard to science education, see Kress, Jewitt, Ogborn, & Tsatsarelis 2001; Lemke 1990; and Ogborn, Kress, Martins, & McGillicuddy 1996. On the notion of affiliation and affinity groups, see Beck 1992, 1994; Gee 2000–2001; Rifkin 2000; and Taylor 1994. For the idea of preparation for future learning, see Bransford & Schwartz 1999, a very important and illuminating paper for anyone interested in learning. On the notion of design and design grammars, see New London Group 1996, a "manifesto" written by an international group of scholars (a group of which I was a member) working in the area of language and literacy studies.

My notion of critical learning combines work on situated cognition (see bibliographic note for chapter 4), especially work on metacognition—see, for example Bereiter & Scardamalia 1989; Bruer 1993: pp. 67–99; Pellegrino, Chudowsky, & Glaser 2001; Schon 1987; and Paulo Freire's 1995 work on critical thinking and literacy as "reading the world" and not just "reading the word." On the concept of the lifeworld, see Habermas 1984.

For discussions of game design relevant to the concerns of this chapter, see Bates 2002 and Rouse 2001.

3

LEARNING AND IDENTITY:
WHAT DOES IT MEAN TO BE A HALF-ELF?

ARCANUM: LEARNING AND IDENTITY

THE LAST CHAPTER ARGUED THAT SEMIOTIC DOMAINS ENCOURAGE people new to them to take on and play with new identities. I discussed the sort of identity as an exploratory problem solver of a certain type that the game *Pikmin* encouraged the six-year-old to take on. All learning in all semiotic domains requires identity work. It requires taking on a new identity and forming bridges from one's old identities to the new one.

For example, a child in a science classroom engaged in real inquiry, and not passive learning, must be willing to take on an identity as a certain type of scientific thinker, problem solver, and doer. The child must see and make connections between this new identity and other identities he or she has already formed. Certainly the child will be at a disadvantage if he or she has one or more identities that do not fit with, are opposed to, or are threatened by the identity recruited in the science classroom (e.g., his or her identity as someone who is bad at learning technical matters, as someone who dislikes school, or as someone from a family that is not "into" science or school—not to mention cases like creationist Christians in biology classes).

This chapter uses learning to play video games as a crucial example of how identities work in learning, an example that illuminates how active and critical learning works in any semiotic domain, including in school. Video games recruit identities and encourage identity work and reflection on identities in clear and powerful ways. If schools worked in similar ways, learning in school would be more successful and powerful because it would become the sorts of active and critical learning discussed in the last chapter. To make the discussion concrete, I base it on one particular video game, a fantasy role-playing game called *Arcanum: Of Steamworks and Magick Obscura*.

I first discuss this game and the sorts of identity work it recruits. Then I turn to learning in school, making comparisons and contrasts with learning in *Arcanum* and games like it. Finally, I continue the list of learning principles that are embedded in good video games, principles that are important for powerful learning in any domain. Let us turn, then, to *Arcanum*.

Arcanum takes place in a massive world called Arcanum, a world made up of a great many countries and towns. Once upon a time magic ("magick") held sway throughout Arcanum. But now technology has arrived, and Arcanum has become a place of both ancient runes and industrial steamworks, a land where magic and machines coexist in a tension-filled and uneasy balance. A variety of races—Humans, Elves, Gnomes, Dwarves, Orcs, and Ogres, as well as Half-Elves, Half-Orcs, and Half-Ogres (each of which have one Human parent)—cohabit this world, each orienting to the conflicts between magic and technology in different ways.

Before you start playing *Arcanum*, you must construct your character. Each race and gender has different natural characteristics. For example, I chose to be a female Half-Elf, whom I named "Bead Bead." Half-Elves, like all other races, have their own unique degrees of strength, constitution, dexterity, beauty, intelligence, willpower, perception, and charisma. Each of these traits will affect how your character—that is, *you*—carries out dialogue and action in the world of Arcanum and how other characters in the world respond to you (e.g., if you are not strong enough to fight in a given situation, you better be intelligent enough to think your way out of the problem, or beautiful or charismatic enough to get others to want to help you).

You can also initially choose from a wide variety of unique backgrounds—things that happened in your character's past. For example, your character might have been a rich debutante who developed strong social skills in her youth suitable now for recruiting help from others or might have been a child of a hero, a parent who has given you extra-special skills with a sword, but whose reputation for goodness you must now live up to, and so on through many other choices.

When the game starts you get five "points" that you can choose to distribute, in any way you wish, to your character, thereby changing his or her "natural" state. For example, Bead Bead, as a female Half-Elf, had a natural strength of 7, but I used one of my five points to make her stronger. As the game progresses and you gain more worldly experience, you gain yet more points to distribute, thereby allowing your character to develop in certain ways and not others.

You can distribute these initial and subsequent points to your character's primary traits, such as strength, dexterity, intelligence, and so forth, but you can also use them to build up a wide variety of other skills, such as ability with a bow and arrow, skill with picking locks, or persuasive skills; ability to cast a wide variety of magic spells or to build a wide variety of technological apparatuses, including weapons; or the ability to heal better or get less fatigued as your character engages in effortful tasks. You can choose to have a character primarily oriented to magic or technology or some mixture of the two.

During game play you talk and interact with a great many other characters in the world of Arcanum. Your actions gain you a reputation as good or evil. Various other characters will join you or not, depending on their own alignments as good or evil and also depending on things like your persuasiveness, beauty, and charisma. Throughout the game, you can get gold and buy clothing, armor, and equipment for yourself and any of your followers, who may run off with your purchases and leave you if you don't treat please them. For example, one of my followers, a rather self-righteous human, kept threatening to leave me if I continued to attempt to pick people's pockets. Rather than quit picking pockets (though I did lay off a bit, at least when he was looking), I reassured him by giving money to poor street beggars, something of which he approved.

Your adventures in Arcanum start with a catastrophe. Your character is a passenger on the *Zephyr*, a large blimp. Two quite odd flying vessels appear and attack the *Zephyr*, destroying themselves in the process. The *Zephyr* bursts into flame and smashes into the ground. Only your character and a dying old man survive the crash. The old man musters just enough strength to give you an engraved ring along with a cryptic message. He pleads with you to take his ring and bring it to "the boy," telling you that a great evil is coming back to destroy everything. After assuring you that the boy "will know what to do," he dies. You are left as the sole survivor of the crash, though you soon meet a mysterious follower of one of Arcanum's religions, a man named Virgil, who, if you wish, will follow and help you.

Thus, your quest begins. The game involves not only the main quest of carrying out the dead man's wishes, a quest that eventually leads to a great many sub-quests that are part of the main quest. It also has lots of side quests, given to you by characters you meet throughout Arcanum, which you can choose to do or ignore. (Though you can gain experience and, thus, more experience points to distribute to your character if you do them.) By the time you finish, your character is very different from the characters other players would have built, and the game you have played is very different from what it would have been had you built your character differently initially and throughout the game.

THREE IDENTITIES:
VIRTUAL, REAL, AND PROJECTIVE

A game like *Arcanum* involves playing with identities in very interesting and important ways. When one plays *Arcanum*, and role-playing games like it, three different identities are at stake. All are aspects of the relationship: "A real person (here James Paul Gee) as a virtual character (here Bead Bead)." They operate all together, at once, as a larger whole.

First, there is a *virtual* identity: one's identity as a virtual character in the virtual world of Arcanum—in my case the Half-Elf Bead Bead. I will represent this identity as "James Paul Gee as *Bead Bead*," where Bead Bead is italicized to indicate that, in this identity, the stress is on the virtual character Bead Bead acting in the virtual world of Arcanum (though I am "playing/developing" her).

In the virtual world of Arcanum, given the sort of creature Bead Bead is (a female Half-Elf) and how I have developed her thus far, there are, at any point, things she can do and things she cannot do. For example, at a certain place in the game, Bead Bead wants to persuade a town meeting to fund the building of a monument to please the town's mayor. To do this, she needs to be intelligent and persuasive. Half-Elves are, by nature, pretty intelligent, and I had built up Bead Bead to be persuasive during the game (i.e., given her points in this area). Thus, she was able to pull off the task at the town meeting (something I very much doubt a Half-Orc could have done, though Half-Orcs have other talents). These traits (her intelligence and persuasive skills) and her accomplishment at the town meeting—for which she received ample praise—are part of my virtual identity as Bead Bead.

The successes and failures of the virtual being Bead Bead (me in my virtual identity) are a delicious blend of my doing and not my doing. After all, I made Bead Bead and developed her, so I deserve—partly, at least—praise for her successes and blame for her failures. Yet Bead Bead is who she is—a female Half-Elf—and must move through the world of Arcanum and be formed, in part, by it, a world I did not create. Thus I am, in this sense, not responsible for her successes or her failures. I suppose this is how many a parent feels about his or her child, save that in this case, I (James Paul Gee) am my own child (Bead Bead).

A second identity that is at stake in playing a game like *Arcanum* is a *real-world identity:* namely, my own identity as "James Paul Gee," a nonvirtual person playing a computer game. I will represent this identity as "*James Paul Gee* as Bead Bead," where James Paul Gee is italicized to indicate that, in this identity, the stress is on the real-world character James Paul Gee playing *Arcanum* as a game in real time (though Bead Bead is the tool through which I operate the game).

Of course, in the real world I have a good many different nonvirtual identities. I am a professor, a linguist, an Anglo American, a middle-age male baby boomer, a parent, an avid reader, a middle-class person initially raised outside the middle class, a former devout Catholic, a lover of movies, and so on through a great many other identities (most of which need not be mentioned here). Of course, these identities become relevant only as they affect and are filtered through my identity as a video-game player playing *Arcanum*. And, indeed, any one of my real-world identities can be so engaged whenever I am playing *Arcanum*. Which of these identities, for instance, was at play—positively or negatively—when I got such joy at having Bead Bead pick rich people's pockets? When I chose to be a female Half-Elf in the first place? When I chose to use my points to make her as strong and good as a male at melee fighting with a sword?

A third identity that is at stake in playing a game like *Arcanum* is what I will call a *projective identity*, playing on two senses of the word "project," meaning both "to project one's values and desires onto the virtual character" (Bead Bead, in this case) and "seeing the virtual character as one's own project in the making, a creature whom I imbue with a certain trajectory through time defined by my aspirations for what I want that character to be and become (within the limitations of her capacities, of course)." This is the hardest identity to describe but the most important one for understanding the power of games like *Arcanum*. I will represent this identity as "James Paul Gee *as* Bead Bead," where the word "as" is italicized to indicate that, in this identity, the stress is on the interface between—the interactions between—the real-world person and the virtual character.

A game like *Arcanum* allows me, the player, certain degrees of freedom (choices) in forming my virtual character and developing her throughout the game. In my projective identity I worry about what sort of "person" I want her to be, what type of history I want her to have had by the time I am done playing the game. I want this person and history to reflect my values, though I have to think reflectively and critically about them, since I have never had to project a Half-Elf onto the world before. But this person and history also reflect what I have learned from playing the game and being Bead Bead in the land of Arcanum. A good role-playing video game makes me think new thoughts about what I value and what I do not.

I, the real-world person, James Paul Gee, a creature with multiple identities, face the fact that I am fixed in certain ways. Though I am, like all human beings, ever changing, at the moment I am who I am (I wish I had more hair, but I don't; I wish I was thinner, but I am not; I wish I was a better game player, but I am not). At least for the moment, I must live with my limitations. Bead Bead, my virtual alter-ego, is a creature who is, at any moment in the game, also fixed in certain ways—she is skilled in certain areas, not others (e.g., while she was pretty good at picking pockets, she was lousy at picking locks). At least for the given moment in the game, I/she must live with her limitations.

The kind of person I want Bead Bead to be, the kind of history I want her to have, the kind of person and history I am trying to build in and through her is what I mean by a projective identity. Since these aspirations are *my* desires for Bead Bead, the projective identity is both mine and hers, and it is a space in which I can transcend both her limitations and my own.

To see more clearly what I mean by a projective identity and how it differs from the virtual identity of being Bead Bead and the real-world identity of being James Paul Gee (however myriad a thing that is), consider that each of the three identities I am talking about can fail (or, for that matter, succeed) in different sorts of ways.

The virtual character Bead Bead (my alter-ego) can fail to defeat another character in battle because, as a Half-Elf, at that point in the game, she just is not strong enough to win. This is a limitation I have to live with if I want to be Bead Bead. Of course, I can mediate on what it feels like—in my role as Bead Bead—to be unable to get what I need or want at a certain point because I am physically too powerless to get it.

The real-world person (James Paul Gee) can fail to use the game controls in an effective way, thereby causing Bead Bead to lose a fight against a weaker creature she could have otherwise beaten; he can fail to save the game at a good time and place (e.g., saving in the middle of a battle that cannot be won is a bad move); he can fail to find his (Bead Bead's) way in a maze because he has poor spatial abilities (a trait Bead Bead therefore inherits). He can even realize that his former Catholic inhibitions will not let Bead Bead take up a madam's offer of a free trip to her (female) brothel. (This is just an example: there is such a brothel in Arcanum, but my former Catholic inhibitions, very real in the real world, did not, in fact, deny Bead Bead a well-deserved night of forbidden pleasure, though, it turns out, she fainted in the middle of things.)

These are limitations in the real-world me as a game player (an identity intersected by a good many other identities), limitations I have to live with if I want to play and eventually get better at games. One sort of limitation video games certainly bring up to real-world baby boomers like me is that they do not reward—in fact, they punish—some of my most cherished ways of learning and thinking (e.g., being too quick to want to get to a goal without engaging in sufficient prior nonlinear exploration).

The projective identity of Bead Bead as a project (mine) in the making can fail because I (the real-world James Paul Gee) have caused Bead Bead (the virtual me) to do something in the game that the character I want Bead Bead to be would not or should not do. For example, on my first try at the game, early on I had Bead Bead sell the ring the old man had given her. This is not a mistake at playing the game (thus not a failure of the real me to play the game properly). It's a move allowed by the internal design grammar of the game and one for which I would have suffered no bad consequences in the game world. It is also not something that Half-Elves can't do or are, for that matter, necessarily too principled or ungreedy to want to do. Thus it is not necessarily a violation of Bead Bead as a virtual identity.

However, the act just seemed *wrong* for the creature I wanted Bead Bead to be (or to have become, however partially, by the end of the game). I felt when I (Bead Bead) had sold the ring that I was forming a history for Bead Bead that was not the one she should have. I wanted her to be a creature who acted more intelligently and more cautiously, a creature who could eventually look back on the history of her acts without regret. I felt I had "let her down" and started the game all over again. Thus, in my projective identity—Bead Bead as my project—I am attributing feelings and motives to Bead Bead that go beyond the confines of the game world and enter the realm of a world of my own creation.

It is not uncommon, even when young people are playing first-person shooter games featuring a superhuman hero (like Master Chief in *Halo*, a game for the Xbox)—a character that, unlike Bead Bead, they usually cannot choose or develop but must take as is—that they will redo a given fight scene because they feel they have "let their character down." They want to pull off the victory more spectacularly as befits a superhero. They feel responsible to and for the character. They are projecting an identity as to who the character ought to be and what the trajectory of his or her acts in the virtual world ought, at the end of the day, to look like.

Likewise, while some young people will let a superhero first-person shooter character kill "civilians" and not just enemies, a good many others will not, since they feel that it just isn't fitting for such a superperson—that is, the person they are projecting into the world—to do such a thing. In fact, I once had remorse when I let/made Bead Bead kill a pesky chicken, an action for which she was also suitably castigated by the self-righteous follower I mentioned earlier. Players are projecting an identity onto their virtual character based both on their own values and on what the game has taught them about what such a character should or might be and become.

This tripartite play of identities (a virtual identity, a real-world identity, and a projective identity) in the relationship "player as virtual character" is quite powerful. It transcends identification with characters in novels or movies, for instance, because it is both *active* (the player actively does things) and *reflexive*, in the sense that once the player has made some choices about the virtual character, the virtual character is now developed in a way that sets certain parameters about what the player can do. The virtual character redounds back on the player and affects his or her future actions.

As a player, I was proud of Bead Bead at the end of the game in a way in which I have never been proud of a character in a novel or movie, however much I had identified with him or her. I can identify with the pride characters in a novel or movie must or should feel, given what they have done or how far they have come. But my satisfaction with Bead Bead is tinged with pride (or, it could have been regret had things turned out differently), at various levels, in and with myself. This feeling is not (just) selfish. In a sense, it is also selfless, since it is pride at things that have transcended—taken me outside of—my real-world self (selves), if I am playing the game reflectively.

IDENTITY AND LEARNING

The theme of this book is that good video games reflect, in their design, good principles of learning. We turn directly to some of these principles in the next section and in following chapters. Now I want to discuss how and why the sort of play with identities at work in *Arcanum* is relevant to learning outside video games.

A game like *Arcanum* is powerfully caught up with playing with identities. However, all deep learning—that is, active, critical learning—is inextricably caught up with identity in a variety of different ways. People cannot learn in a deep way within a semiotic domain if they are not willing to commit themselves fully to the learning in terms of time, effort, and active engagement. Such a commitment requires that they are willing to see themselves in terms of a new identity, that is, to see themselves as the *kind of person* who can learn, use, and value the new semiotic domain. In turn, they need to believe that, if they are successful learners in the domain, they will be valued and accepted by others committed to that domain—that is, by people in the affinity group associated with the domain.

It has been argued that some poor urban African-American children and teenagers resist learning literacy in school because they see school-based literacy as "white," as associated with people who disregard them and others like them. They don't believe that a society that they view as racist will ever allow them to gain a good job, status, and power, even if they do succeed at school-based literacy. Thus they will not envisage themselves in the new identity that success in school-based literacy requires—that is, as the "kind of person" who learns, values, and uses such literacy and gets valued and respected for doing so. Without such an identity commitment, no deep learning can occur. The students will not invest the time, effort, and personally committed engagement that active, critical learning requires. In fact, they resist learning in school in the name of another identity that they see such learning as putting at risk.

The tripartite play of identities that a game like *Arcanum* recruits is at the root of active and critical learning in many other semiotic domains, including learning content actively and critically in school. Let's take good school science learning as an example.

First, let's consider *virtual identities*. In a good science classroom, a virtual identity is at stake. Learners need to be able to engage in words, interactions, and actions that allow them to take on the identity of a "scientist." But what does this mean? There are many different sciences and types of scientists. The teacher must put into motion, in his or her classroom, a set of values, beliefs, and ways with words, deeds, and interactions that represent, for the teacher and the students, what it means to be a particular kind of scientist in this class-room. Doing this means taking up a specific viewpoint on a specific branch of science as a set of cognitive and social practices. Of course, the students are not "real" scientists and are not going to become real scientists any time soon. What is being created here is a virtual identity ("student as *scientist*").

As I did with Bead Bead in *Arcanum*, learners in a science classroom should see the virtual identity (being a particular type of scientist) as partly fixed by the history and workings of the (scientific) semiotic domain being learned and partly open to some choices (compatible, of course, with the domain) that they themselves get to make about this virtual identity. For example, in one fourth-grade classroom in which I have worked, the children did experiments on fast-growing plants, mentored, in part, by the scientist who actually invented such plants (a man with strong views about how scientists ought to think, value, and act) as well as by their teacher (a teacher with strong views about how she wants her students to think, value, and act when they are learning science). In this classroom, the children were expected to act, interact, and use language in ways that were recognizable, in terms of the norms set up in this classroom, as scien-tists doing science. However, the children could also choose a particular style of carrying out their virtual identities as scientists.

For example, the children chose what questions they wanted to ask and what sort of experiments they wanted to carry out to help answer those ques-tions. Some worked in closer collaborations with other children than others did. Some studied texts more thoroughly before experimentation, some more thoroughly afterward. Some experimented to check on the results of previous experiments they found suspicious; others chose to try something for the first time. Some used African American Vernacular English phonology, some did not, though they all used the lexicon and syntax of scientific language about plants when they needed to, which was an important norm in the classroom.

Second, let's consider *real-world identities*. In good science classrooms, the learners' real-world identities are involved ("*learner* as scientist"). All learners in a science classroom bring to that room their real-world identities. As was the case with me playing *Arcanum*, each learner has multiple real-world identities: A given child might be middle-class, male, African American, a Pokemon fanatic, adept at rap music, and have a good many other identities as well. But, too, like me playing *Arcanum*, where these multiple identities are all filtered through my identity as a game player, the multiple real-world identities of learners in a science classroom are filtered through their real-world identities as a learner, a school learner, and a school science learner learning science here and now.

If a child brings to science learning a real-world identity as a learner, a school learner, or a school science learner who is already damaged—and a good many children do—then this identity needs to be repaired before any active, critical learning can occur here and now. Imagine how successful you would be learning to play *Arcanum* if you started with the assumption that you are a failure at learning to play video games and role-playing games in particular. This, in fact, is what has happened to me when I tried to learn real-time strategy games (e.g., *Age of Empires*, *Star Wars: Galactic Battle-grounds*, or *WarCraft III*). I am intimated by anything that is a race against time, and so, thus far, I have been a failure at playing real-time strategy games well and with enjoyment. Some repair work needs to be done.

Furthermore, if children cannot or will not make bridges between one or more of their real-world identities and the virtual identity at stake in the classroom (here, a particular type of scientist)—or if teachers or others destroy or don't help build such bridges—then, once again, learning is imperiled. Children who, for instance, see themselves as members of families that are adept at technical learning have an advantage, since they can build a powerful bridge between one of their real-world identities ("people like us learn technical stuff well—it's no big deal") and the virtual identity at stake in the science classroom ("scientists in the sort of semiotic domain being created in this classroom do not fear or put off technical learning"). If a child cannot or will not build such bridges, then, again, repair works needs to be done.

But how can such repair work be done? It is no easy matter. In fact, often this is what good teaching, especially in socially and culturally diverse classrooms, amounts to. However, good repair work is just a more intense version of good teaching and learning for all types of students, including those who have no need of any particular repair work.

Such teaching and learning is, in my view, a matter of three things:

1. The learner must be enticed to *try*, even if he or she already has good grounds to be afraid to try.

2. The learner must be enticed to *put in lots of effort* even if he or she begins with little motivation to do so.

3. The learner must *achieve some meaningful success* when he or she has expended this effort.

There are three principles here because people will not put in effort if they are not even willing to try in a domain; success without effort is not rewarding; and effort with little success is equally unrewarding.

These three things seem pretty basic. Nonetheless, they are left out of most of the current debates about education, which tend not to engage with issues about the identities learners bring to school and how these identities relate to motivation and effort (or their lack) in relation to specific sorts of pedagogies.

Video games are particularly good at these three things, at least for some types of learners. For instance, when I started playing video games, I certainly brought a fearful and damaged identity as a game player to the task. I had never been good at such things in the past, and my identical twin brother always beat me when we played the early video games. And I felt too old now to have any success. Furthermore, initially I could not conceive of which of my multiple real-world identities could possibly serve as bridge to the sorts of virtual worlds and identities video games set up (e.g., blasting Aliens—I've always liked Aliens).

What enticed me to try in the first place, then? Well, I watched my son play video games, starting with *Winnie the Pooh*, moving on to *Pajama Sam*, *Freddy Fish*, *Putt-Putt*, and *Spy Fox*. I played some of the games myself ("just to help him"). I tried a more adult game, one I picked "randomly" at the store, the little-known game *The New Adventures of the Time Machine*. Of course, its tie to literature (H. G. Wells's book *The Time Machine*) piqued my interest and made playing a video game seem more acceptable, in terms of some of my real-world identities. My engagement with games through my child taught me there was some level at which I could enter this semiotic domain in which I could achieve enough initial success to keep on practicing and getting better. To repair damaged learners in any domain, there must be some such story, though the stories will be as various as the learners.

Even more important, I learned that video games create what the psychologist Eric Erickson has called a *psychosocial moratorium*—that is, a learning space in which the learner can take risks where real-world consequences are lowered.

After all, you can save the game and start back at the save point when you fail. Often you can customize the game to a level of difficulty you can cope with initially. And, of course, you can choose the game you want to play. Although you have to put out a good deal of effort to play any good video game, there is a relatively low cost of failure and high reward for success. None of this is to say that it does not bother or even frustrate players when they die or do not play part of a game well. It does indeed. Of course they care about how well they do—but the cost of caring is not prohibitive, as it so often is in school.

What made me, once I was enticed to try, willing to put in lots of effort and practice with video games? When you have chosen a video game well, the virtual world it allows you to live in is quite compelling. I found the virtual world of *The New Adventures of the Time Machine* simply amazing. I particularly liked how, when a certain wave of light went through the world, all adult characters in the game changed to their child selves and all children changed to their adult selves, so that sometimes the virtual character you are playing, Brendan Wales, is a boy, sometimes a man. What makes a game compelling to me might not make it so to you. Indeed, what made a game compelling to me when I started to play is not what makes a game compelling to me now. But if the virtual world and virtual identity at stake in learning is not compelling to the learner, at some level, then little deep learning is liable to occur, in part because the learner is going to be unwilling to put in the effort and practice demanded for mastering the domain.

What made *The New Adventures of the Time Machine* compelling to me was initially the way in which I could bridge some of my real-world identities to the virtual character I played in the game and the virtual world in which he/I moved. For example, there were the ties to literature (books); academics (Wales is a scientist); problem solving (another tie, at least initially, to my academic identity); a medieval but futuristic world (I once lived for real in the medieval world, though we don't need to pursue the matter further here); and fantasy worlds (I have always been a willing escapee from reality, which is why I have always loved movies and have nothing against Ivory Towers).

Once these ties had drawn me into the game and made me put in lots of effort, it would have been disappointing in the extreme to experience no success. However, it would have been equally disappointing to get the sorts of rewards that much better players get. This would have made me believe the domain was not very deep and rich. So how does one build in success for effort, success that is earned, not given away, but nonetheless ensured, given the effort?

Good computer games are designed so that they adjust to different levels of play and reward each sort of player, if the player is putting in effort, with some appropriate degree of success. For example, in a shooter game, after much exploration, I may uncover a spiffy rifle that I am just thrilled with, since it is so much better than the crowbar I have been using to fend off enemies, while you, much better at the game than I, may have found a tank.

Of course, video games offer players a feeling of achievement in a number of different ways. First of all, they operate according to a very powerful learning principle, a principle we can call the "amplification of input principle." When systems operate according to this principle, they give, for a little input, a lot of output. (Driving a car is a good example: You press a little pedal and off you zoom.) In a video game, you press some buttons in the real world and a whole interactive virtual world comes to life. Amplification of input is highly motivating for learning.

By the way, in the real world, science often operates by the amplification of input principle. In a chemistry experiment, you mix a few chemicals and make a major discovery, cure cancer, or blow up the lab. Think, too, of the monk Mendel and his peas: He putters (in the right way) in the garden and unlocks the key to the origins and development of species on earth. Think even of Newton's laws of motion: Such simple and elegant principles cover so much ground and give so much insight into so many things that one is simply amazed. None of this is to say that great effort is not required. Mendel worked for years (and, by the way, failed his exam to become a high school biology teacher, which was why he was stuck in the garden). It is just to say that there is something very satisfying when what one actually does seems so small compared to what one gets. It's like a miracle.

Video games also offer other rewards than the powerfully amplified outputs they give. When I was enticed to put in effort on *The New Adventures of the Time Machine*, new compelling elements quickly arose, beyond those connected to my real-world identities and the amplification of input I experienced. I discovered that this game, like many other good video games, encourages new ways of learning and thinking for an old baby boomer like me. I discovered new powers in myself. I felt the dawning of a new identity growing, one to be added to my other real-world identities. Of course this is true of all good learning—we gain a new valued identity that gives us new powers; it's the final hook where the repair work is finally done.

This discussion suggests that good science instruction—or good instruction in any content area—must accomplish the same three goals. The learner must be enticed to try. This is done through building bridges to his or her real-world identities and by creating a psychosocial moratorium.

The learner must be enticed to put in lots of effort. This is done by making the virtual world and virtual identity (e.g., being/doing a particular type of scientists in the classroom) at stake in the learning compelling to the learner on his or her own terms. The learner needs to be sucked in.

And, finally, this effort must issue in success at an appropriate level, customized to the learner's stage of development in the semiotic domain being learned. Success for effort at different levels needs to be built in, letting learners know all the while that there will be yet greater successes for yet greater effort. Amplification of input needs to be designed into the teaching and learning. And to ensure the deepest sort of success, the virtual world needs to be built in such a way that learners discover new powers and feel the dawning of new valued identities.

Let us turn to *projective identities* ("the learner *as* scientist"). If learners are to take on projective identities in the science classroom, they must come to project their own values and desires onto the virtual identity of "being a scientist of a certain sort" in this classroom. They also must come to see this virtual identity as their own project in the making, an identity they take on that entails a certain trajectory through time defined by their own values, desires, choices, goals, and actions. This is what creates ownership.

When learners take on a projective identity, they want the scientist they are "playing" to be a certain sort of person and to have had a certain sort of history in the learning trajectory of this classroom. They have aspirations for this scientist, just as I had aspirations for Bead Bead when I played *Arcanum*. Perhaps they want their scientist to have had a history of having been persistent, resilient in the face of failure, collaborative, risk taking, skeptical, and creative. They want their scientist to become this sort of person, whether or not they are themselves anything like this in their "everyday" lives. In good science learning, learners are not just role-playing being a scientist of a certain sort (their virtual identity). They are also proactively building that virtual person as a certain kind of person with a certain kind of history. They are projecting their own hopes and desires onto that person.

The learner's hopes, values, and aspirations for the "character" (the virtual scientist)—and the project the learner makes of that character, the history he or she builds for that character—have their source not just in the learner's real-world identities, though they most certainly partially have their source there as the learner reflects on his or her values, desires, aspirations, and goals. They also have their source in what the learner is learning about the virtual identity and the virtual world (what it means to be a scientist in this classroom). Remember that the projective identity is the interface between one's real-world identities and the virtual identity (e.g., between the real me and the virtual Bead Bead). The projective identity is the space in which the learner can transcend the limitations both of the virtual identity and the learner's own real-world identity.

If learners in classrooms carry learning so far as to take on a projective identity, something magic happens—a magic that cannot take place in quite the same way when playing a video game. The learner comes to know that he or she has the *capacity*, at some level, to take on the virtual identity as a real world identity. However much I might want to do, I myself, in the real world, have no capacity to become the sort of female Half-Elf I wanted and built Bead Bead to be (though I can still adopt some of her persona). But learners in a good science classroom come to feel what it is like to have the capacity to be the sort of scientist (and person) they have wanted and built their "character" in the classroom to be.

Learners do not, of course, have to realize this capacity in actuality and become scientists. They don't even have to feel they could become particularly good scientists—after all, in the projective identity you also learn about your own limitations. Often it is enough that they have sensed new powers in themselves. They will, possibly for a lifetime, be able to empathize with, affiliate with, learn more about, and even critique science as a valued but vulnerable human enterprise.

This is why it is important for teachers to pick the semiotic domains they will teach—and the particular virtual identities and worlds they will create in their classrooms—carefully. If children are learning deeply, they will learn, through their projective identities, new values and new ways of being in the world based on the powerful juxtaposition of their real-world identities ("So, that's what I really feel, think, and value") and the virtual identity at stake in the learning ("So, these are the ways of feeling, thinking, and valuing open to a scientist"). This juxtaposition is the ground on which their projective work has been done. ("So, I want, for this time and place, to have been *this* type of scientist and person and not *that* type.")

LEARNING PRINCIPLES

The discussion has suggested more learning principles that are built into good video games. In this section, I bring these together to continue the list started in chapter 2. After listing principles we have already discussed, I discuss a few others that are related to them:

6. **"Psychosocial Moratorium" Principle**
   Learners can take risks in a space where real-world consequences are lowered.

7. **Committed Learning Principle**
   Learners participate in an extended engagement (lots of effort and practice) as extensions of their real-world identities in relation to a virtual identity to which they feel some commitment and a virtual world that they find compelling.

8. **Identity Principle**
   Learning involves taking on and playing with identities in such a way that the learner has real choices (in developing the virtual identity) and ample opportunity to meditate on the relationship between new identities and old ones. There is a tripartite play of identities as learners relate, and reflect on, their multiple real-world identities, a virtual identity, and a projective identity.

9. **Self-Knowledge Principle**
   The virtual world is constructed in such a way that learners learn not only about the domain but about themselves and their current and potential capacities.

10. **Amplification of Input Principle**
    For a little input, learners get a lot of output.

11. **Achievement Principle**
    For learners of all levels of skill there are intrinsic rewards from the beginning, customized to each learner's level, effort, and growing mastery and signaling the learner's ongoing achievements.

Because good video games are built in such a way that they operate by these learning principles, several other principles also come into play. One thing that designers of video games realize, but that many schools seem not to, is that learning for human beings is, in large part, *a practice effect*.

Humans need to practice what they are learning a good deal before they master it. Furthermore, they tend to lose a good deal of their learning—including school learning—when they cease to practice the skills associated with this learning in their daily lives. This is why it is easy to discover many adults who are no longer very good with school-based science, math, or literacy if they do not, in their work or home lives, practice these on a regular basis.

The fact that human learning is a practice effect can create a good deal of difficulty for learning in school. Children cannot learn in a deep way if they have no opportunities to practice what they are learning. They cannot learn deeply only by being told things outside the context of embodied actions. Yet at the same time, children must be motivated to engage in a good deal of practice if they are to master what is to be learned. However, if this practice is boring, they will resist it.

Good video games involve the player in a compelling world of action and interaction, a world to which the learner has made an identity commitment, in the sense of engaging in the sort of play with identities we have discussed. Thanks to this fact, the player practices a myriad of skills, over and over again, relevant to playing the game, often without realizing that he or she is engaging in such extended practice sessions. For example, the six-year-old we discussed in the last chapter has grouped and regrouped his Pikmin a thousand times. And I have practiced, in the midst of battle, switching Bead Bead to a magic spell and away from her sword in a timely fashion a good many times. The player's sights are set on his or her aspirations and goals in the virtual world of the game, not on the level of practicing skills outside meaningful, goal-driven contexts.

Educators often bemoan the fact that video games are compelling and school is not. They say that children must learn to practice skills ("skill and drill") outside of meaningful contexts and outside their own goals: It's too bad, but that's just the way school and, indeed, life *is*, they claim. Unfortunately, if human learning works best in a certain way, given the sorts of biological creatures we are, then it is not going to work well in another way just because educators, policymakers, and politicians want it to.

The fact is that there are some children who learn well in skill-and-drill contexts. However, in my experience, these children *do* find this sort of instruction meaningful and compelling, usually because they trust that it will lead them to accomplish their goals and have success later in life. In turn, they believe this thanks to their trust in various authority figures around them (family and teachers) who have told them this. Other children have no such trust. Nor do I.

In any case, I have already made my own position clear: Passive learning—rather than active, critical learning—will not lead to much power and empowerment in the contemporary world, however much it may suit one for a low-level service job. Mastering literacy or math as a set of routinized procedures without being able to use these procedures proactively within activities that one understands and for the accomplishment of one's own goals will not lead to learners who can learn quickly and well as they face new semiotic domains, as they will throughout their lives.

Learning how to operate the controls of a computer game outside any understanding of the meaningful activities the controls are used to accomplish in the virtual world of the game and outside one's own goals in that world leads, in a shooter game or a realistic military game, for example, to a quick demise (and, thus, not all that much practice, save at dying again and again). In my view, the same is true—metaphorically speaking—in school.

The achievement principle above (Principle 11) tells us that good video games reward all players who put in effort but reward players at different skill levels differently. But there is more to this matter: Good video games give players better and deeper rewards as (and if) they continue to learn new things as they play (or replay) the game. This means that, in a good video game, the distinction between learner and master is vague (at whatever level of mastery one thinks one has arrived). If players have just routinized their behaviors (i.e., if they operate on "automatic pilot" and keep reacting to problems in the same now well-practiced way), a level of the game will be reached at which the game will realize this and disreward these behaviors. This fact forces players to think about the routinized mastery they have achieved and to undo this routinization to achieve a new and higher level of skill. This higher level of skill will itself, thanks to the large amount of practice that video games allow, become routinized (automatic) as the player perfects it, only to be undone later in the game, or in the same game played a second time at a higher level of difficulty, or in a new game.

Several educators have argued that this cycle of automatization of skills through practice, rethinking this automatization when faced with new conditions in order to learn new skills and transform old ones, and then perfecting these new skills through further practice that once again leads to automatization is the very foundation of intelligent practice in the world. Automatization is good and necessary if one is to engage in fluent and masterful practice. However, it gets in the way of new learning if it does not change and adapt in the face of novel conditions and new opportunities to learn, which requires the learner to bring back to conscious awareness skills that have become unconscious and taken for granted and to think anew about these skills and how they relate to specific sorts of problems. A cycle of automatization, adaptation, new learning, and new automatization is a sine qua non of learning for those who want to survive as active thinkers and actors in a fast changing world that requires the mastery of ever newer semiotic domains. Video games are quite adept at creating and sustaining this cycle.

Finally, all the design features discussed so far work to ensure that a good video game operates within the learner's "regime of competence." By this I mean that the game often operates within, but at the outer edge of, the learner's resources, so that at many points the game is felt as challenging but not "undoable." If learning always operates well within the learner's resources, then all that happens is that the learner's behaviors get more and more routinized, as the learner continues to experience success by doing the same things. This is good, as we have seen, for learning and practicing fluent and masterful performance (which is, indeed, necessary), but it is not good for developing newer and higher skills. However, if learning operates outside one's resources, the learner is simply frustrated and gives up.

While good video games offer players ample opportunity to practice and even automatize their skills at various levels, they also always build in many opportunities for learners to operate at the outer edge of their regime of competence, thereby causing them to rethink their routinized mastery and move, within the game and within themselves, to a new level. Indeed, for many learners it is these times, when they are operating at the edge of their regime of competence, when learning is most exciting and rewarding. Sadly in school, many so-called advantaged learners rarely get to operate at the edge of their regime of competence as they coast along in a curriculum that makes few real demands on them. At the same time, less advantaged learners are repeatedly asked to operate outside their regime of competence.

Additional learning principles follow. These are principles found in good video games, but ones that are hallmarks of deep (active and critical) learning beyond video games as well.

12. **Practice Principle**

Learners get lots and lots of practice in a context where the practice is not boring (i.e., in a virtual world that is compelling to learners on their own terms and where the learners experience ongoing success). They spend lots of time on task.

13. **Ongoing Learning Principle**

The distinction between learner and master is vague, since learners, thanks to the operation of the "regime of competence" principle listed next, must, at higher and higher levels, undo their routinized mastery to adapt to new or changed conditions. There are cycles of new learning, automatization, undoing automatization, and new reorganized automatization.

14. **"Regime of Competence" Principle**

The learner gets ample opportunity to operate within, but at the outer edge of, his or her resources, so that at those points things are felt as challenging but not "undoable."

BIBLIOGRAPHICAL NOTE

There is a massive amount of work on socially situated identities and how they are changing in the modern world. For work compatible with my approach in this chapter, see Alvermann, Moon, & Hagood 1999; Bauman 2000; Beck, Giddens, & Lash 1994; Castells 1996; Foucault 1980; Gee 2000–2001; Gee, Hull, & Lankshear 1996; Giddens 1991, 1992; Hacking 1995, 1998; Martin 1995; Mishler 2000; Rifkin 2000; Sternberg & Grigorenko 1999; Taylor 1989, 1992, 1994. For an early, but brilliant work on socially situated identities, specially relevant to science, see Fleck 1979, originally 1935.

For a discussion of the advantages of many middle- and upper-middle-class students in our schools and the disadvantages of many minority and lower socioeconomic students, see Finn 1999; Gee 1996; Heath 1983; Miller 1995; Varenne & McDermott 1998.

For Erikson's notion of a psychosocial moratorium, see Erikson 1968. Several of the learning principles in this chapter relate closely to principles developed in current accounts of efficacious learning in cognitive science; see, for example, Bransford, Brown, & Cocking 1999 and Pellegrino, Chudowsky, & Glaser 2001. Several of the principles fit very well with Bereiter and Scardamelia's 1989 important discussion of learning and expertise. The importance of gaining and undoing automatization, and its connection to the ongoing learning principle, is well discussed in Bereiter and Scardamelia's book. The practice principle is discussed in sociocultural terms in Scribner and Cole's famous 1981 study. The regime of competence is discussed in diSessa 2000 and is related to Vygotsky's well-known notion of the zone of proximal development; see Vygotsky 1978. diSessa 2000 also discusses amplification of input and contains an extended and important discussion of committed learning.

4

SITUATED MEANING AND LEARNING: WHAT SHOULD YOU DO AFTER YOU HAVE DESTROYED THE GLOBAL CONSPIRACY?

LEARNING AND EXPERIENCE

TRADITIONAL VIEWS OF LEARNING STRESS THE MIND AND NOT THE body. Learning is held to be a matter of grand generalizations, principles, rules, abstractions, and logical computations. This view treats the human mind as if it is pretty much like a digital computer. Digital computers operate by rules that tell them how to manipulate symbols, symbols that have no real meanings to the computer beyond the manipulations the computer carries out on them.

Another view of learning holds that human learning and thinking does not, in fact, always work this way and often does not work this way when humans are thinking at their best. This view holds, rather, that humans learn, think, and solve problems by reflecting on their previous embodied experiences in the world. That is, humans have experiences, store these experiences, and make connections or associations among them.

Of course, humans don't just store these experiences in their minds "as is." Rather, they edit them according to their interests, values, goals, and sociocultural memberships. This editing process helps them structure the ways in which they pay attention to their experiences, foregrounding some things in them and backgrounding others. Furthermore, it is the connections or associations that people make among their experiences that are crucial to learning, thinking, and problem solving.

When people are faced with a new situation in the world, aspects or elements of this situation remind them of aspects or elements of experiences they have had in the past. They use these elements of past experience to think about the new situation. Sometimes they can just apply past experience pretty much as is to the new situation. Other times they have to adapt past experience, more or less, to apply it, in the process learning something new that can, in turn, be applied to future situations.

Let me give you an overly simplified but instructive example of the contrast between learning and thinking as using grand generalizations and learning and thinking as using one's embodied experiences in the world. Let's say that you have experienced in the past a number of white, middle-age, professors who were born outside the middle class but who are now in the middle class. In each case, say, these people displayed a good deal of "class conflict,"—that is, they displayed a certain discomfort with their middle-class identities and associates.

Now consider two ways this information could be stored in your mind. One way would be as verbal generalization, something like:

> (Some? many?) white, middle-age, professors born outside the middle class,
> but now in the middle class, display a good deal of class conflict.

The other way you could store your experiences of such people in your mind is as a set of more or less strong connections or associations among all the elements that compose the experiences. That is, you would associate or connect "being middle age," more or less strongly, with each other element in the experiences, namely, "being a professor," "having been born outside the middle class," "being now middle class," and "displaying a good deal of class conflict." The same is true of all the other elements, each of which must be associated with each other element, more or less strongly. Perhaps you associate "being a professor" strongly with "being middle class"; strongly, but somewhat less strongly, with "being white"; and weakly with "having been born outside the middle class."

You must form such links or associations between any and all of the elements that compose your experiences of these sorts of professors. Doing this makes for complicated diagrams on paper, though the brain realizes such things by forming more or less strong connections among (sets of) neurons in terms of which notions like "being a professor" activate or remind you, more or less strongly, of other notions like "being middle class" or "displaying class conflict." What we are talking about here, in reality, is *patterns* you are discovering in your experiences and storing in your mind.

Now consider what happens when you are faced with an African American, middle-age, professor who was born outside the middle class but who is now in the middle class. What do you conclude? If your mind has stored the verbal generalization above, you conclude nothing, since this person, being African American, does not fall under the generalization, which was, after all, about white professors. A digital computer that has stored this generalization as a set of symbols, confronted with the symbol "African American," will simply not apply the generalization.

On the other hand, if you have stored the sorts of associations or links between elements of your experiences just discussed, then, many of the features or elements of this person's situation will activate or remind you of those associations. For example, the fact that this African American is a professor but was born outside the middle class will bring to mind the likelihood that he or she will display a good deal of class conflict. This is so because your mind associates (fairly strongly) the combination of being a professor and having been born outside the middle class with displaying class conflict. While you may also associate being a professor with "being white," you do not use this association, since in this case you know the person is not white. You suppress it and go with the others that lead you to predict you might find this person displaying some degree of class conflict.

Of course, you might turn out to be wrong. Perhaps this African American professor is quite comfortable with his or her middle-class status. But one has to make guesses and hypotheses to think, act, and problem-solve in the world at all. All the cavepeople who stored the generalization "Tigers are dangerous" and refused to apply it to even the first lion they saw probably died without many offspring. The ones who let the many features lions share with tigers trigger the association between these elements and danger passed on a great many more genes.

If you turn out to be wrong, you will, perhaps, store a negative association between "being African American" and "class conflict" and strengthen your associations between "white" and "class conflict." You will adjust a number of other associations, as well, though all rather tentatively, since so far you have only one case to go on. If you experience many other cases of content middle-class African American professors born outside the middle class, eventually you will revise your associations more confidently.

I pointed out that the view of the mind and learning that favors rules, abstractions, and generalizations is connected to the digital computer as a metaphor for how human thinking and learning work. The view of the mind and learning that favors associations among the elements of our actual (and vicarious) embodied experiences is itself connected to another sort of computer: a so-called connectionist or parallel distributed network computer.

One of several sources of rich evidence that human thinking is deeply rooted in embodied experience of the world comes from studies of human languages. In all human languages, very often abstract notions are encoded in words and phrases that constitute metaphors based in concrete, embodied experience of a material world. For example, consider how we talk about the mind and thinking. We say things like "Why can't you *get* *this* *into* your head," "Keep this *in mind*," or "I can't get the idea *out of* my head." In all the cases we treat the mind as a container that things can go in and out of.

For another example, consider how we talk about argumentation. We say things like "He *destroyed* your point," "She *defended* her own perspective," "She *marshaled* her arguments," or "You need to *challenge* his basic premises," where we treat argumentation as a form of fighting or combat. Or, for a final example, note how we talk about consciousness: "He *came back* to consciousness," "He *lost* consciousness," "He *went* unconscious," or "Try to bring the experience *back to* conscious awareness;" here we treat consciousness as a sort of place we can come to and leave.

There are, of course, a great many more such examples. The argument is that just as language builds abstractions on the basis of concrete images from embodied experience of a material world, so, too, does human learning and thinking. One good way to make people look stupid is to ask them to learn and think in terms of words and abstractions that they cannot connect in any useful way to images or situations in their embodied experiences in the world. Unfortunately, we regularly do this in schools.

In this chapter I discuss the ways in which video games encourage and recruit situated, experiential, and embodied forms of learning and thinking. In this respect good video games incorporate quite good perspectives on how learning, thinking, and problem solving work in the world and should work in schools. I base my discussion, for concreteness, around a particular game, the game *Deus Ex*.

DEUS EX

Deus Ex combines two different genres. It is a first-person shooter in which you fight a variety of enemies from a first-person perspective. It is also a role-playing game in which, like *Arcanum*, you have choices about how to build and develop your character. Before you start playing the game, you choose the name and look of your character. (Your character can be black or white, for instance.) Whatever real name you choose, your character's code name is "J. C. Denton." J. C. is a covert special operative for UNATCO, the United Nations Anti-Terrorist Coalition. Note that this game came out well before the events of September 11, 2001. In fact, the game raises interesting issues about who is and who is not a "terrorist" and under what circumstances.

J. C. Denton is not fully human. He and his brother, Paul, have been "augmented" via a technology that allows them to leverage advanced abilities through the use of "nanite organisms" placed in their blood. Nanites are robots so tiny that they can fit inside individual cells. (They have been said to be the future of robotics, tiny devices that could be used for things like cleaning out clogged arteries or performing other sorts of surgery inside the body—however, I have no idea how far such technology has gone, or will go, in the "real" world.) In this case, nanites have been injected into J. C. Denton's body. This gives him (you) the capacity to gain superhuman powers of various sorts in the game world.

After choosing a real name and look for J. C. Denton, you get a certain number of points with which you can increase his (your) skills. There are 11 skills (computers, electronics, environmental training, lock picking, medicine, swimming, and skills with weapons of different types, including demolition devices, heavy weapons, low-tech weapons, pistols, and rifles). Each of these skills has four levels of mastery (Untrained, Trained, Advanced, and Master). You begin the game with each skill at Untrained Level, except for skill with pistols, which begins at Trained Level. You use your initial points to increase J. C.'s (your) training level in some of the other areas, though you only have enough initial points to increase a few skills a bit. As you play the game, you earn additional points with which you can further increase J. C.'s (your) skills.

Enhancing certain skills and not others, at the beginning and throughout the game, directly affects how you play. For example, if you are at the Expert Level as a lock picker, then you can easily get into places you wouldn't be able to get into otherwise, unless you have found a key. If your Demolition Weapons skills are no good, then you are quite likely to die if you try to disarm a bomb. If your Computer skills are good, you can hack more easily into the myriad of computational devices you find in the world of *Deus Ex*; otherwise you have to gain such information through other sources, if you can.

When I played the game, toward the end, at a point where I knew I was about to face a great many powerful robots and other enemies, I found a very large gun in a dark corner of a military base, quite suitable for blowing robots off the face of the earth. Alas, I did not have any great skill at Heavy Weapons, so stealth and more subtle fighting strategies were the order of the day. (Truth be told, I used the experience points I gained using these more subtle strategies to increase my Heavy Weapons training, went back and got the gun, and had great fun blasting robots with a single shot.)

But choosing J. C.'s skill levels is not the only way in which you can develop him. As I said above, he is "nano-augmented." In fact, he has slots for nano-augmentations distributed around his body. You begin the game with three nano-augmentations already installed: an Infolink that allows J. C. to receive real-time neural communications from commanders and allies; an IFF (Identification: Friend or Foe) system that analyzes people and tells J. C. whether they are hostile or not; and a Light that runs off J. C.'s own biological system.

You can fill the unfilled slots as you find special augmentation canisters in the game world. Canisters contain blueprints for two special abilities, such as having the strength to lift a truck or the ability to see through concrete walls. When you install a canister into the appropriate slot on J. C.'s body, thereby releasing its nanite organisms into his bloodstream, you must choose one, and only one, of the two special abilities associated with that particular canister. Once you fill a slot, that augmentation is permanently installed, and the second option is gone forever. So you must choose wisely. The augmentations you select greatly affect how you (J. C. Denton) develop in the game world and what strategies will be most advantageous against different foes and challenges. You can also find upgrade canisters that allow you to upgrade any augmentations you have already installed, thereby making them stronger or more efficient.

Besides developing J. C.'s skills and nano-augmentations, there are other ways in which the player's decisions affect how the game will unfold. In your role as J. C. Denton, you have conversations with a number of other characters. You can choose different things to say and different ways to respond. How you have carried out a conversation with a given character will affect what that character thinks of you, how he or she reacts to you, and what he or she will later do or not do for or against you. Furthermore, you face other sorts of consequential choices in the world of *Deus Ex*, and how you make such choices affects what happens later in the game.

When you start the game, you enter a futuristic world that has fallen on hard times. Crime, terrorism, and disease are out of all control. No single government or agency can react fast or efficiently enough to control the worldwide devastation. In particular, a horrible plague, known as the Grey Death, is sweeping through cities and countries around the world over, killing millions. There is only one known cure for the disease, a vaccine called Ambrosia, a product that is in short supply and manufactured by the U.S. corporation VersaLife.

One of UNATCO's duties is to administer this cure for the Grey Death. However, the general public does not know that the cure exists. It is kept a secret and given only to politicians, dignitaries, and billionaires to ensure that the world's economy does not crash. Or so the rich and powerful claim. Nothing is ever as it seems at first in *Deus Ex*.

J. C. Denton's first mission takes place on Liberty Island, New York, site of the Statue of Liberty. Inside the statue, a terrorist group knows as the NSF is holding an UNATCO agent hostage. J. C. (you) soon discovers that the NSF is aware of Ambrosia and intends to replicate it and release it to the public. This begins a wild adventure in which you move to various sites and cities across the world (all rendered in great futuristic detail, based on actual architectural maps), uncovering plots and conspiracies, solving a great many problems, and fighting enemies of all sorts.

Deus Ex involves a good many moral dilemmas. For example, you discover, fairly early on, that the NSF are not really the "bad guys" and you and your fellow UNATCO soldiers are not really the "good guys." Yet you have already killed a number of NSF soldiers. If you have been too enthusiastically gung ho in this enterprise, you are left with a very real sense of guilt. In fact, when I returned to the UNATCO base from one of my first missions and told the munitions officer, a seasoned veteran, how I had performed, he told me that I was not a real soldier, because I too readily killed the enemy rather than attempting to sneak past them when I could. He refused to give me more ammunition, telling me to use what I had left more carefully and humanely. Thus, when I discovered that the NSF troops were not really the terrorists UNATCO claimed, I felt all the more guilty.

Later in the game you are forced to choose whether to save your badly wounded brother, Paul, now fighting at your side against UNATCO, or to escape and let him die in order to go on fighting for your current cause. (Indeed, Paul urges you to go on and leave him to protect your retreat.) If you save your brother (and survive yourself, of course), he plays a role later in the story; if you don't, he doesn't, though you later see his body in one of your enemies' bases. When I played *Deus Ex*, I let Paul die and have regretted it ever since. (At the time, I didn't feel I had the requisite game-playing skills to save him—but perhaps that was just a lame self-exonerating excuse.)

By the time *Deus Ex* ends, you know a great deal more than you did at the beginning. You have discovered that the world is, in fact, run by a small number of rich global elites, elites who hide behind and control forces like the U.S. government, many members of which don't themselves fully understand who is actually pulling the strings in the global world. These elites have helped bring on all the devastation in the world, and they benefit by it. At the conclusion of the game, three opposing figures (each of whom has been helping you) try to convince you to engage in a different set of specific final actions that will end the game in three different ways.

One figure tells you the world will always be run by a small elite, though the current ones are selfish, evil, and corrupt. He tells you that you and he and his allies should replace this ruling elite and that all of you will behave more humanely, because you are better people. If you do what he suggests, you will become one of the elite rulers of the world—and, indeed, you (J. C. Denton) are a moral force and incorruptible force, are you not?

Another figure tells you that the world will always be run by a small elite as long as there is a global world tied together through global networked communications. This figure encourages you to engage in actions that will destroy this global communicational infrastructure, returning the world to small and technologically primitive villages that will not be closely connected to each other in any larger system. This, he claims, is the only moral and humane future.

The last figure agrees that the world will always be run by a small elite, especially if the world is a globally interconnected into one big system, as it is. But this figure, who happens to be not a human but a massive and sophisticated artificial intelligence, tells you that the only moral and humane way forward is to have him—a completely dispassionate and rational being—run the world, not human beings, any of whom will simply be corrupted by their passions and by power. Humans have failed, over all of history, to institute a nonviolent, humane world for everyone. Only a purely rational and logical being can make good decisions. The artificial intelligence device tells you to engage in actions that will allow it to rule.

You must choose which ending to bring on. Yourself as an incorruptible elite? Return to small villages? Rational rule by artificial intelligence? I must admit, I was thrilled at the end of *Deus Ex* as I (J. C. Denton) ran from the ruins of the massive global communicational infrastructure collapsing all around me after what I had just done and returned the world to a plethora of small villages. You might have decided otherwise.

Deus Ex has one feature that is characteristic of good video games, though the feature is stronger in this game than in many others: There are nearly always multiple solutions to any given problem. Players can choose strategies that fit with their style of learning, thinking, and acting. This, of course, is highly motivating both for learning and for playing the game and a rich source for reflecting on one's own styles of learning and problem solving (and, perhaps, experimenting with new ones).

STORYING AND LIVING IN THE VIRTUAL WORLD OF A VIDEO GAME

Deus Ex has a rich, ever-twisting and turning story line. However, story in *Deus Ex*, and other video games with rich stories, functions quite differently than it does in books or movies. A book or movie can tell its story from first episode to last or it can begin in the middle of the action and only later get to the initial events in the story. In either case, the reader or viewer knows someone else (the "author") has determined the order in which events in the story will be encountered. This "author" (which, of course, can be multiple people) also determines the sources through which the reader or viewer gains crucial information. For example, a crucial piece of information may be in a conversation between two lovers rather than in a hidden diary. In a video game, on the other hand, some players will gain such information one way and others in another way.

In *Deus Ex*, the player uncovers the story bit by bit as he or she discovers documents, hacks into computers, overhears or engages in conversations, or sees things happen. Different players find different things and discover information relevant to the story line in a different order. Furthermore, the player him- or herself engages in actions that are themselves part of the story line and different players will engage in different actions or the same ones in a different order.

The story line in a video game is a mixture of four things:

1. The game designers' ("author's") choices
2. How you, the player, have caused these choices to unfold in your specific case by the order in which you have found things

3. The actions you as one of the central characters in the story carry out (since in good video games there is a good deal of choice as to what to do, when to do it, and in what order to do it)
4. Your own imaginative projection about the characters, plot, and world of the story

The first and fourth of these items are true of books and movies, as well, but items 2 and 3 are true of video games only.

Thus, in video games like *Deus Ex*, stories are embodied in the player's own choices and actions in a way they cannot be in books and movies. Let's just call them, for short, "embodied stories." When I use the term "embodied," I mean to include the mind as a part of the body. So "embodied" means, for me, "in the body" and/or "in the mind." It's too bad there is no word "emminded" to go alongside "embodied." When I talk about a person's embodied experiences in the world (virtual or real), I mean to cover all the perceptions, actions, choices, and mental simulations of action or dialogue.

This is not to say that stories in video games are better or worse than stories in books and movies. Each form has its own advantages and disadvantages. For example, since stories in video games are embodied in you the player, you (i.e., the character you are playing) cannot die and stay dead (you can die, but then you start the game again from a saved point or from the beginning). Otherwise, the game would be over before its "ending." In a book or movie, you can get quite sad and upset when a character you empathize with dies (you know that the character probably won't being coming back, unless it's a supernatural story, and when characters we like do come back in books and movies, we sometimes cry because it is such a rare, unreal, and special event).

When the character you are playing dies in video game (and it is always, of course, a main character), you can get sad and upset, but you also usually get "pissed" that you (the player) have failed. Perhaps you even feel that you have failed your character. And then you start again, usually from a saved game, motivated to do better. This is part of what it means to call these video-game stories embodied stories. The emotional investments you have in a video-game story are entirely different from the emotional investments you have in a book or movie.

There are all sorts of reasons why stories in video games cannot (yet?) be, in a sense, as deep or rich as stories in good books and movies. For example, a video game must work out different futures based on choices different players have made and different things they have done earlier in the game. This creates a computational problem that books and movies do not face, since in a book or movie the designer always knows what choices have been made earlier. (Although quite simple "choose your own adventure" books are available.) Furthermore, real conversation is beyond the current computational power of a video game, since human beings can make so many different responses to anything said to them. A game like *Deus Ex* carries out conversations by giving the player a choice among several different things to say. Again, creating flexible, unpredictable conversations is a computational problem that books and movies do not face, since they simply script specific set dialogue.

Video games compensate for these limitations by creating what I have called embodied stories, stories that involve and motivate the player in a different way than do the stories in books and movies. One intriguing thing I have found about video-game stories is that I am so involved at the level of action—worrying about where I am, what's to be found there, what I am doing, what good or bad things might happen to me, what needs doing right now—that the larger story line often seems to float somewhat vaguely above me. I can't quite pull all the pieces together, since I'm too busy right now and, in any case, some of the pieces I discovered long ago are a bit hazy now. I can, of course, later (in a safe place) stop and try to put the pieces together, and I can then also usually look things up in notes games often keep for players.

Thus, although every once in a while in playing a game I do pause to consider the bigger picture—I certainly had to, at the end of the game, before I decided to send the world back to small villages—there is also a delicious feeling of being in the midst of things, looking at the world from the ground up and not from a God's-eye perspective. I suppose this is, again, part of what it means to call these stories "embodied stories." But it is also a whole lot like what "real" life is like. (Also, it is a lot like what it feels like to engage in an academic discipline when one does research and doesn't just study things after they have become all cut and dried.)

Again, video-game stories are not better or worse than stories in books and movies. They are different. They offer different pleasures and frustrations.

SITUATED AND EMBODIED MEANINGS

The embodied nature of video-game stories brings out a crucial feature. In video games, meaning (sense, significance) is itself situation-specific and embodied. In the chapter 2 I argued that this is how meaning operates when people actually know what they are doing in a domain and can do more than mindlessly repeat words and other symbols that they cannot situate inside any real practice. Video games are particularly good examples of how learning and thinking work in any semiotic domain when learning and thinking are powerful and effective, not passive and inert.

In games like *Deus Ex*, the meaning of any event, object, artifact, conversation, written note, or any other potentially meaningful sign is up for grabs. You don't really know what it means unless and until you can give it a specific meaning in terms of the world through which you are moving as a character or the actual actions you carry out in that world. Furthermore, as that world and your actions in it change, the meanings of things you have seen or discovered can change as well. That is, meanings in video games are always specific to specific situations. They are always actively assembled (or changed) by the player, on the spot, in terms of images, materials, and embodied actions in the virtual world being mutually created by the game and the player. In other words, meanings in video games are what I called, in chapter 2, "situated meanings" or "situation-specific meanings," not just general ones.

Take something as simple as a numerical code—say five numbers—that you find on a desk or hack from a computer while playing *Deus Ex*. It's pretty clear that this code is nearly meaningless—not completely so, of course, since you know that it's a code of some sort. The code, at this point, just has a decontextualized, general meaning, the meaning "code of some sort." This code means nothing until you find something (e.g., a safe, a locked door, a computer) that it can be used on to some good effect. Then the numbers take on the situated, embodied, action-oriented meaning "opens this safe."

There is a wonderful moment in *Deus Ex* when a completely evil and powerful cyborg woman at the UNATCO command center, a creature who has threatened me (J. C. Denton) throughout a large part of the game, is about to kill me when I have switched sides away from UNATCO. She expects an all-out fight at which I am quite likely to lose badly. But I have found—unbeknownst to her—a code word in a computer that will cause her cyborgian mechanisms to self-destruct should I utter it in her presence. Those who have not found the code must fight her. I, on the other hand, utter the code word and experience a delicious moment of wonderfully embodied and situated meaning (much as I did when I first realized that fractal equations lead to marvelous patterns when you feed them into a computer or actually graph them on a piece of paper, rather than learn just to repeat them and verbally list their numerical properties).

What I have said about a set of numbers found on a discarded note in *Deus Ex* is true, too, of any written note or diary you find in the game. It's true of any words you hear as well. To make sense of them you must fit them into the emerging plot and virtual world you are discovering and helping to build. And you must do this actively, since you have choices about where to go and what to do. Every potentially meaningful sign in a game like *Deus Ex*—whether word, deed, artifact, or action—is a particular sort of *invitation to embodied action* (action actually carried out or simulated in the mind). And the nature of that invitation changes as you experience new situations and engage in new actions in the virtual world of the game.

Even something that seems to have a set and general meaning—a lock pick, for example—takes on different meanings in different situations. For example, at a certain point you may have but one lock pick left. Then that lock pick comes to mean something like: *try other ways into doors, use this lock pick as last resort, because there may be more important doors coming up.* Notice that if you don't assemble some useful meaning for the lock pick, bad effects can happen to you in the virtual world of the game. There is a price to be paid for not thinking at a situation-specific level and in terms of embodied actions in the game.

Of course, one might now say, "Well, that's just how meaning works in video games—it isn't and shouldn't be that way outside of games, say, in school." You already know from the discussion in chapter 2 that I disagree with this view. General, purely verbal meanings, meanings that a person has no ability to customize for specific situations and that offer the person no invitations for embodied actions in different situations, are useless (save for passing tests in school).

This theory of meaning as situated and embodied fits well with some current work that I believe to be at the cutting edge of psychological research on how comprehension of oral and written language works when it works effectively. For example, consider these two remarks:

> . . . comprehension is grounded in perceptual simulations that prepare agents for situated action.
> . . . to a particular person, the meaning of an object, event, or sentence is what that person can do with the object, event, or sentence.

While video games actively encourage such situated and embodied thinking and doing, school often does not. In school, words and meanings usually float free of material conditions and embodied actions. They take on only general, so-called decontextualized meanings. Their meanings just amount to spelling out a word or phrase in terms of still other words and phrases, themselves with only general meanings. People (like the college physics students discussed in the chapter 2) cannot actually *do* anything with these words. (They cannot even simulate or carry out a conversation with these meanings, a conversation in which what they know is used flexibly and adapted differently to specific situations being discussed.)

Imagine you were to design a video game in which the player, a student of architecture, had to learn a new 3-D architectural drafting system, a quite complicated symbol system. (Such a game does exist, though I have not played it.) Certainly learning such a system is equivalent in complexity to taking a class on a new language or a new academic area in school. If this game operated like a good video game, then the player's understandings of this new system—all its words, symbols, and procedures—would have to be embodied in materials, images, and actions in the game's virtual world. Furthermore, the player's understandings would have to change and transform in new and different situations. Additionally, the player would have to actively assemble these understandings on the spot and face real consequences in the virtual world for these assemblies. In fact, it is these consequences that allow the player to test whether the situation- and action-specific meanings he or she has constructed are viable or not.

Compare this to sitting these students down and having them read books, listen to lectures, and discuss these matters apart from any real consequences. In this case, the students would have only general and/or verbal meanings, not embodied ones that they can customize to and for different situations of actual practice. I am not saying that we need to teach these architecture students—or any others—via video games. Good classrooms can teach people how to situate and embody meanings in a variety of different ways, though this may involve getting out of the classroom from time to time.

I suppose we are unlikely to teach people new to drafting via just reading and telling. (Though we do often try to teach adults who already know something about an older drafting system a new one via this route—it works as well as you'd expect, which is not well at all.) But we do routinely try to teach children things like science and math this way in our schools.

Now someone's sure to say: "But we cannot teach children everything they need to learn in school, things like science and math, in ways that make sense in terms of situated meanings and embodied actions. There just isn't enough time, and, after all, they're not all going to become scientists." There is a sort of good common sense in this remark, but the problem is this: There really is *no other way to make sense*. If all you know—in any domain—are general meanings, then you really don't know anything that makes sense to you.

Of course, students in a science classroom do not need to know how to situate meanings in all the contexts a "real" scientist does. And they don't need to be experts at situating meanings in the sort of science they are studying. But they do need to know how *some* important and central situated meanings work in the semiotic domain—to have *some* embodied feel for the matter. Otherwise they have, in reality, no idea how or why words and other sorts of signs in the domain make sense.

Imagine a person who claims to know what the word "democracy" means, because she can give you a dictionary definition of the word or, perhaps, a definition she has gotten out of a social studies textbook. However, faced with the following claim, she can make no intelligent response that speaks in any situated way to the situation the claim is about (i.e., the impact of wealth on elections in some countries):

> A country is not a democracy when candidates must take contributions from wealthy people in order to run for office, since then only wealthy people determine the slate of candidates.

The responder does not have to agree with this claim. But he or she surely has to see the sort of situated meaning being given to "democracy" in the claim. Further, he or she must then either accept that situated meaning or counter it with another situated meaning customized for (i.e., situationally relevant) to the situation the claim is dealing with. This is dialogue as engaged action. If you can't use "democracy" in a situation-specific way in such dialogues, then the word does not make sense to you, no matter how well you can repeat a dictionary definition for the word.

Let me give one more example, again taking a rather mundane word. A faculty colleague of mine who is an avid proponent of phonics instruction in the early grades said to me once, "Kids are coming to college unable to read

the books I assign." He blamed this situation on a lack of early phonics instruction. (The students were victims, he claimed, of Whole Language.)
Thus, he was giving the word "read" the situated meaning: *able to decode print,
that is, translate letters into sounds.*

However, this situated meaning, in fact, does not work well for the very
situation the faculty member was describing. These students can almost certainly decode print, and many can decode it quite well. This is a matter that
can be checked quite easily (by asking them to decode complex nonsense
words out of context). The problem these students have—if they do indeed
have a problem—is that they cannot *comprehend* the complex academic language of college textbooks well. Such language is quite different from "everyday" colloquial language and requires students to have heard and read a good
bit of it before they are very adept at doing so. The faculty member's claim
has a chance of being true only if the word "read" is given a situated meaning
something like: *able to understand text at a level that goes beyond mere decoding
and knowledge of the literal meanings of everyday words and phrases to an understanding of the specialist language of writing that is more technical than everyday
language.*

Let me end this discussion of situated meaning with an example relevant
to science education, an example that will take us away from words toward
situated and embodied meanings for other sorts of symbols. The science edu-
cator Andrea diSessa has successfully taught children in sixth grade and beyond the algebra behind Galileo's principles of motion (principles related to
Newton's laws) by teaching them a specific computer programming language
called Boxer.

The students write into the computer a set of discrete steps in the programming language. For example, the first command in a little program
meant to represent uniform motion might tell the computer to set the speed
of a moving object at one meter per second. The second step might tell the
computer to move the object. And a third step might tell the computer to repeat the second step over and over again. Once the program starts running,
the student will see a graphical object move one meter each second repeatedly, a form of uniform motion.

Now the student can elaborate the model in various ways. For example,
the student might add a fourth step that tells the computer to add a value *a* to
the speed of the moving object after each movement the object has taken (let
us just say, for convenience, that *a* adds one more meter per second at each

step). So now, after the first movement on the screen (when the object has moved at the speed of one meter per second), the computer will set the speed of the object at two meters per second (adding one meter), and, then, on the next movement, the object will move at the speed of two meters per second. After this the computer will add another meter per second to the speed, and on the next movement the object will move at the speed of three meters per second. And so forth forever, unless the student has added a step that tells the computer when to stop repeating the movements. This process is obviously modeling the concept of acceleration. And, of course, you can set a to be a negative number instead of a positive one, and watch what happens to the moving object over time instead.

The student can keep elaborating the program and watch what happens at every stage. In this process, the student, with the guidance of a good teacher, can discover a good deal about Galileo's principles of motion through his or her actions in writing the program, watching what happens, and changing the program. What the student is doing here is seeing in an embodied way, tied to action, how a representational system that is less abstract than algebra or calculus (namely, the computer programming language, which is actually composed of a set of boxes) "cashes out" in terms of motion in a virtual world on the computer screen.

An algebraic representation of Galileo's principles is more general, basically a set of numbers and variables that do not directly tie to actions or movements as material things. As diSessa points out, algebra doesn't distinguish effectively "among motion ($d = rt$), converting meters to inches ($i = 39.37 \times m$), defining coordinates of a straight line ($y = mx$) or a host of other conceptually varied situations." They all just look alike. He goes on to point out that "[d]istinguishing these contexts is critical in learning, although it is probably nearly irrelevant in fluid, routine work for experts," who, of course, have already had many embodied experiences in using algebra for a variety of different purposes of their own.

Once learners have experienced the meanings of Galileo's principles about motion in a situated and embodied way, they have understood one of the situated meanings for the algebraic equations that capture these principles at a more abstract level. Now these equations are beginning to take on a real meaning in terms of embodied understandings. As learners see algebra spelled out in more such specific material situations, they will come to master it in an active and critical way, not just as a set of symbols to be repeated in a passive and rote manner on tests. As diSessa puts it: "Programming turns analysis into experience and allows a connection between analytic forms and their experiential implications that algebra and even calculus can't touch."

diSessa knows what good video games know, but schools often don't: Meaning is material, situated, and embodied if and when it is useful. Abstract systems originally got their meanings through such embodied experiences for those who really understand them. Abstraction rises gradually out of the ground of situated meaning and practice and returns there from time to time, or it is meaningless to most human beings.

THE PROBE, HYPOTHESIZE, REPROBE, RETHINK CYCLE

Because video games so nicely exemplify the nature of meaning as situated and embodied, they are also capable of capturing—and allowing players to practice—a process that is the hallmark of "reflective practice" in areas like law, medicine, teaching, art, or any other area where there are expert practitioners. Playing a good video game like *Deus Ex* well requires the player to engage in the following four-step process:

1. The player must *probe* the virtual world (which involves looking around the current environment, clicking on something, or engaging in a certain action).
2. Based on reflection while probing and afterward, the player must form a *hypothesis* about what something (a text, object, artifact, event, or action) might mean in a usefully situated way.
3. The player *reprobes* the world with that hypothesis in mind, seeing what effect he or she gets.
4. The player treats this effect as feedback from the world and accepts or *rethinks* his or her original hypothesis.

In fact, if you don't engage in this four-step process, you won't get very far in a good video game. For example, in a good but rather standard shooter game (like, say, *Return to Castle Wolfenstein*), you can run around shooting at things a bit without engaging in this process, but soon you will run out of ammo and health and die, probably in the wrong place, all too close to where you started. In a good video game you have to try lots of different things and then you have to think about the results you get, try to make sense of what they mean for you and your progress through the virtual world of the game. In fact, you can't get very far in any real-world practice either if you don't engage in this four-step process (say, in being a good teacher, musician, artist, architect, businessperson, or athlete).

Some consider this four-step process to be the basis of expert reflective practice in any complex semiotic domain. But it is also how children learn, even very young children, when they are not learning in school. It is how children initially build their minds and learn their cultures as they develop early in life. In other words, this four-step process is central to how humans, as biological creatures of a certain sort, learn things when learning is essential for survival and for thriving in the world.

The human mind is a powerful *pattern recognizer*. In fact, humans are quite adept at finding complex patterns where none actually exists (witness astrology), a problem I will deal with in the next chapter. The young child does something (this is the probe); for example, he or she tries to crush a soft cloth book lying on the floor. The child, usually unconsciously, reflects on what he or she is doing while acting ("reflection-in-action") and after having acted ("reflection-on-action"). Such reflection involves listening to the world as it "talks back" to your action, giving you feedback about the success or failure of that action in terms of your own goals and desires.

Based on this feedback, the child forms a hypothesis (a guess) about a pattern that may exist (a set of relationships), say: "Books are soft, they squish, but don't break." His or her next action (the reprobe) is treated as a test of this pattern—do things really work this way or not? Perhaps the child now tries to crush a book made of paper laying next to the cloth book on the floor and finds that it doesn't squish, but rips and tears. Based on this test, the child reflects again in and on action, accepting or re-forming his or her hypothesis about what the pattern is (say, now, hypothesizing, that cloth books squish and paper ones tear).

The child, through action and reflection, becomes a "self-teacher," "training" his or her own mental networks of associations (the patterns the mind stores). Here the network of associations is something like: book—cloth—squish; book—paper—tear, a larger pattern made up of two smaller subpatterns. Note that the child's pattern already captures the fact that there are two types of book. Indeed, the child may already have another subpattern for book that is something like: book—cardboard—bends, doesn't break, exemplifying yet another category of book.

As the child forms more associations around the node book (e.g., with things like fun, pictures, being read to by his or her parents, etc.), the child builds up an interlocking set of patterns (call this all the "book pattern") and subpatterns (elements like book—cloth—squish, or book—parent—being read to—feeling loved). Of course, subpatterns in the book pattern are also subpatterns in other larger patterns to which they are linked. For example, the subpattern book—cloth—squish is also a subpattern in the larger "squish pattern" (the pattern that captures how squishiness works in the world).

This forming of associations is crucial not just to the development of the child's mind. It also constitutes aspects of the child's emerging identity as a cultured being of a certain sort connected to a certain sort of family, social group, and community. For example, the six-year-old playing *Pikmin* in chapter 2, when he was two, took his first hike in a forest. He saw a chipmunk on a fallen tree and said "Henry's forest," referring to a chipmunk in a *Thomas the Tank Engine* book he had at home, a book devoted to an animated railroad engine named Henry who is helping to reforest an area after it has burned in a forest fire.

What is happening here is that, as part and parcel of his embodied experience in the world, this child is creating a link (association) in his mental networks (patterns) between "real" chipmunks and "book" chipmunks, between the real world and the world of books. If such episodes continue (and they did, of course), the real world and books become integrally linked into the same sets of associations or patterns for such a child. Books and the real world don't stand apart or opposed.

Since the initial patterns we form in life are a basis on which we form all the rest of our later patterns (because they determine the hypotheses we originally make and revise, setting a certain trajectory to our mental development), children like this have links between the real world and books as a foundational part of who they are in mind, body, and culture. It is not surprising that they often orient to books and literacy when they go to school in powerfully different ways from children who have formed quite different patterns of association and built their viewpoints on the world on that basis.

Of course, there is no simple deterministic story to be told here. People can transform their mental associations when sufficiently powerful learning experiences encourage them to do so. What I am referring to here is a certain "set" or "direction" given to a child's cognitive, social, and cultural development. Nonetheless, for some children, who have failed to interlink literacy into their embodied experiences of the world and their social groups, powerful learning experiences may be required in school to set some new directions in respect to literacy. Unfortunately, such children are often the ones who get literacy in school completely detached from anything otherwise meaningful to them, as they are skilled-and-drilled to death on things like phonics.

As children build up their concepts—like their concept of book—as a set of complexly interlinked patterns and subpatterns, they use these patterns to situate meanings that are appropriate to specific situations. They pull out the subpatterns that are appropriate (useful) for the situation they are in, adapting them to the current situation. If no such subpattern exists already, they cobble together a new subpattern from bits and pieces of existing ones and adapt this to the current situation.

For example, if a child wants something hard and flat to draw or color on, he or she will situate a meaning for *book* something like *hard flat surface good for supporting a piece of paper*, drawing on a pattern like "book—paper pages—hard covers—covers won't bend," and others, and adapting them to the current need. Of course, such adaptations, based on experiences in the world, in turn form new subpatterns in the child's mind. Our experiences in the world build patterns in our mind, and then the mind shapes our experience of the world (and the actions we take in it), which, in turn, reshapes our mind. Concepts are never set and finished. They are like a large tree that always seeks to rise higher (i.e., attain more generality) but that must always send into the ground deeper roots (i.e., return to embodied experience).

This view of the mind, as I pointed out earlier, is quite different from the traditional one in psychology. In the traditional view, concepts are like general definitions in the mind (like definitions for words in dictionaries). In the traditional view, the mind thinks through stored "facts" and grand generalizations that are like statements in logic (like "All books have covers"). In the view I am developing here, the mind thinks and acts on the basis of something like stored images (simulations) of experience, images that are complexly interlinked with each other (thereby attaining some generality) but that are always adapted to new experiences in ways that keep them tied to the ground of embodied experience and action in the world.

These two viewpoints on the mind have different consequences for how people think schools should operate. If you believe the traditional view, you think schools should teach children to memorize facts and should overtly tell them important generalizations. If you believe the other view, you think schools must give children embodied experiences in and through which they can form networks of associations that must continually be rechecked against the world. Of course, as I show in the next chapter, in this view, children still need active teachers who are guiding the hypotheses they make and the patterns they form from their embodied experience. Otherwise children, ever creative beings, may very well hit on wonderful patterns that, in the end, don't work in the semiotic domains to which they are exposed in school.

The four-stage probe/hypothesize/reprobe/rethink process that underlies the formation of the child's mind is not different in kind from the process by which expert practitioners operate. This four-stage process is, of course, basic to good science, whether carried out by children in a good science classrooms or "real" scientists in a lab, since science is one important form of expert practice. Ironically, though, the process that is basic to young children's learning and to adult's expert practice is usually discounted and unused in school learning.

For example, it is currently fashionable, in some circles, to teach young children to decode print via scripted direct instruction (so-called DI). This is a return to a pedagogy that was popular in the 1960s. In this sort of instruction, the teacher reads a written script and overtly tells children what they need to know about decoding. The children repeat the script over and over, drilling on phonics. Though it may not sound like it, this sort of thing can be done with enthusiasm, and children can learn to decode this way. There are now even calls for such scripted direct instruction in areas like science and math.

The problem is this: Children in these sorts of pedagogies are not learning to discover and test patterns for themselves (which still, of course, requires the guidance of a good teacher). They are learning to store discrete facts and elements of knowledge, not deeper patterns. If all people have in their minds is a list of facts, then, when they are faced with a new situation, and nothing on the list applies, they must simply memorize another fact. This fact, in turn, will apply, like all the others they have stored, only to situations just like the one that triggered it in the first place. If people have a pattern in their mind, however, when they are faced with a new situation, they can reflect on how this pattern can be revised to cover the new situation. Now they have a new and more powerful pattern in mind, one that might actually cover novel situations the person has not yet encountered.

Let me give an example of this contrast between a list and a pattern, though the discussion of a child building up the concept of a book already makes much the same point. Say you knew that a bedroom could contain the following things: a bed, lamps, tables, a chest of drawers, a carpet, and pictures. What you have is a list. Now, say you see or hear about a bedroom used by a college student with a hot plate and small refrigerator in it (perhaps it's a room in a large house rented by a group of students). If all you have is a list, you just add this to the list: bedrooms can also have hot plates and small refrigerators in them. There is no real need to think about the matter, since lists are, in any case, indefinitely extendable.

But, now, say that you start not with a list but with a pattern, a visual picture of a typical bedroom. Patterns in the mind are not actually pictures, of course. They are systems of neural elements standing for things like beds, carpets, lamps, and the like, systems that are associated with each other through stronger or weaker links in terms of which each system (e.g., the one standing for beds) more or less strongly activates the others (e.g., the systems standing for chests of drawers and night tables). But mental patterns operate, for our purposes, enough like pictures to make the point.

To make our mental pictures a bit more like neural patterns in the mind, let's imagine that elements in the picture can be more or less clearly focused depending on how strongly or weakly they are associated with the main items in the picture. So we could imagine that in the typical bedroom picture, the bed is in clear and sharp focus, but there is a rather less well focused plant in the room, thereby noting that plants are less strongly associated with typical bedrooms than are beds. Perhaps, in your picture, a television is somewhere in between in focus between the bed (very clearly focused) and the plant (not so clearly focused).

If you have such a picture in mind when you see the college student's bedroom with a hot plate and small refrigerator in it, you have to revise your picture. Perhaps you change your original picture to be one not of a typical bedroom but the bedroom of a working adult. This amounts to associating "working adult" with the other elements in your picture. Note, too, that this picture is not, like a list, indefinitely extendable—it now can't have a hot plate and small refrigerator in it. Further, you create a new picture of a typical bedroom of a college student, a picture that does have a hot plate and refrigerator in it.

If later you come across a similar bedroom, another one with a hot plate and refrigerator, but now one used by a working adult, you will find that your college student bedroom picture, by and large, fits. You need revise it only a bit to be the picture of a financially strapped person, rather than just a college student. You will then also revise your picture of the typical bedroom of a working adult to be the picture of the typical bedroom of a middle-class-working adult. You might even reflect on the fact that college students often live like financially strapped persons even when they come from well-off homes, a reflection that can lead to further mediation on the ways in which class, age, and institutions interact in our society. Patterns prepare you for future learning in a way that lists don't.

What's really happening here is that you are creating pictures (patterns), subdividing them, and adding and subtracting things from them (and refocusing items) as you confront new situations. You are, in reality, learning how to situate the meaning of the word or concept "bedroom" to fit different situations, including situations you may not have seen before. Lists require no such thinking and learning. Patterns are experiential *theories* (here a theory of bedrooms) that we change with more experience, more probing and reprobing of the world. Lists are just get bigger with time, taking more effort to remember, and making less and less real sense at any deep explanatory level.

APPRECIATIVE SYSTEMS

So far I have argued that the probe/hypothesize/reprobe/rethink cycle is typical of how both young children and professional practitioners learn and think, though not necessarily how students learn and think in schools. But what differentiates the young child learning from the expert practitioner learning? What differentiates them, I believe, is the way what I call their *appreciative systems* work.

When the child acts and reflects, probes the world and gets a result, on what basis does the child determine the "significance" and the "acceptability" of the result? The very form of this question makes it clear that children must *evaluate* the answer coming back from the world, must determine whether they "like" it or not, whether it is "good" or not from their perspective. Otherwise, why use the answer in their reflections and subsequent interactions with the world and, indeed, in their own minds as they build up their mental networks of associations?

Children can determine what they "like," what is a "good" result, only in terms of an *appreciative system*, that is, their set of goals, desires, feelings, and values in respect to the domain being engaged with. The appreciative system is where affect and cognition merge and come together. The children revise the hypotheses they have formed based on the goals, desires, feelings, and values encapsulated in their appreciative system. Young children who are thrilled by their power to destroy things will evaluate the tear of the brittle page of a book as a good result and seek other brittle things to tear.

Expert practitioners in a given semiotic domain—whether teaching, science, law, business, architecture, art, or what have you—have to form an appreciative system relevant to that domain in terms of which they can evaluate action (probes) in the domain. That is, they must form the sorts of goals, desires, feelings, and values that "insiders" in that domain recognize as the sorts members of that domain (the affinity group associated with that domain) typically have. This process is much more specialized than the everyday learning a small child does. Furthermore, if learning in the domain is to be active and critical, the learning process and the appreciative system to which it gives rise must be open to a good deal more *conscious* reflection and critique than is typical of small children mastering their early worlds.

This is not to say that individuals do not merge and color these "social" goals, desires, feelings, and values (stemming from the affinity group associated with the semiotic domain) with their own personal idiosyncratic goals, desires, feelings, and values. They most certainly do. They also merge and color them with those connected to other semiotic domains of which they are members and other identities, including cultural identities that they have in the real world. The appreciative system, then, is the place where not only the affective and cognitive merge and come together, it is the place where the social, cultural, and the personal merge and come together as well.

Nonetheless, the affinity group connected to the semiotic domain being learned norms and disciplines what counts as an "acceptable" and "recognizable" and "competent" appreciative system in the domain and what does not. The newcomer learns what counts as competent goals, desires, feelings, and values in the domain in terms of which he or she can properly evaluate the results of his or her probes within the world of the domain. In a sense, the learner is forming what we might call "taste" in the domain.

In any domain—whether playing video games or learning some branch of science—the learner can learn in such a way that no real appreciative system is operative. In this case, the learner just does what he or she is told in a rote way. On the other hand, the learner can be actively enough involved in learning the domain to form an appreciative system that norms and guides his or her thought and action in the domain, but this system can remain largely unconscious and not reflected on in any very overt way. This is active but not yet critical learning.

In critical learning, the learner comes not just to form an appreciative system through practice and interaction with the affinity group associated with the domain but to reflect overtly on the goals, values, feelings, and desires that compose this system, to compare and contrast this appreciative system to others, and to make active and critical choices about the system. Of course, these choices must either remain within the confines of what the affinity group associated with the domain will recognize as acceptable or transform what the group finds acceptable. In either case, the learner is taking on a projective identity—actively, reflectively, and critically interfacing, at a metalevel, his or her real-world identities with the new identity being formed in the new semiotic domain.

When a player plays a video game like *Deus Ex* actively and critically, the player forms a viewpoint on what counts as playing well or not. It is not just a matter of getting through a crisis or solving a problem, of just surviving to get to the end of the game. The player cares about how his or her character (his or her virtual self) has fared. As I played more and more of *Deus Ex* and got better at the game, I found myself repeatedly playing scenes to do them better—to have my character look better and to be able myself to look back on the history of that character's interaction in the virtual world with a certain pride (pride that I could feel both in terms of my virtual identity as the character and my real identity as a player).

I was forming an appreciative system, one on which I could overtly reflect if and when I wished to. When I did engage in such overt reflection, asking myself why I cared about this or that outcome and what exactly my values in the game world were, I learned a good deal about myself, about the virtual world of the game, and about the design of this and other related games.

People do not usually form appreciative systems by themselves. Even in my case, where I was playing alone and not in a multiplayer game, I formed my appreciative system through multiple routes that went beyond my private play. As I got into the game (one of the first I played), I read about it on a variety of Internet sites. I looked at chat room sites devoted to the game and saw how others talked and felt about playing it and games like it. I eventually read magazines devoted to video games as well. I consulted several different walkthroughs of the game, intrigued both by how the writers had played through a given part and how they talked about such play.

And, of course, players who play with others, often on teams against other teams, and often getting on chat rooms to talk about their play, have their appreciative systems formed even more directly by the affinity group associated with the game. My appreciative system in regard to games like *Deus Ex* has changed and, I think, deepened as I have played more such games and had more interactions with the affinity group associated with such games via the Internet, magazines, books, and face-to-face verbal interaction (e.g., I learned a good deal when I talked about and played the Xbox shooter *Halo* with a young lawyer, a member of a generation that grown up playing video games).

When players not only form but overtly reflect on their emerging and ever-changing appreciative systems, they gain insight into and opinions about the design of the genres of video games in regard to which they have formed appreciative systems. It is not uncommon for players to voice these opinions in reviews and in comments on Internet sites devoted to games. Indeed, some players use software that often comes with a game to build their own new extensions to the game or whole new games.

As I play shooter games now—games like *Max Payne, Red Faction, Halo, Return to Castle Wolfenstein*—I find myself comparing and contrasting them. I find myself, however silently, critiquing elements of the game as "nothing new," "nice touch," "a nostalgic nod to *Half-Life*" (an earlier, vastly popular shooter), "brilliant integration of graphics and action," "problem well-integrated into the plot line, not just a puzzle," and a great many more (some expressed in language not printable here—especially in regard to the jumping in *Half-Life*). My appreciative system is tied in an important way to knowledge about and perspectives on shooter games as *designed entities* having their own sort of "design grammar." It is a "language" I am beginning to think and speak, even to think and speak creatively in the sense that I can critique such games and imagine new and different ones. In the end, then, while I don't have the skills to build a game, I think a good deal, while playing (reflection in action) and afterward (reflection on action), about what new and better games "ought to" look like.

It is my contention that active, critical learning in any domain should lead to learners becoming, in a sense, *designers*. Some, like the players who build their own extensions to games, will actually design new things. Others, like me, will design in thought and talk and let it inform their play. But there is no design and designing, in the sense I am talking about, without forming an appreciative system for a given semiotic domain. And no appreciative system is formed without probing, hypothesizing, reprobing, and rethinking through embodied action in a domain in connection with the affinity group associated with the domain.

I have said enough already, in this respect, about schools. But let me note that talk about appreciative systems, design and designing, and reflection in and on embodied action in association with an affinity group are matters that hardly ever appear in discussions about school or in educational research. Perhaps that's one reason why so many young people learn to play complex video games so much faster and better than they learn anything comparably complex is school.

WRITTEN TEXTS

With all my talk of situated and embodied meanings, probing the world, and designing things, some will ask what has happened to good old-fashioned printed texts. Video games have, I believe, a great deal to teach us about how reading printed texts actually works when people understand—again, in situated, embodied, active, and critical ways—what they read.

A game like *Deus Ex* has a great many texts inside the virtual world it creates, texts you find along the way, like notes, e-mail, diaries, and messages you have hacked from various computers. These texts help you not only to piece together the ongoing story but to make decisions about actions you will or will not take. In some games, such as *Clive Barker's Undying*, the number of extended texts you find gets quite large and is a central part of playing (and enjoying) the game.

However, video games are deeply connected to written texts in a different way as well. They are surrounded by a great many different types of written texts. For instance, there are a large number of reviews of games in magazines and on Internet sites. Furthermore, players often can and do add their own reviews to the official review written for a particular Internet site (and players appear to show no deference whatsoever to the official reviewers).

Games come with manuals (often, but not always, fairly small—the one for *Deus Ex* is 20 pages). They also often come with a booklet, written as a diary, or notes, or otherwise set as part of the virtual world of the game, that give the back story or background information for that virtual world. For example, *American McGee's Alice*, a game where Alice has gone insane and returned to a nightmarish Wonderland, comes with a booklet entitled "Rutledge Private Clinic and Asylum Casebook," which contains Alice's physician's daily notes on her treatment.

For many games, publishers offer highly colorful and detailed strategy guides that tell players all about the game (its characters, maps and geography of the world, weapons, enemies, objects to be found, fruitful strategies to follow, etc.). Such guides also give a complete walkthrough for the game. A number of Internet sites offer (usually free) a variety of different walkthroughs written by players themselves. These sites also offer hints from players and "cheats" for the games. (Cheats are ways to manipulate the game's programming to do things like give yourself extra life or more ammunition.)

These texts are all integrated into the appreciative systems associated with the affinity groups connected to video games. Different players and groups have different views about whether, when, and how to use these texts. For example, consider walkthroughs. These documents often run to 70 or more single-spaced pages and are written according to a tight set of rules about what they should contain and look like (including a list of each date on which the walkthrough was revised). Some players shun walkthroughs entirely, though they may write them. Others argue that walkthroughs can and should be used, but only to get a hint when one is thoroughly stuck. Indeed, the writers of the walkthroughs themselves often recommend that players use them this way. (Imagine producing a 70-page, single-spaced document and advising people to look at it only when and where they are stuck.)

Of course, if children had walkthroughs in school when they studied things like science, we would call it "cheating" (let alone if they had "cheat codes"). But, then, imagine what a science classroom would look like where learners wrote extensive walkthroughs according to strict norms and debated when and how to use them, debates that became part and parcel of the learners' growing appreciative systems about what it means to "do science (well)." And, indeed, in a sense, real scientists do have walkthroughs. They know (through talk with others and through texts) the case histories of how relevant related discoveries in their field were made. They also have opinions about how closely one should consult or follow these histories.

It is now a piece of folk wisdom that "young people" don't read things like manuals but just start playing games. To the extent that this is true, it is partly because, I explain in the next chapter, video games are so good at teaching people to play them by actually starting to play them. Yet I would argue that these young people are reading and using print in the way it is and should be used when people actually understand what they read in a useful and situated way. Baby boomers—perhaps too influenced by traditional schooling—often try to do otherwise to their regret and frustration, when they insist on reading a manual before they have any embodied understanding of what the manual is about.

Very often players quickly look over the instruction booklet that comes with a new game before starting to play. Experienced players often can tell at a glance how the controls will work and anything special they may need to pay attention to as they start to learn to play the game by actually starting to play it (or doing the game's on-disk training, if it has one). If the game is a new genre for them, they may have to pay a bit more attention. But, in any case, the problem with the texts associated with video game—the instruction booklets, walkthroughs, and strategy guides—is that they do not make a lot of sense unless one has already experienced and lived in the game world for a while. Of course, this lack of lucidity can be made up for if the player has read similar texts before, but at some point these texts originally made sense because the player had an embodied world of experience in terms of which to situate and spell out their meanings.

The same thing is most certainly true of the sorts of texts that show up in learning content areas like science and math in school, especially in the later grades, high school, and college. A biology textbook does not make a lot of sense unless and until one has experienced and lived in the world of biology as practice for a while. And again, this lack of lucidity is mitigated if the student has already read a good many similar texts. However, at some point these texts also originally made sense because the student had an embodied world of experience (in reality or, at least, simulated in his or her mind) in terms of which to situate and spell out their meanings.

When I give talks on video games to teachers, I often show them a manual or strategy guide and ask them how much they understand. Very often they are frustrated. They have no experience in which to situate the words and phrases of the texts. All they get is verbal information, which they understand at some literal level, but which does not really hang together. They cannot visualize this verbal information in any way that makes sense or makes them want to read on. I tell them that that is how their students often feel when confronted with a text or textbook in science or some other academic area if they have had no experiences in terms of which they can situate the meanings of the words and phrases. It's all "just words," words the "good" students can repeat on tests and the "bad" ones can't.

When you have played a video game for a while, something magical happens to the texts associated with it. All of sudden they seem lucid and clear and readable. You can't even recall how confusing they seemed in the first place. At that point, players can use the text in a great variety of ways for different purposes. For instance, they can look up details that enhance their play. (I recently looked up information on the different guns in *Return to Castle Wolfenstein* and discovered I was using a less accurate one than I could have been using, and I also got a crucial hint on how to keep the better gun from overheating.) Or they can fill out their knowledge of the places, creatures, and things in the virtual world in which they are living. They can troubleshoot problems they are having in the game, with the game, or with their computer. They can get hints or compare their play to how others have done.

Let me take the booklet that comes with *Deus Ex* as an example of what I mean by saying that texts associated with video games are not lucid unless and until one has some embodied game experience in which to "cash out" the meanings of the text. The book contains 20 small pages, printed in double columns on each page. In these pages, there are 199 bolded references that represent headings and subheadings. One small randomly chosen stretch of headings and subheadings that appears at the end of page 5 and the beginning of page 6 says: *Passive Readouts, Damage Monitor, Active Augmentation & Device Icons, Items-at-Hand, Information Screens, Note, Inventory, Inventory Management, Stacks, Nanokey ring, Ammunition.* Each of these 199 headings and subheadings is followed by text that gives information relevant to the topic and relates it to other information throughout the booklet. In addition, the booklet assigns 53 keys on the computer keyboard to some function in the game, and these 53 keys are mentioned 82 times in relation to the information contained in the 199 headings and subheadings. So, although small, the booklet is packed with relatively technical information.

Here is a typical piece of language from this booklet:

Your internal nano-processors keep a very detailed record of your condition, equipment and recent history. You can access this data at any time during play by hitting F1 to get to the Inventory screen or F2 to get to the

Goals/Notes screen. Once you have accessed your information screens, you can move between the screens by clicking on the tabs at the top of the screen. You can map other information screens to hotkeys using Settings, Keyboard/Mouse.

This makes perfect sense at a literal level, but that just goes to show how worthless the literal level is. When you understand this sort of passage at only a literal level, you have only an illusion of understanding, one that quickly disappears as you try to relate this information to the hundreds of other important details in the booklet. First of all, this passage means nothing real to you if you have no situated idea about what "nano-processors," "condition," "equipment," "history," "F1," "Inventory screen," "F2," "Goals/Notes screen" (and, of course, "Goals" and "Notes"), "information screens," "clicking," "tabs," "map," "hotkeys," and "Settings, Keyboard/Mouse" mean in and for playing games like *Deus Ex*.

Second, though you know literally what each sentence means, together they raise a plethora of questions if you have no situated understandings of this game or games like it. For instance: Is the same data (condition, equipment, and history) on both the Inventory screen and the Goals/Notes screen? If so, why is it on two different screens? If not, which type of information is on which screen and why? The fact that I can move between the screens by clicking on the tabs (but what do these tabs look like; will I recognize them?) suggests that some of this information is on one screen and some on the other. But, then, is my "condition" part of my Inventory or my Goals/Notes—it doesn't seem to be either, but, then, what is my "condition" anyway? If I can map other information screens (and what are these?) to hotkeys using "Setting, Keyboard/Mouse," does this mean there is no other way to access them? How will I access them in the first place to assign them to my own chosen hotkeys? Can I click between them and the Inventory screen and the Goals/Notes screens by pressing on "tabs"? And so on—20 pages is beginning to seem like a lot; remember, there are 199 different headings under which information like this is given.

Of course, all these terms and questions can be defined and answered if you closely check and cross-check information over and over again through the little booklet. You can constantly turn the pages backward and forward. But once you have one set of links relating various items and actions in mind, another drops out just as you need it and you're back to turning pages. Is the booklet poorly written? Not at all. It is written just as well or as poorly as—just like, in fact—any of a myriad of school-based texts in the content areas. It is, outside the practices in the semiotic domain from which it comes, just as meaningless, however much one could garner literal meanings from it with which to verbally repeat things or pass tests.

Of course, you can say, "Oh, yeah, you click on F1 to get to the Inventory screen and F2 to get to the Goals/Notes screen" and sound like you know something. The trouble is this: In the actual game, you can click on F2 and meditate on the screen you see at your leisure. Nothing bad will happen to you. However, very often you have to click on F1 and do something quickly in the midst of a heated battle. There's no "at your leisure" here. The two commands really don't function the same way in the game—they actually mean different things in terms of embodied and situated action—and they never really *just* mean "click F1, get screen." That's their general meaning, the one with which you really can't do anything useful until you know how to spell it out further in situation-specific terms in the game.

When you can spell out such information in situation-specific terms in the game, then the relationships of this information to the other hundreds of pieces of information in the booklet become clear and meaningful. And, of course, it is these relationships that are what really count if you are to understand the game as a system and, thus, play it at all well. *Now* you can read the book if you need to to piece in missing bits of information, check on your understandings, or solve a particular problem or answer a particular question you have.

When I first read this booklet before playing *Deus Ex* (and having played only one other shooter game, a very different one), I was sorely tempted to put the game on a shelf and forget about it. I was simply overwhelmed with details, questions, and confusions. When I started the game, I kept trying to look up stuff. But I understood none of it well enough to find things easily without searching for the same information over and over again. In the end, you have to just actively play the game and explore and try everything. Then, at last, the booklet makes good sense, but by then you don't need it all that much.

There is much discussion these days about how many children fail in school—especially children from poor homes—because they have not been taught phonics well or correctly in their early years. But the truth of the matter is that a great many more children fail in school because, while they can decode print, they cannot handle the progressively more complex demands school language makes on them as they move up in the grades and on to high school.

School requires, in respect to both oral and written language, forms or styles of language that are different from and, in some respects, more complex than everyday oral language used in informal face-to-face conversations. The forms of language used in texts and discussions in science, math, social studies classes, and other content areas, go by the general name of "academic language," though different varieties of academic language are associated with different content areas in school.

Academic language, like the language in the *Deus Ex* booklet, is not really lucid or meaningful if one has no embodied experiences within which to situate its meanings in specific ways. For example, consider this academic-language quote from a high school science textbook:

> The destruction of a land surface by the combined effects of abrasion and removal of weathered material by transporting agents is called erosion. . . . The production of rock waste by mechanical processes and chemical changes is called weathering.

Again, one can certainly understand this at some literal word-by-word, sentence-by-sentence way. However, this is not "everyday" language. No one speaks this way at home around the table or at a bar having drinks with friends. But this language is filled with all the same problems the language of the *Deus Ex* booklet was for me when I had not lived through any experiences in terms of which I could situate its meanings. Without embodied experiences with which to cash out its meanings, all the above academic text will do—as the *Deus Ex* booklet did to me initially—is fill one with questions, confusion, and, perhaps, anger.

For example: I have no idea what the difference is between "abrasion" and "removal of weathered material by transporting agents," which I would have thought was one form of abrasion. What's a "transporting agent"? What's a "mechanical process"? I am not really clear on the difference between "mechanical processes," especially in regard to weather, and "chemical changes." And what chemicals are we talking about here—stuff in rain?

Since the first sentence is about "erosion" and the second about "weathering," I suppose these two things are connected in some important way—but how? They must be two forms of "destruction of a land surface," given that this is the subject of the first sentence. But, then, I would have thought that producing "rock waste" was a way of building, not just destroying, land, since rock waste eventually turns into dirt (doesn't it?) and thus, I would have supposed, eventually into potentially fertile land. But this is a geology text, and they don't care about fertile land (or do they?). The word "land" here has a different range of possible situated meanings than I am familiar with.

Of course, I can turn the pages of the book back and forth clarifying all these points. After all, these two sentences are meant to be definitions—though not of the words "erosion" and "weathering" in everyday terms but in specialist terms in a particular semiotic domain.) And, of course, I do need to know that they *are* definitions, and I may not even know that if I have had little experience of specialists trying to define terms in explicit and operational ways so as to lessen the sort of ambiguity and vagueness that is more typical of everyday talk. Since they are definitions, they are linked and cross-linked to a myriad of other terms, descriptions, and explanations throughout the book, and I can follow this tangled trail across the pages, back and forth, losing bits of the connections just as I need them and page turning yet again.

However, once I have experienced the sorts of embodied images, actions, and tasks that engage geologists—including their ways of talking and debating, their reasons for doing so, their interests, norms, and values—then the text is lucid and useful. Confusion, frustration, and anger disappear. Given such understanding, everybody would pass the test and we couldn't fail half the class and reward a small set of "winners,"—people who can repeat back verbal details they remember well when they don't fully understand them in any practical way.

MORE LEARNING PRINCIPLES

Let me conclude this discussion by listing further learning principles that our discussion of learning and thinking in video games in this chapter has implicated. Once again, in this list, I intend each principle to be relevant both to learning in video games and learning in content areas in classrooms. After listing principles we have already discussed pretty thoroughly, I discuss a few others that are related to them.

15. **Probing Principle**
    Learning is a cycle of probing the world (doing something); reflecting in and on this action and, on this basis, forming a hypothesis; reprobing the world to test this hypothesis; and then accepting or rethinking the hypothesis.

16. **Multiple Routes Principle**

There are multiple ways to make progress or move ahead. This allows learners to make choices, rely on their own strengths and styles of learning and problem solving, while also exploring alternative styles.

17. **Situated Meaning Principle**

The meanings of signs (words, actions, objects, artifacts, symbols, texts, etc.) are situated in embodied experience. Meanings are not general or decontextulized. Whatever generality meanings come to have is discovered bottom up via embodied experiences.

18. **Text Principle**

Texts are not understood purely verbally (i.e., only in terms of the definitions of the words in the text and their text-internal relationships to each other) but are understood in terms of embodied experiences. Learners move back and forth between texts and embodied experiences. More purely verbal understanding (reading texts apart from embodied action) comes only when learners have had enough embodied experience in the domain and ample experiences with similar texts.

Now let us turn to four related learning principles, which are implicated in the discussion of video games and learning in this chapter although they were not discussed directly. The Intertextual Principle is concerned with the fact that after players have dealt a good bit with a certain type or genre of video game and the texts associated with them, they can begin to see these texts themselves as a family or genre of related texts. They understand any one such text (say a strategy guide for a fantasy role-playing game) intertextually in relationship to other related texts they have read connected to such games. Now they are "cashing out" texts not just in terms of embodied action in the games they have played (they are most certainly doing that as well) but also in terms of other texts they have read in the family or genre. Reading "new" texts becomes easy.

The Multimodal Principle is concerned with the fact—clear in all of the discussion about video games in this book so far—that, in video games, meaning, thinking, and learning are linked to multiple modalities (words, images, actions, sounds, etc.) and not just to words. Sometimes, at a particular point in a game, multiple modalities support each other to communicate similar meanings (e.g., "go in this direction"); sometimes they communicate different meanings, each of which fits together to form a bigger, more meaningful and satisfying whole (e.g., "I have just entered an evil place, better be real careful").

The "Material Intelligence" Principle is really a subpart of the Multimodal Principle. In a video game, objects and artifacts store some of the thinking and knowledge a player gains. So, in fact, does the environment the player moves through. For example, in *Deus Ex* if you haven't got a lock pick, you may have to think a great deal to get into a given door. If you have a lock pick, the lock pick stores your knowledge of how to get in the door, and you don't need to store the knowledge yourself. You can devote your thinking and problem-solving skills to other matters, thereby powerfully extending the amount of overall thinking and problem solving that is being accomplished, since the lock pick is doing some of it, along with lots of other "potent" material items.

In video games players soon learn how to "read" the physical environments they are in to gain clues about how to proceed through them. The shapes and contours of the physical environment, and the objects lying around, come to guide the player (of course, one can be fooled from time to time) in making good guesses about how to proceed. For instance, at one point in *American McGee's Alice*, you (playing as Alice) are lost among rocks and wild streams. However, you can see far off at the top of a mountain a bit of a mansion. Furthermore, the environment contains some contours of rocks and hills that suggest ways up. And finally, shining on a few rocks ahead of you are red jewels that you have already learned give you more health if you pick them up. Their placement clearly suggests moving toward them. The whole layout of the environment, then, helps you guess intelligently about how to proceed.

It is certainly good you get this help from the material environment and objects in it—good that the material environment and objects in it are part of your intelligence—because all along the way you have more than enough to do thinking about how to fight Wonderland's now-deranged characters who want to stop your progress (and about how to solve a good many other problems).

Of course, in good science instruction in classrooms, children should come to see that, in science, too, objects, artifacts, and the ways in which the environment is set up can store knowledge and power. This, in turn, can allow them to think about other things and solve other problems that, when combined with the knowledge and power stored in the material objects and environment, truly extends their reach. Indeed, good teachers set up scientific environments that guide learners and surround them with empowering objects that extend their individual efforts.

For example, just staring at and playing with pendulums in the real world is not actually a good way to "discover" the laws of the pendulum's movement. Galileo actually discovered these laws not by staring at a swinging chandelier, as the myth has it, but by using geometry and drawing, on paper, arcs and circles and paths of movement along them and figuring our their geometrical properties. Geometry is a powerful tool that stores much knowledge and skill that the learner does not have to invent for him- or herself. So, too, is the computer program diSessa uses to teach students Galileo's theorems about motion. Of course, we often expect children to learn science without the tools, artifacts, and material guidance that actual scientists have and have gained from the history of their science. There is real intelligence built into geometry and diSessa's Boxer program, as there is "player intelligence" built into the objects and environments in *American McGee's Alice*.

Finally, the Intuitive (Tacit) Knowledge Principle is concerned with the fact that video games honor not just the explicit and verbal knowledge players have about how to play but also the intuitive or tacit knowledge—built into their movements, bodies, and unconscious ways of thinking—they have built up through repeated practice with a family or genre of games. It is common today for research on modern workplaces to point out that in today's high-tech and fast-changing world, the most valuable knowledge a business has is the tacit knowledge its workers gain through continually working with others in a "community of practice" that adapts to specific situations and changes "on the ground" as they happen. Such knowledge cannot always be verbalized. Even when it can be verbalized and placed in a training manual, by that time it is often out of date.

Of course, conscious knowledge is important for critical learning, as I have pointed out several times already. But, too often, unlike video games and good workplaces, schools do not honor the tacit and embodied knowledge people build up through practice and adaptation to change "on the spot" as it happens amid practice (and not in pure speculation). Yet such knowledge is crucial in a great many domains and is a large part of why learners feel competent in a domain and feel as if they share real membership with the affinity group associated with a domain. The child learning science who has built up no tacit knowledge—no "craft knowledge"—cannot really feel competent either. But the child who has built up such knowledge is liable to be turned off by school when such knowledge is not valued and mindlessly repeating facts and numbers that one understands in no embodied way gains one an A.

I once helped run an after-school science club for middle-school students who were quite unaffiliated with school and school-based learning and literacy. We taught these children how to do science and how to talk about what they were doing and discovering with each other. We taught them to act and talk like knowers, not just passive observers. When we checked up on one of the young boys who had flourished in our club (had even won a prize in his school's science fair), his high school teacher told us something quite interesting: "It's funny, he is really good at actually doing the science when we run an experiment or do other things, but he has a bad grade, because he keeps failing my multiple-choice tests." This teacher did not value how much science this child knew in a tacit way tied to practice. He could hardly leverage this knowledge— and bring some of it to conscious and critical awareness—if he did not honor it. When profit is on the line, good businesses no longer make this mistake.

Next I list the principles we have just discussed.

19. **Intertextual Principle**

    The learner understands texts as a family ("genre") of related texts and understands any one such text in relation to others in the family, but only after having achieved embodied understandings of some texts. Understanding a group of texts as a family (genre) of texts is a large part of what helps the learner make sense of such texts.

20. **Multimodal Principle**

    Meaning and knowledge are built up through various modalities (images, texts, symbols, interactions, abstract design, sound, etc.), not just words.

21. **"Material Intelligence" Principle**

    Thinking, problem solving, and knowledge are "stored" in material objects and the environment. This frees learners to engage their minds with other things while combining the results of their own thinking with the knowledge stored in material objects and the environment to achieve yet more powerful effects.

22. **Intuitive Knowledge Principle**

    Intuitive or tacit knowledge built up in repeated practice and experience, often in association with an affinity group, counts a great deal and is honored. Not just verbal and conscious knowledge is rewarded.

BIBLIOGRAPHICAL NOTE

The discussion in this chapter about thinking as founded in pattern recognition from our embodied experiences of the world draws broadly on so-called connectionist views of the mind. See P. M. Churchland 1989; P. S. Churchland 1987; P. S. Churchland & Sejnowski 1992; Clark 1989, 1993, 1997; Margolis 1987, 1993; Rumelhart, McClelland, and the PDP Research Group 1986. For related work that has deeply influenced me, see Barsalou 1999a, b; Glenberg 1997; Glenberg & Robertson 1999; Hutchins 1995; Nolan 1994. The quote about comprehension being grounded in perceptual simulations is from Barsalou 1999, p. 77. The quote about meaning being about what a person can do is from Glenberg 1997, p. 3.

For the idea that abstract notions are rooted in metaphors for embodied experience, see Lakoff 1987; Lakoff & Johnson 1980. On situated and embodied meanings, see Brooks 2002; Brown, Collins, & Dugid 1989; Clancey 1997; Clark 1997; Gee 1996, 1999b; Lave 1988; Lave & Wenger 1991; Rogoff 1990; and Tomasello 1999.

For Galileo's use of geometry to solve the problem of pendulums and how children are asked to engage in an actually harder task in school when they must solve the same problem without geometry, see Edwards & Mercer 1987. For diSessa's work and a discussion of Boxer, see diSessa 2000, quotes are from pp. 32–33, 33, 34. The probe, hypothesize, reprobe, rethink cycle is deeply related to Donald Schon's work, see Schon 1987; see also Gee 1997. The discussion of "appreciative systems" (a term Schon uses) was inspired by Schon's work. On the idea that learners ought to be designers, see New London Group 1996. The quote about the destruction of land surfaces is taken from a textbook quoted in Martin 1990.

Intertextuality is a major theme in Bakhtin's influential work; see especially Bakhtin 1986. Material relevant to the material intelligence principle and the intuitive knowledge principle is discussed in diSessa 2000; the intuitive knowledge principle is also much discussed in terms of how knowledge functions in modern workplaces; see Gee, Hull, & Lankshear 1996. For multimodality, see Kress & van Leeuwen 1996, 2001.

5

TELLING AND DOING:
WHY DOESN'T LARA CROFT
OBEY PROFESSOR VON CROY?

OVERT INFORMATION
AND IMMERSION IN PRACTICE

IN TERMS OF HUMAN LEARNING, INFORMATION IS A VEXED THING. On one hand, humans are quite poor at learning from lots of overt information given to them outside the sorts of contexts in which this information can be used. This problem can be mitigated if the learners have already had lots of experience of such contexts and can simulate the contexts in their minds as they listen to or read information. Humans tend to have a very hard time processing information for which they cannot supply such simulations. They also tend readily to forget information they have received outside contexts of actual use, especially if they cannot imagine such contexts.

On the other hand, humans don't learn well when they are just left to their own devices to operate within complex contexts about which they know very little. Children who know no physics and have no mathematical tools but who are nonetheless left to discover Galileo's principles of motion on their own by mucking around with ramps and balls are likely only to be angered and frustrated. In fact, since Galileo used his deep knowledge of geometry to discover these principles, the children are actually being asked to engage in a harder task than the one Galileo (a genius if there ever was one) faced, since they lack both his prior knowledge and sophisticated tools.

The dilemma then is this: For efficacious learning, humans need overt information, but they have a hard time handling it. They also need immersion in actual contexts of practice, but they can find such contexts confusing without overt information and guidance. This is just the dilemma between overt telling versus immersion in practice that has characterized educational debates for years. Educators tend to polarize the debate by stressing one thing (telling or immersion) over the other and not discussing effective ways to balance and integrate the two. They tend to associate support for overt telling in education with conservative politics and support for immersion in practice with liberal politics. Needless to say, they have not solved the problem.

The makers of video games—good capitalists that they are—have no such luxury. If they don't solve this problem, no one is going to learn to play their games. And if no one can learn their games, no one will buy them. If only for good old "Darwinian" reasons (the survival-of-the-fittest theories of learning on the market), the games that survive and flourish on the market have solved the problem. Indeed, different games solve it in different ways. This is just a specific example of a point I am trying to make quite generally in this book: Good video games incorporate good learning principles, because otherwise there would be no video games, because too few people would have purchased them.

In this chapter—through a discussion of two good video games—I take up some of the ways in which video games deal with overt information and guidance on one hand and immersion in practice on the other. Their solution to our dilemma is to deny there are two hands here and to see overt information and immersion in practice as two fingers on the same hand.

LEARNING TO BE LARA CROFT

Lara Croft, the heroine of the *Tomb Raider* series of games (and now a movie), is one of the most famous video-game characters in the world. Lara is the pampered aristocratic daughter of Lord Henshingly Croft, and she has wanted for nothing in her (virtual) life. When Lara was a young girl, a lecture by the noted archaeologist Professor Werner Von Croy triggered in her a lifelong desire for travel to remote places in search of adventure. Some time after hearing that lecture, when Lara was 16 and away at boarding school, she came across a copy of *National Geographic* magazine that featured an article by Von Croy. From the article, Lara learned that he was preparing for a new archaeological tour across Asia.

Lara showed the article to her parents and demanded to accompany Von Croy on his expedition. Lord Henshingly then wrote Von Croy offering him financial assistance if he would let Lara join him. Von Croy replied that he remembered Lara's incessant but insightful questions at his earlier lecture. Her company as an assistant was welcomed, as was the offer of financial support. Thus, Von Croy became Lara's mentor. *Tomb Raider* games depict Lara as an adult using the skills she learned as a young girl from Von Croy and pursuing danger, knowledge, and adventure across the world.

Lara—one of the few female lead characters in video games—is one of the most physically agile characters in the world of such games. The player can manipulate Lara to engage in more physical maneuvers than most other heroes in adventure and shooter games. She can walk, run, do both standing and running jumps, jump back, crouch, duck, roll, climb, cling to ledges and maneuver along them, and even jump and swing on vines and branches. She (the player) uses all these skills to defeat enemies and to explore the treacherous landscapes of ancient tombs and temples, deserts, jungles, and foreign cities.

So far what I have described—the story of Von Croy and Lara—is only back story, a story that gamers are told (in the booklet that comes with a game or in bits and pieces they have learned while playing the games) but haven't experienced for themselves. However, *Tomb Raider: The Last Revelation*, a game late in the series, returns to this back story as part of the game. The first episode in *Tomb Raider: The Last Revelation* shows Lara as a 16-year-old being trained by Professor Von Croy after they have just broken into an ancient and sacred royal tomb in Cambodia. The player now actually gets to live and play Lara's apprenticeship when she was a girl.

This first episode is a real part of the game. (An episode is like a chapter in a book.) The player must search for treasures and avoid many pitfalls and dangers, just as in any other episode, though things are easier here than they are in the later episodes. At the same time, however, this episode is also meant as a training module where the player is explicitly coached on how to play the game. This coaching is done in a fascinating way. As Von Croy trains Lara to be an adventurer, he is also simultaneously training the player to operate the computer controls and play the game. While similar things appear in other games, they are handled here in a particularly nice way.

After an opening video showing Von Croy bursting into the ancient Cambodian tomb (a very large building with many levels and twisting paths) and a display of the words "Cambodia 1984," we hear Von Croy say, "And so we breech the sanctum of the ancients, the first footfalls in this tomb for centuries." We then immediately see the young Lara next to him, looking around in awe, and hear her say, "This place gives me the creeps, [pause] after you." This sort of not-so-respectful patter is typical of Lara, a rather spoiled and self-satisfied young girl.

Von Croy proceeds to tell Lara to be careful, that not all is as it seems. Concealed traps and pitfalls are everywhere. She is to stay close to him and follow his instructions. Since good men have died for the information contained in this tomb—and bad ones have "bartered the information for their own ends"—Von Croy insists that "[f]or this we must respect it, we will not deviate from its route and you will not deviate from my instruction." Altogether, Von Croy comes across as an intimidating and dominating professor.

But, of course, Lara is not cowered by him. She has, after all, just said that he gives her the creeps even more than the old tomb itself. The game encourages the player not to be too deferential to Von Croy either. Even though Von Croy has told Lara (the player) to stay close and not deviate from the straight route ahead, the only way that the player (Lara) can find hidden treasures (like golden skulls) is to wander away from him and explore things a bit. In fact, as Von Croy is commanding Lara to stay close, a willful player (as Lara) is probably looking behind a group of pillars to see if they hide anything interesting. If players are not willful in this way, by the end of the episode they will have missed lots of good stuff and probably will play it over again.

The player is placed, by the very design of the game, in the same psychological space as Lara—learning from Von Croy but not subordinating oneself entirely to his old-fashioned professorial need for dominance. The game's design encourages the player to take on a certain sort of attitude and relationship with Von Croy—and, more generally, a certain sort of personality—that represents, in fact, just the sort of person that Lara is.

When I played the game, I was a bit intimidated by Von Croy. Based probably on a lifetime of (trying to look as if I am) following the orders of authority figures like deans, I found myself wanting to follow his orders to the T. But I also wanted the treasures and found myself guiltily sneaking down paths off Von Croy's route and thereby becoming more like Lara and less like myself.

The game has a neat way to ensure that even inept players will discover that they can find good things if they are willing to disobey the professor. For example, when I was playing the game, at one point Von Croy ordered Lara to jump across a cavern; in doing so, she fell in the water below, due to my ineptness in controlling her (via the computer's keys). She can climb back up again and try the jump again (indeed, she needs to do this to follow Von Croy and eventually complete the episode). But, low and behold, as I (Lara) swam toward land, I (Lara) discovered a golden skull in the water. A player cannot help but think: What if I purposely disobey orders and jump and climb other than where I am told? What other good things will I find? Soon one is just a bit more like the willful and spoiled Lara herself (and practicing yet more jumps and climbs). In such video games, players get practice in trying out new identities that challenge some of their assumptions about themselves and the world. A good science class should do the same.

STRANGE LANGUAGE: VON CROY TEACHES LARA HOW TO PLAY A VIDEO GAME

After Von Croy has told Lara to follow closely and has pushed a hidden stone in a wall to lower a floor-full of sharp spikes ahead, they come to a small obstacle. Von Croy says, "The first obstacle, a small hop to test your—how do you say—pluck. Press and hold walk, now push forward."

Now this is, if you think about it, a strange thing to say. However, it does not seem the least bit strange when one is actually playing the episode. Von Croy is talking to the virtual character Lara, a character who walks and jumps in the virtual world but has no computer whose keys she can press, push, or hold. However, the player who is playing as the character Lara does have a computer and must learn to manipulate its keys to make Lara come alive. (I played *Tomb Raider: The Last Revelation* on a computer, but *Tomb Raider* games are also available, and probably more often played on, game platforms, which, of course, have controls of their own—controls on a hand-held controller—that the player needs to learn.) Thus, Von Croy's remark perfectly melds and integrates talk to Lara and talk to the player. This melding is part of what marries the player's real-world identity as a player and his or her virtual identity as Lara.

But things are even yet more interesting here. When Von Croy says, "Press and hold walk," he means for the player to press and hold the Shift key on the computer, which is the key that makes Lara walk rather than run. (When she walks she automatically stops at ledges; when she runs, she runs past them and falls. It is easier to have her walk up to dangerous ledges than to run up to them.) When Von Croy continues with "now push forward," he means for the player, who is now holding down the Shift key, to press the Arrow key pointing up on the computer, which is the key that moves Lara forward. When the player does this combination of keystrokes, Lara walks up to the obstacle and automatically stops at its edge. She is now ready to jump.

At this point Von Croy says, "Come, come, child, do not fear, this is merely an appetizer for the perils ahead. Push forward and jump together." This tells the player to press the Up Arrow key (move forward) and the Alt key (the key that makes Lara jump) together. When the player does so, Lara easily jumps over the obstacle.

Here Von Croy is using the functional names for the keys, the actions they carry out in the virtual world, actions like "walk," "forward," and "jump," rather than the computer names for the keys, things like "Shift key," "Up Arrow key," and "Alt key." So, then, how does the player know what keys to press? A player knows this in three ways.

1. The player can do as I did and look in the booklet that comes with the game. This means that when the player is listening to Von Croy, he or she is simultaneously looking up the computer key equivalents of his commands (another way in which the virtual and real worlds are married).

2. The player can make intelligent guesses from having played other *Tomb Raider* games or games like them.

3. The player can do as my child does in similar circumstances and press all the keys until he or she gets the right result and thereby finds the right key.

Throughout the first episode, Von Croy continues to talk this way, telling the player (Lara) about even more complicated actions that he or she (and Lara) can do, saying things like: "This gap is wider and the edge is treacherous. First walk to the edge. Then press forward and jump together. When you are in midair, press and hold action. You will grab the outcrop." By the end of the episode, the player has both finished the first episode of the game (and it's a very long game, like most good video games) and learned how to operate the basic controls. The player also has learned some basic strategies of how to explore the virtual world and avoid certain dangers.

LARA AND LEARNING

Why is this "strange" language not actually strange when one is playing the game? In a good many video games, players hear such language, language that "confuses" the virtual world (e.g., "walk") and the real world of the player at the computer (e.g., "press the walk key"). Such language, in fact, represents a very basic and crucial learning principle, one regularly ignored in schools. Learners cannot do much with lots of overt information that a teacher has explicitly told them outside the context of immersion in actual practice. At the same time, learners cannot learn without some overt information; they cannot discover everything for themselves.

The solution is to give information in context and to couch it in ways that make sense in the context of embodied action. Consider a simple real-world example. Telling someone "When your car is skidding, turn the wheel in the direction of the skid" works less well than saying "When your car is skidding, look in the direction of the skid." (Of course, when the driver looks in that direction, he or she will turn the wheel in that direction.) The latter formulation couches the information in a way that allows it to be integrated with embodied action both in the learner's mental simulation and in actual action on the spot.

In good classroom science instruction, an instructor does not lecture for an extended period and then tell the learners to go off and apply what they have learned in a group science activity. The learners won't remember most of what they have heard. And, in any case, none of it will have made much sense in a situated and embodied way that is actually usable. Yet good science instructors don't just turn learners loose to engage in activities with no help at all.

Rather, as group members are discovering things through their own activity, the good science instructor comes up, assesses the progress they are making and the fruitfulness of the paths down which they are proceeding in their inquiry, and then gives overt information that is, at that point, usable. The instructor gives group members information that facilitates their further movement down a fruitful path they are already on, or sends them down a related but more fruitful path than the one on which they have hit, or gets them to think about an aspect of the phenomenon they are investigating that they have not yet considered but for which they are ready and ripe. And, indeed, after such embodied inquiry, there are even times when learners need and are ready for lectures. They are now able to give a good many of the words and phrases in the lecture situated and embodied meanings through the their own mental simulations of former and future actions.

However, there is more at stake in Von Croy's "mixed" language—language that mixes talk to Lara about the virtual world and to the player about the game's controls. Such language is one among many devices in a good video game that encourages the player to relate, juxtapose, and meld his or her real-world identity (actually, multiple real-world identities) and the virtual identity of the character he or she is playing in the virtual world of the game. Such a process also encourages the player to adopt what I called in chapter 3 a projective identity.

I argued earlier that projective identities are the heart and soul of active and critical learning. Children who take responsibility for the sort of classroom virtual scientist they are and will become throughout the school year and relate this proactively to their real-world identities (some of which may have started as virtual identities in other play or school domains) are engaged in real learning, learning as a refashioning of self. Of course, no child can do this if no such virtual identity and world—a world of imagined scientists and science enacted in words, deeds, and texts—is present in the classroom.

But let me return to our game. As is typical of training modules in good video games, this first training episode of *Tomb Raider: The Last Revelation* does not tell the player everything he or she needs to know and do in order to play the rest of game. All the episode does is give the player enough information and skill to play and learn from the subsequent episodes. Since each episode gets more difficult, the player is, in fact, always both playing and learning. Indeed, the distinction between playing (doing the actual activity) and learning is blurred in a video game, as is the distinction between master and beginner, since players always willingly face new challenges as a game progresses (games get harder as they progress) and as new games do new things, make new demands, and get better and better at challenging players in creative ways.

When the second episode of *Tomb Raider: The Last Revelation* begins, Von Croy challenges Lara (you) to put your newly acquired skills to the test in a race against him through unfamiliar territory to grab a sacred stone in another part of the temple. Unfortunately, after he says, "We will race for the Iris, on the count of three: one, two," he takes off without saying "three," giving himself a good head start.

If you've found and collected all eight golden skulls in the first episode, Von Croy chooses the Path of the Heretical, a more difficult test. If you haven't found all the skulls, then he chooses the Path of the Virtuous, an easier test. This is typical of good video games and represents several of the learning principles discussed earlier: A good video game adapts to the level of the player, rewards different players differently (but rewards them all), and often stays at the edge of the player's regime of competence.

It is also interesting and an important fact that the game rewards the player for finding the golden skulls. Finding them requires the player to disregard Von Croy's commands to stay close and follow his every command. The player is encouraged by the very design of the game to be more Lara-like—playful and willful—leaving behind his or her own fears and hesitations about authority and the risks of exploration.

LEARNING IN A SUBDOMAIN OF THE FULL DOMAIN

The third episode of the game starts with Lara, now an adult, off adventuring in Egypt. Von Croy, older as well, returns from time to time in the story. By now the player has learned and lived through Lara's back story—even learned where and how she got her famous backpack (indeed, the player playing Lara as a teenager has picked it up). So, are the first two episodes "training" ("learning") or a "real" part of the game? They are, of course, both. In a good video game, the player learns to play the game by playing in a "subdomain" of the real game. This is an important learning principle and, again, one regularly ignored in school.

Many video games have an explicitly labeled training module. For example, many shooter games (like *Tom Clancy's Ghost Recon*, *Half-Life*, *Deus Ex*, or *Max Payne*) have such modules where instructors—sometimes sergeants shouting at you, sometimes more gentle instructors, even peaceful-looking female holograms as in the training module for *Half-Life*—talk to the player just as Von Croy talked to Lara (you). These modules are not episodes in the game, but the player moves through the same sorts of landscapes, performs the same sorts of actions, and engages with the same sorts of artifacts as in the "real" game (except the only way you can get killed in the training module is by blowing yourself up while trying to learn how to use dynamite and similar items, something I have done on more than one occasion).

Once the game proper starts, the first episode (sometimes several early episodes) is almost always something of a training module, even though it may not be labeled explicitly as such. In this episode, things are less hectic and demanding than they will get later on. (This is not to say that things aren't hectic and demanding, enough to provide a feel for the game world and what is to come). *System Shock 2* provides a particularly good example of this sort of first episode.

In the first episode, the player is rarely under any sort of time pressure and generally pays only a small price for mistakes. Usually no demanding enemies—often none at all—attack the player. Furthermore, this episode usually offers a concentrated sample of the most basic and important actions, artifacts, and interactions that the player will need to deal with throughout the game.

Nonetheless, these early episodes are very much part of the game and its story. *Tomb Raider: The Last Revelation* combines the training module and the early episodes as places where demands are lowered enough so that lots of fundamental learning can be done "on site" in the "real" world (i.e., in this case, the "real virtual world") of the game (and not, say, in books or through lots of overt instruction out of context).

By saying that in a good video game, players learn to play the game by playing in a "subdomain" of the real game, I mean that training modules and early episodes, where fundamental learning gets done, are built as simplified versions of the same world in which the player will live, play, and learn throughout the game. Learning is not started in a separate place (e.g., a classroom or textbook) outside the domain in which the learning is going to operate. At the same time, the learner is not thrown into the "real" thing—the full game—and left to swim or drown.

Because good video games have training modules, early episodes as further training in the fundamentals, and more advanced learning throughout as one is ready, all done in the game's virtual world, something interesting happens to the learner. Let me tell you a little story to make the point: Once when I was giving a talk about video games and learning, there were two excellent game players (and computer experts) in their mid-20s in the audience—dragged to the talk by the academic whose research they assisted. After my talk, this academic asked them publicly what they thought about what I had said. Were the sorts of learning principles I had talked about really operating in these games? The two players both said that, yes, they were aware that such principles were at work when they were playing video and computer games, but that they had never thought of what they were doing as "learning."

This is what is magical about learning in good video games—and in good classrooms, too—learners are not always overtly aware of the fact that that are "learning," how much they are learning, or how difficult it is. Learners are embedded in a domain (a semiotic domain like a branch of science or a good video game) where, even when they are learning (and since the domain gets progressively harder, they are always learning), they are still in the domain, still a member of the team (affinity group), still actually playing the game, even if only as a "newbie."

TRANSFER AND BEYOND IN VIDEO GAMES

Of course, there are times in a video game where players recognize that they are learning. These are the times—and, as the game progresses, such times become more common—where learners see that their now-routinized mastery, developed earlier in the game and in playing similar games, breaks down. They face a new challenge for which their now-routinized skills don't work. In cases like this, a form of learning happens that is just the sort we want to encourage in school but often have little success doing: transfer of prior knowledge mixed with innovation. Let me make this point with an extended example from my own game playing.

By the end of the first-person shooter game *Return to Castle Wolfenstein*, I had learned a strategy for killing Nazi "Super Soldiers" (robotlike, mechanically and biologically enhanced beings who can take and give a great deal of damage) of which I was quite proud. In fact, I had gotten quite good at this strategy.

Here is what I did: I positioned myself quite far from a Super Soldier, behind good cover, and then sniped at him using a long-distance rifle with a good scope, ducking below cover each time the Super Soldier fired back. After many shots, the Super Soldier died, and I had suffered little or no damage. Suffering little or no damage is important—it does little good to win a battle but have so few health points left that you will easily die in the next battle, even with a weak opponent, before you can find a health kit to heal yourself. In a closer battle with a Super Soldier, even if I won, I tended to take lots of damage, which left me too weak for the fights to come. However, I do know other players who learned good strategies for defeating the Super Soldiers up close without taking too much damage.

At the end of *Return to Castle Wolfenstein*, the player (playing U.S. Office of Secret Actions' Agent Major B. J. Blazkowitz—a very famous video-game character, because he originally appeared in one of early first-person shooter games, *Wolfenstein 3D*, a game some consider the "mother" of all first-person shooter games) must face Heinrich I, an ancient deadly knight the Nazis have risen from his grave through dark mysterious rituals. Heinrich is one heck of a Super Soldier. He can cause zombies to rise from the ground to attack you (Blazkowitz). Furthermore, he can cause a myriad of spirits to fly through the air, find you wherever you are trying to hide, and attack you. If you get close to Heinrich, he can cause rocks from surrounding pillars and arches to fall on you; he can pull you in closer to him by swiping his sword on the ground; and he can easily kill you with one blow of his massive sword.

Trying to hide behind cover and snipe Heinrich does not work—trust me, I tried it many times. The flying spirits find you every time and kill you. So, I discovered that my routinized strategy was no good. At this point, the game forced me—at its very end, to boot—to try other things and learn something new, or not finish it.

Of course, in such a situation, players can call on experiences they have had in other games, adapting them to the current circumstances, or they can try something entirely new. The first strategy, calling on previous experience, is an example of what learning theorists call "transfer." An example of transfer at work would be a case where a student applies something he or she has learned about reasoning in biology to a new problem faced in a social studies class. Transfer does not always work and can be dangerous. (Maybe social studies is better off not being done in the style of biological thinking; then again, maybe not.) Transfer requires active learning and, if it is not to be dangerous, critical learning.

At one time, cognitive psychologists considered transfer to be a fairly easy phenomenon. Then they went through a stage of thinking that people were, in fact, quite bad at transfer and it was, for all practical purposes, impossible to trigger transfer in school learning. Now they believe transfer is crucial to learning but not at all easy to trigger in learners, especially in school. Getting transfer to happen typically requires making the learners overtly aware of how two different problems or domains share certain properties at a deeper level. That is, it requires thinking at a design level, thinking about how two problems or domains are structured or "designed" in similar ways, ways that may be obscured by the more superficial features of the problems or domains.

Facing Heinrich, and having failed many times, I decided to call on what I had learned in playing other video games. I tried a strategy I had learned from *American McGee's Alice* when trying to kill "bosses" (particularly powerful enemies). I moved wildly around, zigzagging around and away from Heinrich, stopping only quickly to shoot him a couple of times with my most powerful weapons, moving again to avoid his fire and the zombies and spirits he sent after me, all the while frantically searching for health kits laying among the fallen rocks and rubble that would repair the damage I was taking.

This strategy had worked to kill bosses like the Duchess, the Centipede, and the Queen of Hearts in *Alice*. It almost worked here. I survived longer than I had in all my other attempts. But, alas, Heinrich got me in the end. I went down with more pride and dignity (remember, in my projective identity, I care about such things), but I went down nonetheless.

Since some of the *Alice* strategy seemed to work, I needed to think about what in it to keep and what in it to change. Here is where transfer marries innovation. In this type of situation, the player has to think of something new (new to the player, at least; others may have already hit on it) in the context of keeping what is useful from past experience. This is a key moment for active and potentially critical learning. It is the place where previous experience is, at one and the same time, recruited and transformed, giving rise to newer experiences that can be used and transformed in the future.

Here is what I did. First I used another instance of transfer and did something I have done in a good many shooter games: I ran out of a tunnel I was in, quickly pounded Heinrich with four rockets from my rocket gun, and then ran quickly back into my tunnel. Often in shooter games some of your enemies will follow you into the tunnel or other such narrow space, and they become easier targets, since they are not all spread out and you see them coming at you in a direct line. Some of Heinrich's key helpers (three Dread Knights and the Nazi who had brought him back to life) ran after me, and I easily killed them.

Heinrich was momentarily without helpers, though that would soon change. Now I knew I had to run out and face him—he was not about to follow me back to the tunnel and would have killed me there, in any case, by sending his spirits at me from afar (his version of my sniping strategy). The *Alice* strategy wasn't going to work without some serious modification. What to do? There is, of course, only one way to proceed: Think and try something. If you die, you go back to the drawing board.

I figured that I had to do my wild moving-around strategy from *Alice*, but closer in to Heinrich. If I stayed close, the flying spirits flew over my head for the most part (since they are really a device to stop people from trying to kill Heinrich from a distance). Yet if I stayed too close, he would draw me into him by hitting the ground with his sword and then, as I flew toward him, he would slay me with one blow. What seemed to be called for was a more constrained version of the *Alice* strategy, stressing moving toward and quickly away from Heinrich in straight lines more than the wider and more circular motion I had used in *Alice*. (Other players have had success with circular strafing when fighting Heinrich, but I am no good at tightly controlled circular movements.)

I ran out of my tunnel and tried my new part-transfer, part-innovation strategy. After four direct battles with Heinrich, interrupted by wild runs to find health kits to repair my damage, I had him seriously weakened. Things appeared to be working and I had gotten farther than ever before. But by then I had just less than half my health, even after I had used the last health kit to be found.

Then something happened that can be added to transfer and innovation as a learning strategy: a lucky discovery. As I used the last health kit, I realized I was out of ammunition for my Venom gun and switched to my Telsa gun, which fires electric rays. I had found the last health kit behind some boxes and, as I stood behind them, I noticed that the rather slow-moving Heinrich was moving toward the boxes to finish me off. Thus, I ran quickly around the boxes and around behind Heinrich, who was now staring over the boxes at where I had been standing. His back momentarily turned to me, I ran right up to him and blasted him from behind with the Telsa.

It was risky, but he had already taken enough damage that this finished him off. He died in a rage and I immediately saw a cut scene (a short video). The Super Soldier project and the Heinrich project had been Himmler babies. In the cut scene I saw Himmler looking through binoculars. He had obviously been watching my battle with Heinrich from atop a far away hill.

Himmler says with dismay, "This American, he has ruined everything." His aide then says, "Herr Himmler, the plane is waiting to take you back to Berlin." Himmler is reluctant to go; he obviously does not want to have to explain his failure to Hitler. The aide pushes him: "Sir, the Fuehrer is expecting your arrival." Himmler walks very slowly back to the car. It's quite satisfying to have finished off Heinrich and to have pissed off Himmler at one and the same time.

Though this example may seem trivial—with its talk of Super Soldiers and risen dead—it represents several components of one very important type of active learning.

1. The learner realizes that a more or less routinized strategy does not work and quits using it.
2. The learner transfers skills and strategies from previous experience by seeing underlying similarities between that experience and the current problem (*American McGee's Alice* and *Return to Castle Wolfenstein* are, at the surface level, quite different games, though both are shooter games—*Alice* is a third-person shooter and *Wolfenstein* is a first-person shooter.)
3. The learner learns that, while school sometimes sets up problems so that earlier solutions transfer directly to later ones, this rarely happens in real life. The learner adapts and transforms the earlier experience to be transferred to the new problem through creativity and innovation.
4. The learner also uses (and is prepared to use) what he or she discovers—often "by accident"—on the spot, on the ground of practice, while implementing the new transformed strategy (as I did when I circled behind Heinrich looking for me over the boxes). This requires reflection not after or before action but in the midst of action. The learner remains flexible, adapting performance in action.

SYSTEM SHOCK 2

System Shock 2, like *Deus Ex*, combines elements of a role-playing game with a first-person shooter. As a story, it also combines genres, combining the science fiction of star travel, the action of a war movie, and the horror of a movie like *Alien*. *System Shock 2* takes place in the same fictional world as the original *System Shock* did, a universe in which humans have already colonized the solar system. In the first game, a super-powerful artificial intelligence system called SHODAN went crazy and killed many people onboard the Citadel Space Station.

After SHODAN was stopped by the intrepid efforts of whoever played the first game, the governments of Earth came together in the United National Nominate (UNN). The UNN has struggled to control the megacorporations that have held power for a long time—the largest of which, the TriOptimum Corporation, was responsible for SHODAN's creation. This power struggle between government and the corporations has resulted in an uneasy truce in which the UNN holds power officially, but the corporations still hold a great deal of de facto power through their own armies and police forces.

Into this already tension-filled situation comes a new source of potential problems: TriOptimum, despite government efforts to keep corporations out of such projects, has built a new spaceship, the *Von Braun*, capable of faster-than-light travel. Indeed, the *Von Braun* is making its maiden voyage far beyond the solar system. The new technologies aboard the *Von Braun* have not been well tested and don't work as they should. The major problem is the ship's central computer, XERXES. XERXES is quite "buggy" and is having all sorts of problems (shades of SHODAN). Furthermore, the crew, made up of both UNN and TriOptimum personnel, has separated into two warring factions that mistrust and hate each other.

When the *Von Braun* passes the Tau Ceti star system, it receives, and decides to respond to, a distress call coming from Tau Ceti. At that point, something goes terribly wrong on the ship. This is the disaster to which you awake when you—a military officer frozen for the long voyage—are called out of cyber-slumber to help solve the problem.

When you start playing *System Shock 2*, you start out a few years before the Von Braun's voyage. You arrive at a military recruitment station (in a first-person view, so you can't see yourself, just the world around you). There you choose from one of three career paths: the Marines, the Navy, or the OSA (a special service that teaches psychic powers). This determines the basic statistics (e.g., how strong you are) and skills (e.g., how good you are at hacking into computers) with which you will start the game. Marines are weapon and combat oriented. Navy personnel are less skilled with weapons and are more oriented toward technology and research. They have skills necessary to hack security programs and to engage in research about the creatures and objects they find. OSA personnel are sort of like a psychic CIA and have developed psychic powers that allow them to do a variety of special things (e.g., Kinetic Redirection, which allows you to pull distant objects toward you, or Remote Electron Tampering, which deactivates all active security alarms).

Overall there are nine different skills and five different statistics in *System Shock 2*. Each character type starts with some of these and not others, different for each type. The nine skills are: Hacking (makes you more effective at breaking into enemy computers), Repair (allows you to fix broken items), Modify (lets you add new features to your existing weapons), Maintenance (helps you keep your weapons in working order), Research (lets you research new technologies and enemy physiologies), Standard Combat (makes you an expert in the use of conventional weapons like pistols and shotguns), Energy Weapons (improves your use of energy weapons like lasers and EMP rifles), Heavy Weapons (helps you use larger weapons like Grenade Launchers and Fusion Cannons), and Exotic Weapons (gives you more skill with the special bioweapons you discover during the game). The five statistics are: Strength, Endurance, Psionics, Agility, and Cybernetic Affinity.

Having made your choice, you sign up for a four-year hitch. In each of the first three years you are given a choice of different postings, different for each character type, each of which will enhance your character's skills and stats in certain ways. You don't actually play these initial postings but see videos and read about what you have gained by each experience you have chosen. Thus, by the time the game play starts in earnest, your own choices have shaped the sort of character you are going to be.

Your initial choice of character and the three postings you have chosen set your initial distribution of skills and stats, the ones with which you will enter the first episodes of the game. Once you get into the game, you find and are sometimes rewarded with (by other characters in the virtual world) cybernetic modules. You can use these modules at upgrade units to buy improvements in your different skills and stats. The higher the skill level you are attempting to purchase, the more cybernetic modules it costs you.

Since cybernetic modules are hard to come by, you can become a real expert in only a few areas (whether skills or stats or some combination). Thus, you must pick intelligently rather than squandering modules on a little of this and a little of that. Since some of the best items and weapons in the game require you to get the maximum score you can achieve in a specific skill or stat before you can use them, if you spend all of your cybernetic module points trying to become a generalist, you won't be able to use these neat items or weapons by the end of the game.

Once you have completed your first three postings, the game proper starts. You are in your fourth posting and find yourself awakened from a cryo-slumber on the *Von Braun* with no memory of recent events. You immediately see that things have gone badly wrong. Pipes are broken, debris is all over the floor. Bodies are scattered across the ground and you hear crashing noises and screams everywhere.

You are soon contacted via e-mail by Dr. Janice Polito, the Senior Systems Analyst onboard the *Von Braun*, and told that you have been cybernetically enhanced so that you can receive messages from her and others on your built in "PDA" (Personal Data Assistant). Your cyber-enhancements also allow you to use special skills and tools. She tells you that everything has gone wrong, though you get no details now. She says only that you need to reach her as quickly as possible on level four of the ship. It is no easy task getting there, since much of the ship is destroyed and XERXES appears to be trying to foil your every attempt.

As you travel around the corridors of the ship, there are three ways you learn more about the situation, and, thus, can begin putting the story together.

1. You occasionally get messages on your PDA from Dr. Polito telling you about things that have just happened and giving you advice on what you must do next.
2. You find small computer disks scattered around the ship that hold the log messages of the crew. As you pick these up and read them, the story slowly unfolds and you also get more information on how to proceed.
3. The cybernetic system that's been installed in you can pick up psychic signals. When your system comes in contact with these, it interprets them as light and sound. The result is that occasionally, as you move through the ship, you see "ghosts" of people in the actions they took prior to their deaths.

Using these clues, you must figure out what has happened to the crew of the *Von Braun* and how you're going to stop the menace.

Whatever has taken control of the ship has found a way to infect the crew and turn them into zombies. Other creatures you run into, as you move through the ship, include giant spiders, cybernetic nursemaids, and stealthy cyber-assassins. As you get to the higher decks of the ship, you encounter giant security bots and gun turrets that can mow you down in seconds. All of these creatures have been designed with AI that allows them each to behave differently and seemingly intelligently.

There are many different ways to approach the many fights and problems you face in *System Shock 2*. And, of course, you can play the game as different characters—Marine, Navy, or OSA—each of which can be designed in different ways by your choices at the beginning and throughout the game. So, in reality, there are even different types of Marine, Navy, and OSA characters. Each different set of choices gives the game a different feel, so you can play it a number of times as if it were a different game. While you will, on the second go-round, know where many of the items are hidden, there's still a big difference between a Heavy Weapons expert blowing up whole groups of foes, a Hacker bypassing security systems and doors rather than fighting, and a Psi master using mind power to get through problems.

System Shock 2, like all good video games, recruits a number of the learning principles we have already discussed. Players make choices that allow them to play the game according to their own favored styles or explore new ones. There are multiple routes to solve problems. Players get multiple and multimodal sources of information to enable their own discoveries about the story, the virtual world, and the problems they face. *System Shock 2* also has training modules and early episodes that, like *Tomb Raider: The Last Revelation*, exemplify important learning principles.

TRAINING MODULES AND EARLY EPISODES IN *SYSTEM SHOCK 2*

When you are at the recruitment station at the beginning of *System Shock 2*, you can choose to go into several rooms that constitute the game's training modules. Here you hear talk much like the talk that Professor Von Croy addressed to Lara Croft in *Tomb Raider: The Last Revelation*. A disembodied voice welcomes you when you enter the first training room and tells you that you are about to engage in a virtual training course using a "simulated cyber-interface identical to an actual military-grade cyber-interface." The voice then says: "Move the mouse, see how it changes where you look? That means you're in Shoot Mode. Hit the Tab key. This puts you in Use Mode where you can use your mouse to interact with items in the world."

Once again we see here a language that mixes references to you as a virtual character in the virtual world of the game (e.g., "actual military-grade cyber-interface") and references to the computer in the real world on which you, a real person, are playing the game. You begin to learn to play the game by engaging in a language that already fuses your real-world identity and your virtual identity. The training modules continue this way until you know just enough, and not more, to start playing the game "for real" and thereby continue your learning through actual game play. There is no attempt to make you remember information ahead of time and outside embodied experience of specific situations.

When you start the game proper, you find yourself coming awake to a disaster. Dr. Polito tells you to get out quickly before the chambers you are in run out of oxygen. Then you must reach her. There is a great deal of commotion all around you. You find destruction, smoke, burning steam, loose electrical wires, and dead bodies everywhere as you seek a way out. You feel panicked, but you come to realize there is no reason for real panic. This first episode—as in many good video games—is both a real part of the game and part of your training. It is not really timed and nothing very bad can happen to you. You are meant to learn as you proceed. You get to experience the "feel" of the game—in this case, the pervasive panic and dread that spreads throughout—but without any bad consequences that will deter your learning.

One way you learn in this first episode and other early episodes of the game is by coming upon Information Kiosks as you travel through the lower levels of the *Von Braun*. Each of these is labeled "TriOptimum Information Terminal" along the side and says "A service of the TriOptimum corporation, presented for your convenience" at the top. When you highlight the kiosk by placing your mouse cursor on it, a message at the bottom of the screen says: "right click to use information kiosk." When you right-click the mouse, the kiosk opens up a message that gives you information about playing the game related to where you are at that time and to actions you will need to take at that point or very soon thereafter. This is just-in-time and on-demand information, situated in the sorts of contexts in which it makes sense and can be used.

For example, one information kiosk contains the following information: "Your PDA contains every email, log and info kiosk note you find onboard. It also contains an automatic note-taking utility, which keeps you informed of pressing tasks while onboard. You can access the PDA by left clicking on the Log icon on the right info bar." Very soon after reading this message, you find a log on a nearby body with a code in it that you need to get through the next door. Thanks to the Information Kiosk, you know how to access the log and the needed code. During the early episodes, you gain a wide variety of such situated information from these kiosks, though you can pass them by if you feel you don't need any more information and know how to use the basic controls of the game. In essence, a game manual has been spread throughout the early episodes of the game, giving information when it can be best understood and practiced through situated experience.

Dr. Polito's early messages also give you situated information about how to play the game, and clues about the basic story. For example, when you find a power cell on the ground, she sends you a message (which you hear orally, thanks to your cyber-enhancements, and which is also written in a little box on the screen) that tells you that the power cell is dead but that there should be a recharger nearby. She then says, "Just use it and it will recharge all the power-driven devices in your possession." After you have recharged the cell, Dr. Polito tells you that you can open a nearby airlock door by plugging the recharged power cell into the power unit associated with the door. She then says, "Be quick about it, the vacuum seals won't hold up much longer." (Since this is the first episode, even if you are clumsy and slow, you will still make it.)

When you do get out of the decompressing chamber—before all the oxygen is gone—Dr. Polito praises you and rewards you with cybernetic modules with which you can upgrade your skills and stats. She explains how to do this at upgrade units that just happen to be in the very next room. She also tells you to use your cybernetic modules carefully, that they are "hard to come by." In fact, she only gives you four modules, and you cannot upgrade much with these. Thus even at the outset you must choose very carefully what new skills or stats you want and then build on these.

Dr. Polito then gives you further messages that help you on your way to find her. Of course, things don't always work out as she says—for example, XERXES has shut down the main elevator and closed certain exits. In these cases, you and Dr. Polito have to change strategies and seek for new ways to proceed. As you move on, things get progressively harder. You eventually face enemies—zombies—that try to (and can) kill you. You engage in your first fights, using strategies available to your character type and based on the choices you have made about skills and statistics.

These early fights are easier than ones to follow, allowing you to explore different strategies and get better at your chosen strategies, so that you can handle the more difficult battles. The game stays at the outer edge of what I called in chapter 3, the player's "regime of competence." Things are challenging, but not undoable. And, of course, you learn to save the game at crucial points, so when you do die, you don't have to start all over again, just from the last saved point.

The early episodes of *System Shock 2* also engage a number of other learning principles that are typical of good video games. First of all, such games *order* the sorts of situations and problems with which they confront the player. It's not just that easier ones come earlier. Even more crucially, earlier situations and problems are designed to lead a player to discover and practice fruitful patterns and generalizations in regard to skills and strategies. These patterns and generalizations turn out to be useful ones both for playing the rest of the game and as the basis for more complicated patterns and generalizations later when one faces more complex situations and problems.

Too often in school—especially in progressive pedagogies that stress immersing children in rich activities without a good deal of teacher guidance—children confront cases early in their learning that are not very helpful. Since the children are in a rich environment with little guidance, nothing stops them from starting with complex cases rather than easier and more basic ones. Such complex cases, thanks to the fact that all children are powerful pattern recognizers, often lead children to hit on interesting patterns and generalizations that are, in fact "garden paths." Such garden-path patterns and generalizations are not fruitful for the future, however interesting and even intelligent they are for the present. In fact, they may very well lead children to miss easier, more basic and useful patterns and generalizations that would have facilitated finding the correct patterns and generalizations later for more complex cases.

The issue here is not starting children (or game players, for that matter) with easy cases. The issue is starting them with cases that are basic or fundamental in the sense that they lead the learner to discover and practice what are, in fact, fruitful patterns and generalizations. Fruitful patterns and generalizations are ones that allow the learner to make real progress in the domain and that can serve as the correct basis for more complicated patterns and generalizations that need to be discovered later by confronting more complex and less basic situations and cases.

To take a simple example from *System Shock 2*, consider that the first enemies one confronts are zombies that can be killed by whacking them with a crowbar. When the player later discovers that more powerful enemies are not easily killed by using the crowbar, he or she quickly hits on a strategy of using the crowbar to kill easier enemies, saving better weapons (and weapons wear out in this game) and ammunition for more powerful ones.

But now suppose the first enemies confronted were, say, the cyber-assassins that leap and jump away from the player and shoot arrows from afar while hiding behind objects. Not only would this frustrate the player early in the game before he or she had developed much skill, but the player also would have to use sophisticated weapons and movements. Should the player learn how to engage in such tactics and then apply them to zombies—enemies that are less powerful but that, in our current hypothesis, the player is seeing later, after he or she has learned to deal with the cyber-assassins—then the player will surely kill them, but will waste weapons and ammunition that are in short supply. The player will feel successful and powerful. But this strategy ultimately will lead him or her to a dead end when confronted with other creatures more powerful than the zombies when the player is low on good weapons or ammunition.

This is an all-too-simple case. In fact, games like *System Shock 2* design their early situations and problems in a quite sophisticated way to lead to fruitful learning. When later the player is confronted by harder situations and problems, he or she has just the right basis on which to make fruitful guesses about what to do. This is not to say that these situations and problems are not hard or that the player hits on the "right" answers quickly or without a good deal of thought and effort. (Remember, in a good video game there are always several different "right" answers.) It's just that the harder situations and problems are not, in fact, impossible, as they too often are in school when children confront them with no basis or a very misleading one. (Moral for teachers: Order your cases to subserve fruitful generalizations.)

Good video games do more than order the situations and problems the player faces in an intelligent way, at least in the early parts of the game. They also offer the player, in the early episodes, what I call a *concentrated sample*. By this I mean that they concentrate in the early parts of the game an ample number of the most fundamental or basic artifacts and tools the player needs to learn to use and actions the player needs to learn.

This is much like creating a foreign language classroom in which the teacher concentrates the most fundamental words, phrases, and grammatical forms into the early lessons. These words, phrases, and grammatical forms appear in this classroom sample more often and more concentrated together than they would be in the "real world." This allows the learner to overpractice the most basic and central parts of the language's vocabulary and grammar, setting a good foundation for later learning and learning in the real world.

To take one simple example: Finding and using health kits, or otherwise getting healed, is an important part of many shooter games. These kits heal the damage the player's character has sustained thus far in the game, returning the character to full health or, at least, giving back health. Shooter games are usually generous with health kits early on, allowing their discovery and use to become rather routine and allowing the player lots of health with which to learn by exploring and taking risks in the early part of the game. Later they become much more scarce, but by then the player has become adept at finding and using them.

Many times the early parts of games are replete with things to find, places and situations to explore, and things to do that teach players the range or types of artifacts to be discovered, places and spaces to be encountered, and actions to be expected. Players gain a good "feel" for the game and its controls. By the time they get past the early parts, they are more adept and ready for more advanced learning. Further, against a background of knowing what is normal or to be expected, players can assess and reason well about new and more special cases they encounter later.

What all this means is that good video games have a special way of dealing with what we would call in school the basics. When players start a new genre of game—say a real-time strategy game after having played only shooter games—they have no way of knowing what is a basic skill and what is a more advanced one. They don't yet know which skills will be used over and over and combined with others to make more complex skills.

Players discover what are basic skills "bottom up" by playing the game and others like it. Things they use and do repeatedly and combine in various ways turn out to be basic skills in the genre—and these things are different in different genres. Ironically, by the time new players are aware of what are basic skills in a given type of game—what are the basic elements that are used repeatedly and combined and often concentrated in the earlier episodes— they have already mastered them. Players come to realize that basic skills are simply the most common genre features of a game, learned by playing the game. For example, the player learns that finding and using health kits (regardless of what form they take) is a basic skill (and genre feature) in a shooter game (and does not exist in "realistic" military games, like *Operation Flashpoint*, where one shot maims or kills you for good).

But basic skills can be learned by playing the game—and not through decontextualized skill and drill—because the games are well designed in the ways in which they construct their training modules and early episodes and in the ways in which they order cases and concentrate their samples early on. Neither players of games nor children in school can learn by "playing" (i.e., immersion in rich activities) if they are forced to operate in poorly designed spaces.

And the real world—that is, the world without game designers or good teachers, themselves designers of virtual worlds in classrooms—is not in and of itself well designed for learning. Leaving children to the mercies of the real world by just letting them loose to think and explore is not education.

LEARNING PRINCIPLES

The discussion has suggested a variety of learning principles that are built into good video games. Here I bring these principles together. As in earlier chapters, the order of the principles is not important. And, once again, I intend each principle to be relevant both to learning in video games and learning in content areas in classrooms.

23. **Subset Principle**

Learning even at its start takes place in a (simplified) subset of the real domain.

24. **Incremental Principle**

Learning situations are ordered in the early stages so that earlier cases lead to generalizations that are fruitful for later cases. When learners face more complex cases later, the learning space (the number and type of guesses the learner can make) is constrained by the sorts of fruitful patterns or generalizations the learner has found earlier.

25. **Concentrated Sample Principle**

The learner sees, especially early on, many more instances of fundamental signs and actions than would be the case in a less controlled sample. Fundamental signs and actions are concentrated in the early stages so that learners get to practice them often and learn them well.

26. **Bottom-up Basic Skills Principle**

Basic skills are not learned in isolation or out of context; rather, what counts as a basic skill is discovered bottom up by engaging in more and more of the game/domain or game/domains like it. Basic skills are genre elements of a given type of game/domain.

27. **Explicit Information On-Demand and Just-in-Time Principle**

The learner is given explicit information both on-demand and just-in-time, when the learner needs it or just at the point where the information can best be understood and used in practice.

28. **Discovery Principle**

Overt telling is kept to a well-thought-out minimum, allowing ample opportunity for the learner to experiment and make discoveries.

29. **Transfer Principle**

Learners are given ample opportunity to practice, and support for, transferring what they have learned earlier to later problems, including problems that require adapting and transforming that earlier learning.

BIBLIOGRAPHICAL NOTE

On the issue of telling versus immersion, see the discussion and citations in Gee 2001. For further discussion of this issue in relation to learning in real domains and subdomains of real domains, see Beaufort 1999; Coe, Lingard, & Teslenko 2001; Dias, Freedman, Medway, & Pare 1999; Dias, Pare, & Farr 2000. These works are also relevant to the bottom-up basic skills principle developed in this chapter.

For accounts of transfer that fit the perspective on learning developed in this book, see Beach 1999 and Bransford & Schwartz 1999. The incremental learning principle plays an important role in some connectionist models of learning, see, for example, Elman 1991a, b; see also Karmiloff-Smith 1992. The explicit information "on-demand" and "just-in-time" principle has played a large role in writings on learning and thinking in modern workplaces, see Gee, Hull, & Lankshear 1996. On the learning principles in this chapter generally, see Gee 1994 and the citations there.

6

CULTURAL MODELS:
DO YOU WANT TO BE THE BLUE SONIC
OR THE DARK SONIC?

CONTENT IN VIDEO GAMES

CHAPTER 2 DISCUSSED A CASE WHERE A GRANDFATHER SAID THAT A six-year-old playing *Pikmin* was wasting his time, because he wasn't learning any "content." But, of course, video games *do* have content. *RollerCoaster Tycoon*, for instance, is about building, maintaining, and making a profit from an amusement park. *Medal of Honor Allied Assault* is about World War II and includes an absolutely hair-raising invasion of Omaha Beach, reminiscent of the opening scenes of the movie *Saving Private Ryan*. *Civilization III* is about world history and the dynamics of building and defending a society from the ground up. A great many video games, such as *Half-Life*, *Deus Ex*, and *Red Faction*, are about conspiracies where powerful and rich people or corporations seek to control the world through force and deception. In fact, the content of video games is nearly endless.

One of the things that makes video games so powerful is their ability to create whole worlds and invite players to take on various identities within them. When players do this, two things can happen: On one hand, their presupposed perspectives on the world might be reinforced. For example, if someone thinks war is heroic, *Return to Castle Wolfenstein* will not disabuse him or her of this viewpoint. If someone thinks that the quality of life is integrally tied to one's possessions, *The Sims* (a best-selling game where you build and maintain whole families and neighborhoods) will not disabuse him or her of this perspective, either.

On the other hand, through their creation of new and different worlds and characters, video games can challenge players' taken-for-granted views about the world. Playing through the invasion of Omaha Beach in *Medal of Honor Allied Assault* gives one a whole new perspective on what a full-scale battle is like. The movie *Saving Private Ryan* did this as well, but the game puts the player right in the midst of the action, pinned to the ground, surrounded by deafening noise and wounded, sometimes shell-shocked, soldiers, and facing the near certainty of a quick death if he or she makes one wrong move. As players make choices about people, their relationships, and their lives in *The Sims* (and sometimes players have made real people, such as their friends, into virtual characters in the game), they may come to realize at a conscious level certain values and perspectives they have heretofore taken for granted and now wish to reflect on and question.

This chapter is about the ways in which content in video games either reinforces or challenges players' taken-for-granted perspectives on the world. This is an area where the future potential of video games is perhaps even more significant than their current instantiations. It is also an area where we enter a realm of great controversy, controversy that will get even more intense as video games come to realize their full potential, for good or ill, for realizing worlds and identities.

SONIC THE HEDGEHOG AND CULTURAL MODELS

Sonic the Hedgehog—a small, blue, cute hedgehog—is surely the world's fastest, most arrogant, and most famous hedgehog. Originally Sonic was the hero in a set of games for the Sega Dreamcast game platform. However, now that the Dreamcast has been discontinued, he has shown up on the Nintendo GameCube in the game *Sonic Adventure 2 Battle*. Sonic can run really really fast. He can go even faster—like a blurry blue bomb—when he rolls into a ball. Either way, he can race around and through obstacles, dash into enemies, and streak through the landscape, leaping high in the air over walls and barriers.

The back story for *Sonic Adventure 2 Battle* is that the sinister Dr. Eggman, while searching the remnants of his grandfather's laboratory, uncovers a dark form of his arch-nemesis, Sonic, namely a black hedgehog named Shadow. Together the two conspire to unleash the Eclipse Cannon, a weapon of mass destruction. The government, unable to tell the blue Sonic from the dark Shadow (they look alike) arrests Sonic for Shadow's evil do-ings. Sonic escapes and has to free the world of Dr. Eggman and Shadow's evil to clear his name.

Players can play *Sonic Adventure 2 Battle* in two different ways. They can be "good" and play as the blue Sonic, or they can be "bad" and play as Sonic's look-alike, Shadow. If they choose Sonic, they play as Sonic, together with his friends Knuckles (a boy echidna) and Tails (a boy squirrel), trying to stop Dr. Eggman and Shadow from taking over the world. If they choose Shadow, they play as Shadow, together with his friends Rouge (a girl bat) and Dr. Eggman, trying to destroy the world. Players can switch back and forth, playing part of the Sonic quest and then changing to play part of the Shadow quest.

The six-year-old from chapter 2 also plays *Sonic Adventure 2 Battle*. When he originally got the game, he first played a few episodes from the Sonic quest and then started playing episodes from the Shadow quest. When he was playing as Shadow, he commented on the fact that "the bad guy was the good guy"—an odd remark. What he meant, of course, is that when you are playing as a virtual character in a video game, that character (you) is the hero (center) of the story and in that sense the "good guy" no matter how bad he or she might be from another perspective. This boy had never before played a game where the hero (himself) was, in terms of the story behind the virtual world, a bad or evil character.

Of course, video games are just as easy to design to allow you to play a sinner as a saint. Indeed, this fact has generated a good deal of controversy. While the video game world is replete with heroes who destroy evil, it also contains games where you can be a mob boss, a hired assassin, or a car thief. For example, in the notorious *Grand Theft Auto 2*, you play a budding young criminal, striving to make a name for yourself in a near-future world filled with drugs, guns, and gang wars. Your city is populated by three different gangs, each of which runs a different section of the city. Each gang has a set of pay phones that you can use to take on odd jobs stealing cars. The problem is that a gang will assign you work only if it respects you. You earn this re-spect by driving over to a rival gang's turf and shooting as many of their members as you can. Here you are certainly not a "good guy" in any tradi-tional mainstream sense. (*Grand Theft Auto 2* was followed by the highly suc-cessful sequels *Grand Theft Auto III* and *Grand Theft Auto: Vice City*.)

What our six-year-old discovered was that there are (besides still others) two different models of what counts as being or doing "good." In one model, what counts as being or doing good is determined by a character's own goals, purposes, and values, as these are shared with a particular social group to which he or she belongs. Shadow and his group (Rouge and Dr. Eggman) have a set of goals, purposes, and values in terms of which destroying the world is their valued goal.

If you want to play *Sonic Adventure 2 Battle* from Shadow's perspective you must act, think, and value (while playing) from this perspective, a perspective that makes Shadow "good" or "the hero." After all, you are fighting numerous battles as Shadow and feel delight when winning them and dismay when losing them. It would be absolutely pointless to play as Shadow but purposely lose battles because you disapprove of his value system. If you played that way, Shadow would die quickly in the first episode and you'd never see anything else in the Shadow part of the game.

In the other model, what counts as being and doing good is determined by a wider perspective than just a character's own goals, purposes, and values, as these are shared with a particular social group. Rather, what counts is determined by the values and norms of a "wider society" that contains multiple, sometimes competing, groups as well as more or less generalized rules and principles about behavior. In terms of this model, Sonic is fighting for social order and the survival of the majority, things that are considered good from the perspective of many different groups and in terms of rather general principles of right and wrong.

By "models" of what it means to be and do good, I do not mean "professional" philosophical positions on ethics or theological ones on morality. I just mean "everyday" people's conceptions. The first model, which we might call the group model, can be captured by something like the following: "I am acting like a good person when I am acting in the interests of some group of which I am a member and which I value." The second model, which we might call the general model, can be captured by something like this: "I am acting like a good person when I am acting according to some general conception of what is good and bad, a conception that transcends my more narrow group memberships."

These two models regularly come into conflict in real life and cause all sorts of interesting issues and questions to arise. Some people readily believe that their group interests and values are or ought to be the general good. Others think that general conceptions of good really just hide the narrow interests of particular groups in a society that has cloaked them as general goods. Yet other people believe their interests and values represent future, rather than present, general conceptions of good and may see going against current conceptions of good as a necessary evil for a greater future good. And, of course, there are multiple ideas about what general conceptions of good and bad are.

The six-year-old, in playing *Sonic Adventure 2 Battle*, has been confronted with these two models. He has realized that when you act in (or think in terms of) the role of someone else (even a hedgehog), this involves not merely taking on a new identity but sometimes thinking and valuing from a perspective that you or others may think "wrong" from a different perspective. He also has learned that experiencing the world from that perspective (in one's mind or in a video game) does not mean that he accepts it in the sense that he wants, in his real-world identity, to adopt the values and the actions that this perspective underwrites.

These two models of what it means to be good are examples of what I will call *cultural models*. Cultural models are images, story lines, principles, or metaphors that capture what a particular group finds "normal" or "typical" in regard to a given phenomenon. By "group" here I mean to single out anything ranging from small groups to the whole of the human race with everything in between. Cultural models are not true or false. Rather, they capture, and are meant to capture, only a partial view of reality, one that helps groups (and humans in general) go about their daily work without a great deal of preplanning and conscious thought. After all, if many things were not left on "automatic pilot," we would spend all our time thinking and never acting.

So, for example, something like "People are good people when they are acting so as to help their group (family, church, community, ethnic group, state—pick your group)" is a cultural model for many different groups. It is a version of what I called the group model of good. Something like "People are good when they are acting according to general principles of morality (pick your principles)" is another cultural model that many groups use, though they may accept different cultural models about what are typical general principles of morality. This is a version of what I called the general model of good. And, of course, the two models can and sometimes do come into conflict.

Since cultural models are usually not conscious for people and since people rarely, if ever, try to formulate them definitively and once and for all in words, there is no exactly right way to phrase them. If forced to formulate them, people will put them into different words in different situations. The best researchers can do, then, is study people's behavior and words when they are acting as members of a certain sort of group and acting within certain sorts of situations and eventually conclude that, given what they do and say, they must accept a certain cultural model for a given phenomenon, a cultural model we formulate in words the best we can. Of course, when they are acting as members of different groups in different situations they may not act according to the cultural model we have hypothesized but in terms of another one.

Social groups do not usually pay much overt attention to their cultural models, unless one is threatened. Of course, when cultural models are challenged or come into conflict with other such models, then they can come to people's conscious awareness (even to the conscious awareness of the group as a whole). If someone comes to think that the actions he or she is taking for the family's good conflict with general conceptions of morality (not even necessarily the person's own general conceptions), this can give rise to discomfort and conflict, discomfort and conflict that can be resolved in various ways.

A number of pervasive cultural models about gender have become conscious to people thanks to the fact that these models have been openly challenged in society. For example, a cultural model that holds that unmarried women are unfulfilled "spinsters" because they do not have families has long been challenged by feminists, single women with children, lesbian couples with children, and perfectly fulfilled single women with good careers with which they are satisfied. Of course, all these people existed before, but as long as they did not speak out and make themselves visible, they were easily rendered invisible and marginal by traditional cultural models. Once they did speak out, those models and the social work they did came to people's consciousness and had to be overtly defended or changed.

The world is full of an endless array of ever-changing cultural models. For example, what do you think of a teenage child who tells his or her parents to "F_ _ _ off?" Perhaps you apply a model like "Normal teenagers rebel against their parents and other authority figures" and are not too concerned. Perhaps you apply a model like "Normal children respect their parents" and conclude the teenager is out of control. Who is to say what a "normal" or "typical" teenager is or does? Different cultural models hold different implications.

What do you make of a toddler who throws a tantrum when you, in a hurry to get your chores done, open a heavy car door that he or she wants to try to open, no matter how long it takes? Perhaps you apply a cultural model like "Young children go through sometimes-difficult 'stages' in their urge for growing self-reliance and independence" and conclude your child and the situation you are in is quite "normal." Perhaps you even encourage the child. Or perhaps you apply a model like "Young children are naturally willful and selfish and need discipline to learn to get along with and cooperate with others." Again, you would conclude you have a "normal" child, but one in need of discipline.

When you see a beggar on the street, your first reaction might stem from a cultural model like "People are responsible for themselves and when they fail it's their own fault" and go on your way, ignoring the person's pleas for money. Or you might apply a model something like "Down-and-out people are victims of problems that have overwhelmed them in a harshly competitive society" and give the person some money. Or you might apply a model like "Giving people money just encourages them to seek more help from others rather than seek to help themselves" and give the beggar an address of a foundation that can help him or her get a (probably quite bad) job.

When you have an argument with someone, do you apply a model something like "Arguments are a sort of verbal conflict" (helped along in this case by metaphors in our language like "I *won* the argument" or "I *defeated* her positions")? When you are in a romantic relationship, do you apply a model something like "Relationships are a type of work" (helped along in this case by metaphors in our language like "I've put a lot of *work* into this relationship" or "He has *worked hard* to be a good lover")? When you talk about people's jobs, do you apply a model something like "Working with the mind is more valuable to society than working with one's hands" and find yourself valuing even an academic who debates how many angels can sit on the head of a pin over your plumber? Perhaps the answer is no in all these cases, in which case you operate, at least sometimes and in some places, with different cultural models.

There are several important points to be made about cultural models. They are not just in your head. Of course, you store images and patterns in your head that represent cultural models, but they are also represented out there in the world. For example, the cultural model that said that "Young children go through sometimes-difficult 'stages' in their urge for growing self-reliance and independence" exists in a lot of self-help guides on babies and childrearing. The words and images of the magazines, newspapers, and other media all around us represent many cultural models. The models also are represented and acted out in the words and deeds of the people with whom we interact and share memberships in various groups.

Different cultural models are associated with different groups in the larger society, though some are also shared widely by many, perhaps all, groups in that society. For instance, the cultural model about children going through "stages" toward independence is associated more closely (though not exclusively) with the modern middle class, and the cultural model that said "Young children are naturally willful and selfish and need discipline to learn to get along with and cooperate with others" is associated more closely (though not exclusively) with the traditional working class.

Cultural models, which cannot be stated in one definitive way, are stories or images of experience that people can tell themselves or simulate in their minds, stories and images that represent what they take to be "normal" or "typical" cases or situations. In this sense, they are like theories, theories about things like children, childrearing, relationships, friendship, being and doing good, and everything else. These theories are usually unconscious and taken for granted. However, like all theories, even overt ones in science, they are not meant to be detailed, blow-by-blow descriptions of reality. Reality is too complex to be described accurately in every detail. Rather, cultural models and formal theories both are meant to capture general patterns in such a way that we can do things in and with the world, whether this is to accomplish a goal with others or to make successful predictions in an experiment.

Cultural models are picked up as part and parcel of acting with others in the world. We act with others and attempt to make sense of what they are doing and saying. We interact with the media of our society and attempt to make sense of what is said and done there, as well. Cultural models are the tacit, taken-for-granted theories we (usually unconsciously) infer and then act on in the normal course of events when we want to be like others in our social groups. People who have no cultural models would have to think everything out for themselves minute by minute when they attempt to act. They would be paralyzed. And they certainly would not be social beings, since part of what makes us social beings is the set of cultural models we share with those around us.

Cultural models can be used for many different purposes and they can sometimes conflict with each other. For example, the anthropological psychologist Claudia Strauss found that working-class men she studied behaved in their daily lives according to what she called a bread-winner model. This model can be phrased something like this: "Men take care of their families even if this means sacrificing their own interests." On the other hand, Strauss found that many upper-middle class people operate with a cultural model that stresses their own self-development over the interests of those around them, including their own families. When such people were faced with moving to take a new and better job, they often did so, even if this damaged their families and relationships. The working-class men Strauss studied, when faced with the same choice, gave up the new career opportunity for the benefit of their families.

These working-class men also used what Strauss and others have called the success model to judge their own behaviors. This model says something like "In the United States, anyone can get ahead if they work hard enough." The working-class men saw that they did not hold jobs the wider society considered successful and used this model to condemn themselves, saying they had not worked hard enough or weren't smart enough. They used the success model to judge themselves negatively even though this model exists in some degree of conflict with the bread winner model on which they led their lives in action, a model that would not let them take the "selfish" steps often required by the success model.

Since this conflict did not surface to consciousness for these men, it did not come out into the open. They simply felt bad about themselves, at least when forced to think about themselves in relation to the society as a whole. In other settings, of course, they may have felt quite differently—remember, people take on different identities in different situations and all people are members of many different groups.

Are cultural models, then, "good" or "bad"? They are good in that they allow us to act and be social in the world without having to constantly reflect and think. They are bad when they operate so as to do harm to ourselves or others but go unexamined. Certain circumstances can, however, force us to think overtly and reflectively about our cultural models. We certainly don't want or need to think overtly about all of them. But we do need to think about those that, in certain situations or at certain points in our lives, have the potential to do more harm than good.

Sonic Adventure 2 Battle forced the six-year-old overtly to realize and confront two different, and sometimes conflicting, cultural models of what constitutes being and doing "good." Of course, this realization was only beginning. Many other experiences, not the least in video games, will give this child other opportunities to think more about these two models. And, indeed, they are models that bear a good deal of thinking about, since they have done and have the potential to do a lot of harm in the world.

UNDER ASH

The sort of thing that the six-year-old experienced can go much further and deeper. Consider the case of Arab children. After the terrorist attacks of September 11, 2001, a number of video games came out, initially on the Internet and thereafter as packaged games, featuring U.S. soldiers killing Arabs and Muslims. These games, for obvious reasons, were not entirely palatable to Arab children. In response, the Syrian publishing house Dar Al-Fikr designed a video game called *Under Ash*. Its hero is a young Palestinian named Ahmed who throws stones to fight Israeli soldiers and settlers. The game, of course, involves the player deeply in the Palestinian cause and Palestinian perspectives.

In the game, Ahmed initially must reach Jerusalem's Al-Aqsa mosque, an important Islamic holy site, avoiding or fighting Israeli soldiers and settlers along the way. Once he reaches the mosque, Ahmed has to help injured Palestinians, find weapons, and expel Israeli soldiers. There are many other episodes to the game, including ones where Ahmed infiltrates a Jewish settlement and where he serves as a guerrilla warrior in southern Lebanon. As is typical of such video games, Ahmed only attacks those he does not consider "civilians." (In this case, occupation forces, settlers, and soldiers do not count as "civilians.") "Civilians" (all others) are left unharmed.

Of course, it is clear that in video games who does and does not count as a "civilian" is based on different perspectives embedded in the game's virtual world. I was originally surprised (which shows I was operating with a different cultural model) that settlers (since they are not in the army) didn't count as civilians. But then I realized that this game accepts a cultural model in terms of which the settlers are seen as the "advance" troops of an occupation army.

The general manager of the company that produced *Under Ash*, Adnan Salim, considers the game, one that is violent in just the way many U.S. shooter games are, "a call for peace." In an Internet site devoted to the game, Salim says that "Slaying and shedding blood have been the worst of the Human's conducts [*sic*] since the beginning of creation." I got Salim's views from Google's (a search engine) cache of www.underash.com/emessage.htm.

(A cache is a snapshot that the people at Google took of the page as they "crawled the web.") This site, like several others devoted to *Under Ash*, no longer exits. Opponents of the game have destroyed many sites devoted to it. I have no idea whether this was true of this site or not. Salim goes on to say that "[i]n spite of the Human's endeavor and struggle to get rid of the crime of murder since he appeared on Earth, Israel has been practicing collective killing and eradication."

On the other hand, he claims that:

Under Ash is a call to humanity to stop killing and shedding blood. After all its awful experience and global destructive wars, the whole world has become aware of the fact that wars never solve problems. . . .

Under Ash is a call to dialogue, coexistence and peace. Justice is the deeply-rooted human value that God Almighty enjoined . . . On the other hand, nations perish, states stabilize and civilizations collapse according to the amount of aggression, injustice and harm they practice. . . .

Under Ash is a call to justice, realizing truth, preventing wronging [*sic*] and aggression. God made all mankind as equal to each other as the comb teeth. . . .

Such is the philosophy of *Under Ash*. The idea on which it was based repulses violence, injustice, discrimination and murder, and calls for peace, justice and equality among people.

This idea, accompanied by the best available technology, is still handy to our youth, trying to dry up their tears; heal their wounds; remove all the feelings of humiliation, humbleness and wretchedness from their souls, and draw the smile of hope and the sense of dignity and efficiency on their faces.

If you find these remarks odd in regard to a violent video game (remember that there was no outcry in the United States over shooter games where the enemies were Arabs), that is because these remarks and the game itself take for granted a number of cultural models foreign to many Americans (just as American games and remarks about them take for granted different cultural models). For example, consider that Salim says that, after having experienced the violence of global wars, the world: "turned back to the patient dialogue around the table of negotiation which resulted in the establishment of a *European Union* among nations which previously hated one another and went on fighting for centuries. Then they agreed to coexist peacefully within a union under whose authority none is harmed and every one benefits."

One cultural model that seems to be at work here is something like this: "The experience of violence will make people seek peace." In terms of this model, we can see the guerrilla fighter as trying to push more powerful entities (i.e., states), entities that the guerrilla cannot defeat outright, to settle their differences through negotiation rather than war. A cultural model something like "The experience of overwhelming violence will make less powerful entities give up and give in to more powerful entities" seems at play in both some U.S. video games and much U.S. media devoted to warfare in the modern world. Note that like all cultural models, these are not "true" or "false." (History is replete with examples and counter-examples to both.) They are meant to help people make sense to themselves and others and to engage in joint activity with others with whom they share these cultural models.

Now, you might very well not want to play *Under Ash*. If you did play the game, you would be placed in a situation where you took on the virtual identity of a character whose cultural models about many things are different from yours. If you not only adopted this virtual identity while you played but took on what I called in chapter 3 a projective identity vis-à-vis your virtual identity (Ahmed), you would surely come to understand what it feels like to be among those angry young people who are "trying to dry up their tears; heal their wounds; remove all the feelings of humiliation, humbleness and wretchedness from their souls, and draw the smile of hope and the sense of dignity and efficiency on their faces."

Would this mean you would, all of a sudden, want to kill Israeli settlers or even that you would support the Palestinian cause over the Israeli one if you had not before? Certainly not. But it would mean that, far more interactively that you could in any novel or movie, you would have experienced the "other" from the inside. Even more interesting, since the cultural models built into the game are not yours, you would be able to reflect on them in a more overtly conscious way than young Arabic players for whom the models are taken for granted (as U.S. game players take for granted different models that fit their own sense of reality). In turn, this might make you contrast these models to ones you have taken for granted and bring them to consciousness for reflection.

What if *Under Ash* allowed you to play through the game twice, once as Ahmed and once as an Israeli settler, just as *Sonic Adventure 2 Battle* allows you to be Sonic or Shadow, or *Aliens vs. Predator 2* allows you to be a Marine fighting off the Aliens and Predator or either an Alien or Predator trying to survive by killing the Marines? My guess is that if you had taken on both the projective identity of you as Ahmed and you as Israeli settler, you would find the whole thing much more complex than you do now and would be a bit more reluctant to take the death of either side for granted. Such complexity is bad, I admit, for people and states trying to wage war.

Video games have an unmet potential to create complexity by letting people experience the world from different perspectives. Part of this potential is that in a video game, you yourself have to act as a given character. As you act quickly, and not just think leisurely, and as you (while playing) celebrate the character's victories and bemoan his or her defeats, you must live in a virtual world and make sense of it. This making sense of the virtual world amid not just thought but also action in the world amounts to experiencing new and different cultural models. Furthermore, you may experience these models much more consciously—and render some of your own previous models conscious by contrast in the process—than is typical of our daily lives in the real world. In the next section I turn to an example that is less esoteric for Americans than *Under Ash*.

I am well aware that this potential of video games—if and when it is more fully realized—is liable to be very controversial. An Israeli or Palestinian who has lost a loved one to violence is not going to want to play both sides of my make-believe *Under Ash* game. Indeed, the Israeli and Palestinian may each revel in playing "their" side and getting virtual revenge. Each may think it immoral to "play" the other side, to take on such a perspective on the world even in play. I, too, think that certain perspectives are so repugnant that we should not take them even in play. But who decides? And if we are willing to take none but our own side, even in play, then violence would seem inevitable.

We do not have to imagine games that most of us would find entirely repugnant, regardless of our political perspectives. Such games actually exist. For example, a game called *Ethnic Cleansing*, put out by the Virginia-based National Alliance, has players killing African Americans, Latinos, and Jews as they run through gritty ghetto and subway environments. The game is quite sophisticated technologically. (It was built using free game development software called Genesis 3D.) Hate groups like the National Alliance have long recruited members through the use of web sites, white-power music, and books and magazines. However, there is concern, for just the reasons we have discussed, that interactive media like video games are a more powerful device than such passive media. But if they are, then they are potentially more powerful for both good and ill.

Whether we like it or not, new technologies make it easy to design realistic and sophisticated video games that allow players to be almost any sort of person or being living in almost in sort of world that any designer can imagine. Eventually this capacity will be used to allow people to live and interact in worlds where violence plays no role and is replaced by conversation and other sorts of social interactions. (*The Longest Journey*, a game whose lead character is an 18-year-old woman named April Ryan, is one such game; *Siberia*, whose protagonist is a female lawyer wandering around a town full of automatons, is another.)

The same capacity that will allow us to enact new identities and learn to act according to new cultural models can also allow us to renew our hate or even learn new models of hate. In the end, who is to decide what identities you or I can enact and whether enacting them will be a good or bad thing for us? Publicly the issue usually is couched in terms of children and teens, where parents surely bear a major responsibility, but the average video-game player is in his or her late 20s or early 30s. I don't want politicians dictating what identities I can enact in a virtual world. At the same time, I worry about people who play *Ethnic Cleansing*. But any attempt to stop the flow of identities that new technologies allow presents the danger of locking everyone into their most cherished identities, and that has brought us a great deal of ethnic cleansing of its own. I have no solid answers to offer, only the claim that video games have the potential to raise many such questions and issues.

GOING TO WAR

Both *Return to Castle Wolfenstein* and *Operation Flashpoint: Cold War Crisis* are shooter games played out in military settings. *Castle Wolfenstein* is a first-person shooter. (You see only the weapon you are holding, unless you look in something like a mirror when you then see yourself.) *Operation Flashpoint* can be played either in the first-person or in the third-person (where you see your character's body as if you were just a bit behind him). In *Castle Wolfenstein* you play Major B. J. Blazkowitz in World War II fighting against the Nazis. In *Operation Flashpoint* you start the game as Private David Armstrong, though you (Armstrong) go up in rank during the game. Private Armstrong is involved as a U.S. soldier representing NATO in a war against a resistance movement on an island nation.

While all this makes these two games sound similar, they are in a great many respects entirely different. In *Return to Castle Wolfenstein*, Major William J. "B. J." Blazkowicz is a highly decorated Army Ranger recruited into the Office of Secret Actions (OSA) and given the task of going to Castle Wolfenstein to thwart Heinrich, the reincarnation of a tenth-century dark prince, Henry the Fowler (also known as Heinrich), and an army of genetically engineered super soldiers.

As in most shooter games, your character (B. J. Blazkowitz) can take a great deal of damage before he dies. It takes a number of bullets to kill him, and he can find health kits throughout the game to replenish his health. While he faces tough enemies, the fact that he can dish out a great deal of damage with special weapons (like a Venom Gun, which fires dozens of bullets at once) and sustain a good deal of damage makes you, the player, feel like quite a superhero. Indeed, when you have successfully finished the game, you see a cut scene (video) where Blazkowitz's superiors in Washington are discussing what a great job he has done and how he is currently taking some well-deserved R and R, imagining him relaxing on some tropical isle. But then the video cuts away to a dramatic scene where we see Blazkowitz jumping from a ledge, machine gun in hand, entering the fray in yet another battle against multiple Nazis, a sly grin on his face. This is *his* form of R and R.

Games like *Return to Castle Wolfenstein* trade on several pervasive cultural models that are part of their allure. They play on cultural models that treat heroes as superhuman people and that see warfare (for the "right" cause) as heroic. Also they play on a cultural model that is quite pervasive particularly among males, namely one that sees fighting (and even losing) against all odds—standing alone against the horde no matter what—as romantic (a model often triggered when people watch a bad sports team against a good one). And, of course, they play on cultural models, pervasive particularly in United States, that romanticize the individual against the group.

There is nothing particularly wrong with this. People get pleasure out of seeing their cultural models confirmed and, in the case of video games, actually getting to act them out. After all, a good many of these models have been picked up not so much from one's actual experiences in the world as through experiences with books and the media. However, I believe there is something wrong when these sorts of models are never challenged or overtly reflected on.

Some modern shooter games have begun to play against these sorts of pervasive models in interesting ways. Games like *Thief: The Dark Project* and *Metal Gear Solid 2: Sons of Liberty*, in their entirety, and parts of *Deus Ex* and *No One Lives Forever 2: A Spy in H.A.R.M.'s Way*, and a good many other modern sophisticated shooter games, stress stealth and cunning over fighting. A shooter game like *Anachronox* and many fantasy role-playing games (like *Baldur's Gate II: Shadows of Amin*) stress teamwork. At times *Anachronox* plays to hilarious effect against cultural models about heroism and individuality.

In fact, these trends are strong enough that games like *Duke Nukem* and *Serious Sam* bill themselves as nostalgic returns to the "good old days" of shooters where you just rushed in and shot up everything around you. (Duke Nukem's motto in his more recent game, *Duke Nukem: Manhattan Project*, is "It's my way or . . . Hell—it's my way.") In many a modern shooter game that's a strategy that will lead quickly to your death. Finally, we can mention that the very popular *No One Lives Forever* games star a female James Bond figure and parodies (in a very playful way) the conventions of the Bond genre and 1960s.

But none of this prepares you for a game like *Operation Flashpoint: Cold War Crisis;* a realistic military game that quickly disabused me of all the cultural models about warfare I had picked up from books and movies. Its contrast with games like *Return to Castle Wolfenstein* is so stark that a player cannot help but be confronted consciously with the cultural models heroic shooter games reinforce.

Operation Flashpoint is set in the Cold War period just as Soviet President Mikhail Gorbachev is elected into power. The game follows a fictional story line centered around the battle between a disgruntled rogue Soviet military group that has seized control of an island community and a NATO peacekeeping force, sent in at the request of the Soviets. The player assumes the role of Private David Armstrong in over 30 missions that have you assaulting small towns as a member of a large squad, commandeering vehicles, launching sniper attacks, and, later, serving as a squad leader. In the early parts of the game, you follow a computer AI-controlled leader as you and other squad members try to survive to later missions, where you move up the ranks, eventually becoming a battle-hardened commander.

Operation Flashpoint is fully realistic. One bullet is usually enough to kill or disable you pretty fully. Opposing soldiers can shoot at you from far away, can snipe you from hiding places that are hard to discover, and often appear as small deadly spots on the horizon, not as larger-than-life foes confronting you face-to-face. There are no health kits to be found, only the very occasional medic on the battlefield if you are lucky enough to find one and get to him quickly enough. Very often, if you are not very careful, you get shot and die without even having seen what direction the bullet came from.

Needless to say, if you try to be Rambo in *Operation Flashpoint* and run out heroically firing all guns, you will, as a review on gamezilla.com put it, "find yourself in a black body bag being shipped to the USA, next day air." Cooperation from and with your computer-controlled squadmates is a must for survival. Many times there are more of the enemy than there are of you, and they are well trained. When things go wrong—and they often do—you can hide from enemies, for example, in bushes, especially when you are in camouflage. But once you fire, there's a good chance the enemy will hear it and attack your position, with predictable results. (You die.)

Playing *Operation Flashpoint: Cold War Crisis* let me experience what it would be like to have quite different cultural models about warfare. Early on, I found myself (as Private Armstrong) with my squad following my commander as we skirted the edges of forests and open fields in search of the enemy. I really had no idea how I should move. My inclination as an "everyday" person was to stand up and move forward briskly. I died, shot from afar. In fact, I never saw the enemy soldier who shot me.

Replaying the game, I watched how my (computer-controlled) squadmates moved. Often they moved forward in a crouching position, staying low to the ground. They rarely moved in straight lines and frequently stopped and checked the horizons all around them. When they sensed any danger, they hit the ground and crawled forward for a while. Progress was punishingly slow. You had to develop a sense of possible danger everywhere, knowing that the enemy might very well see you before you saw them. For long periods nothing happened and a sense of boredom overcame me. Then all of a sudden information would come over my radio or the commander would shout out orders and there would be firing and mayhem. Often I barely had time to get excited before I died, having failed to think beforehand of possible avenues of protection or retreat.

During the game's early episodes, as I moved (ever more skillfully and "paranoidly") with my squad, I went into missions with high expectations and optimism. After all, we were the "good guys," weren't we? We were in a well-trained professional army with highly qualified officers (I was, after all, only a private), weren't we? But time and again, things did not go as planned. We had to change plans, retreat and regroup, or even be evacuated in defeat. Winning was no simple matter, and every step forward seemed to portend two possible steps backward. While I often got orders directly from the commander of my squad or over my radio, I didn't always know what the "big plan" was, if there was one, only what my group was supposed to accomplish and that changed under the conditions of the actual battle on the field.

Speaking of orders: As I said, I often got them under conditions where I had to act fast. But many times these orders left me in quandaries. In one case, for example, an officer got killed only moments after ordering me to move in a certain direction and take up a certain position. Should I follow the order now that he just got shot—which, of course, didn't inspire great confidence? In other cases, there were clearly much safer—and sometimes, from my perspective, smarter—things for me to do than follow the order to the T. What to do? How exactly need I follow orders? What room is there for my own judgment? Sometimes when I hesitated, I got yelled at. At other times, I was too far away for the officer to observe the details of my behavior.

When we did accomplish our goals in fine fashion, I did not know how much or how little I had contributed to the "victory." For example, once we assaulted an enemy position on the outskirts of a town. I and others were ordered to move forward under fire, while some of our fellow soldiers stayed behind sniping at the enemy positions from farther back. I moved forward, firing my gun and evading return fire. We "won," but I never knew if I had disabled any of the enemy or contributed to the task (partly because I was not the first soldier over the top—see the next paragraph). The whole squad got praised, but I didn't know how good (or bad) to feel about the matter.

Finally, early on, I discovered an important but very uninspiring principle. I have already pointed out that I learned a good deal by observing my squadmates—for example, how to move. But I also learned that the safest position is to move with but behind other squadmates. The people in front have to make the snap decisions and take the fire first. But it felt very "unmanly" staying behind the others. I particularly liked moving behind (not too close, though) some of the officers on the field who seemed to know the most about how to proceed and often made the best decisions.

Enough said; this is not war as romantic and heroic. Here are some of the cultural models I was beginning to pick up about warfare from playing this game, none of which is remotely part of the experience of playing *Return to Castle Wolfenstein:*

- War is, for the most part, boring.
- Soldiers need to move as if they are constantly paranoid.
- When war is exciting, it is also confusing.
- Following orders is a vexed matter.
- Things don't go as planned.
- Situations on the ground don't resemble people's generalities and plans about them.
- No one really knows what people at the top know and whether they really know what they're doing.
- The guys next to you on the actual battlefield often do know what they're doing.It's hard to know what you can take credit for as an individual.
- "Manly" behavior often gets you dead quickly, Rambo-type behavior even quicker.

These are cultural models, because they are images, principles, or story lines that I don't really "know" are true. I picked them up from my own experience, and one's experience is always limited, local, connected to particular groups and situations, and never scientifically "valid." Such models help organize and make sense of experience and help one move on and get on with the job at hand (in this case, staying alive long enough to go on fighting a war). Of course, people and game players differ. In my case, I have never had the slightest desire to be a real soldier, and playing *Operation Flashpoint* certainly does not inspire me to change my desires in this regard. It does make me worry about media depictions of war and gives me loads of sympathy for anyone who has to fight one, especially bottom up in the ranks. (The U. S. Army has created a massive multiplayer realistic game called *America's Army* but I do not know what effect it has on players, save to say a number have wanted to sign up.)

CULTURAL MODELS IN SCHOOL

Cultural models play a crucial role in school. Let me give you a specific example from a science classroom. High school students taking a physics class were having a discussion about whether a ball rolling on a level plane would keep moving at constant speed. They had previously heard from their teacher Galileo's arguments that under ideal conditions (i.e., leaving out friction and assuming no force acts to accelerate or retard the ball's progress) the ball would keep moving at a constant speed.

During the discussion, one student asks, "What's making the ball move?" Another answers, "The forces behind it." The student who asked the question responds, "The force that's pushing it will make it go." Yet another student says, "Where'd that force come from, because you don't have a force" (which, of course, is Galileo's and modern physics' assumption), and another student answers, "No, there is force, the force that's pushing it, but no other force that's slowing it down." The teacher comments that some students say there are no forces on the ball, while others say there is "a force that's moving it." One student now says, "There's an initial force that makes it start, giving it the energy to move."

What is happening here—and it happens in many physics classrooms—is that some (most) of the students are assuming that things in motion stay in motion either because some force is constantly acting on them (they are being "pushed" by this force) or because they have stored up energy from some initial force (a "push") that acted on them, a stored energy that is a kind of "impetus" (which itself is like an internal force acting on the object, one that gradually "runs down"). However, in terms of the semiotic domain of physics, any object stays at rest or in constant motion unless some force acts to change its state. When its state is changed, it stays in the new state (in motion or at rest) until some other force changes this state. In physics, there is no need to explain why things stay in constant motion or at rest. Thus, there is no need to appeal to any "impetus" moving objects have stored up (a "force" that doesn't exist). We only need to explain the situation when things in motion accelerate or slow down or things at rest move. In these cases, we must assume some force has acted on the object.

Of course, in the real world, things rarely stay in constant motion for any length of time, since forces almost always act on them to change (speed up or slow down) their motion. And when things stay at rest in the real world, often it takes a number of forces to keep them that way and oppose forces that are attempting to change them. Galileo was assuming an ideal world, for instance a world with no friction between surfaces and nothing in the environment to perturb the motion of the ball. Furthermore, the ball is assumed to be rolling horizontally on level plane to make the force of gravity irrelevant to the problem. (If the ball were falling down it would be accelerating, thanks to gravity.) He wanted to think about things in a certain idealized way so that the basic pattern or fundamental principle at work would show itself clearly, namely, the principle that things at rest stay at rest and things moving at a constant speed stay moving at a constant speed unless some force acts on them to change their state.

This is a new and different way of looking at the world. In physics, things moving at constant speed or at rest don't need explaining. What needs explaining is change. In the world of our "everyday" experience, since things are always changing, what often has to be explained is how certain things resist these changes to remain in a constant state.

Physicists want to think in terms of such ideal worlds so that they can discover elegant mathematical models that can later be applied to the real world. When they are applied to the real world, we have to think about things that were left out of the model (like friction). Such elegant models, when these other things are added in, make a multitude of correct predictions about the real world.

Most other academic disciplines operate in a similar way. They leave out a myriad of details to formulate a basic pattern that later can be made more complex to apply in different ways to different situations. For example, some branches of economics operate with the assumption that people are always rational when they act within free markets. This lets these economists think about and discover principles about how markets work in an ideal sense. Of course, when they want to make predictions about the real world, they have to add in adjustments for different situations where people display different kinds of irrational behavior or where markets are not fully free. Their idealized assumption is good if, when they add back in these different adjustments (different ones for different situations), they are able to make good predictions.

Ironically, this way of proceeding—i.e., leaving out a lot of details to get to the basic pattern—is not all that different from how cultural models work. People form cultural models from their experience by leaving out many of the details to capture what they take to be the typical cases. Scientific models are formed through the socially organized process of scientific investigation (e.g., formal research and peer review), not through largely unconscious encounters with daily life. Furthermore, scientific models and cultural models exist for different reasons. Scientific models attempt to explain how some aspect of the world works as an answer to a formal and consciously formulated question, and sometimes the aspects of the world that they deal with are not ones we experience in our everyday lives (e.g., atoms). Cultural models exist to help us get on with our "everyday," less specialized and often less consciously reflected on social and cultural business and our everyday lives in the material world.

In the high school physics class, the cultural models of some students were in conflict with the scientific models used by physicists. They did not realize this and could not turn off (for the time being) their conflicting cultural models and begin to think and act through the physicists' models. Let me discuss for a moment, then, one of the conflicting cultural models that these students were using.

A number of studies in science education have found that students often bring to the physics classroom, in one form or another, a conception that *motion is caused by force*. They believe that if an object is moving, then there must be a force on it causing that motion. It is common to read in this literature that this is a "misconception," a mistake commonly made by people who don't know physics. The problem is that often students continue to make this "mistake" even after they have taken a good deal of physics and learned that it is a "mistake."

The reason why the idea that motion is caused by force is so hard to remove is that it is not, in reality, a "mistake." Rather, it is a type of cultural model, a model built up from our experiences in the material world. Most or all humans hold a model something like this: "Things keep working because they are continually supplied with some form of power or agency." Like all models, this model is neither wrong nor right. Rather, it works in a lot of situations. Because it does, we usually can get by perfectly well by assuming it without much conscious thought. For example, we assume (correctly in this and the following cases) that a car keeps running because its engine keeps powering its wheels. Lights keep working because electricity keeps flowing into them. Humans move because, at one level, they (continuously) "will" it and, at another level, because the energy reserves from their food fuel their cells and limbs.

While it is fair to say this is a physical model, it applies to social affairs as well and, thus, is also a social model. In fact, it is really just a cultural model that applies both to the physical and the social world. We assume that students keep working because something is motivating them or that relationships last because people put effort into them. In general, people do what they do and keep doing it, when they do keep doing it, because they are "agents" empowering themselves (through will or desire or whatever) to do and keep doing. The model that says, "things keep working because they are continually supplied with some form of power or agency" is deeply rooted in our physical and social experience. Of course, different cultural groups have different cultural models about what sorts of things can or cannot be sources of power or agency (e.g., spirits).

This cultural model—in its specific physical instantiation as *motion is caused by force*—happens to be wrong in physics, no matter how accurate it may be in a great many other areas. However, you do not get people to realize it is wrong in physics and then pick up other models that work better in physics, if you don't realize the power of this model or if you abuse people for holding it (e.g., tell them they are stupid or misguided). You must bring the model to consciousness and juxtapose it to other ways of thinking appropriate for the new situation, without implying that the model is wrong in all situations.

You must also make the way physicists think—a way that does not use this cultural model, at least when they are doing physics—sensible and clear by letting students understand it not just as words but in terms of embodied thought and action in the same physical world in which they got their original model. After all, just as people's cultural models come from their everyday experience of the world, physicists' scientific models come from their experiences (in problem solving, thinking, dialoging, and carrying out experiments in and on the world) within the semiotic domain of physics as it applies to the world. This domain, like all specialized domains, looks at and operates on the world in a different way from "everyday" people do, but it operates in and on the material world nonetheless.

Students bring to their classes a great many cultural models. For example, cultural models about what counts as "good English" (e.g., something like "Educated people speak good or correct English") cause lots of trouble when students are trying to learn linguistics and discover that, to a linguist, a dialect of English that says things like "My puppy be following me everywhere I go" is just as rule governed and "good" as a dialect that doesn't say such things. (In fact, this sort of construction, using a form like "be" to mean that something happens repeatedly or habitually, is not at all uncommon across the world's languages.)

However, students also bring to classrooms cultural models about school subject matter (e.g., what "physics" as a school subject is) and about learning (e.g., what learning is or should be like in school). For example, in regard to physics or other academic domains, many students bring with them a cultural models that say: "Learning is a matter of mastering a set of facts." They may bring, as well, a model that says: "Learning is a matter of memorizing information from teachers and books."

These models are not "wrong"—indeed, a great many schools operate so as to reinforce them daily. Nonetheless, if you have gotten this far in this book, you know that I believe they are in many situations unfortunate models of learning. However, if students are to adopt different models of content learning in school, teachers need to know that these unfortunate models exist. Students need to think about them, why they have them, where they do and do not work, and new and different models and why they might want to adopt these in word and deed. Of course, the newer models I am advocating involve the sorts of active and critical learning I have been stressing throughout this book.

CULTURAL MODELS OF LEARNING
AND VIDEO GAMES

Good video games have a powerful way of making players consciously aware of some of their previously assumed cultural models about learning itself. In fact, good video games expose a whole set of generational models of what constitutes typical ways of learning. Since the baby-boomer models are still quite prevalent in schools as teachers, administrators, and parents, children today are most certainly exposed to them and often adopt these models uncritically and unconsciously, at least when they are at school.

Consider, for instance, the famous game *Metal Gear Solid* (a game that has a sequel called *Metal Gear Solid 2: Sons of Liberty*). In this game you are Solid Snake (one of the most famous video game characters of all time), a genetically enhanced antiterrorist, who has been called on to infiltrate an Alaskan military base that has been taken over by terrorists. The terrorists are also genetically enhanced and some are foes Solid Snake has confronted in the past (in earlier games), such as his brother Liquid Snake. The terrorists have fitted a massive robot called "Metal Gear" with nuclear warheads and are threatening to fire them at the United States if their demands are not met. As Solid Snake goes about infiltrating the military base and ultimately trying to destroy Metal Gear, he finds out a great deal about himself and about love and loyalty. In fact, in the middle of the game, if Solid Snake does not give in under torture, his great love and fellow warrior, Meryl, survives, and they eventually head off into the sunset together at the end of the game. (If he does give in and ask for the torture to stop, Meryl does not survive and the game has a different ending.)

Early in the game, you (as Solid Snake in a third-person view) are standing in the shadows looking at a massive building with many doors and balconies, fronted by a courtyard with many additional rooms coming off it. There are searchlights fixed atop the building and guards everywhere. You must sneak past the searchlights, staying in the shadows, get into the building, and move unseen through it to your goal.

If the player is inclined to move as straightforwardly and efficiently as possible toward the goal, this game and almost all other video games, will punish this inclination. The player needs to take the time to explore, even if this means moving off the main line toward the goal and delaying getting there. If Snake does not head right to his goal of entering the main building but instead moves carefully into a side room off the courtyard, he finds important items (e.g., weapons, ammunition, tools). When he sneaks into the back of a truck parked in the courtyard, he not only avoids the searchlights, he also finds more good things. As he sneaks around the perimeter of the courtyard and the edges of the building, he can check out less obvious ways into the building.

Even when he gets in, lingering over grates in the floor of an overhead duct he is moving through allows him to overhear important information and see various things (including Meryl in a cell with not too many clothes on). Sneaking to other nooks and crannies in the building allows him to gain crucial information. All the while Snake is receiving, via a communication device that only he can hear, orders to move forward and information about how to do so.

When I played the game, I was tempted to rush guards, guns firing, to clear my path, since they seemed like such clear and straightforward targets. But, of course, if there were more of them than there was of me, I usually died or took too much damage. Even when there was only one and he seemed an obvious and easy target, often an alarm sounded, set off by a hidden camera triggered when I had snuck out into the open behind the guard, an alarm that quickly brought a good many other guards to his rescue.

This and other games have brought home to me that I hold cultural models about learning something like this: "The final goal is important, defines the learning, and good learners move toward it without being distracted by other things" and "Good learners move quickly and efficiently toward their goal." I also hold other models: "There is one right way to get to the goal that the good learners discover (and the rest of us usually don't)" and "Learning is a matter of some people being better or worse than others, and this is important."

These models all get entrenched in school repeatedly. They are linear models that stress movement ever forward toward greater skill until one has mastered one's goal. They are competitive models, as well, that stress better and worse and sorting people into categories along the lines of better and worse.

Video games tend not to reward these models. They stress both nonlinear movement—exploring all around without necessarily moving forward toward one's ultimate goal and the mastery defined by that goal—as well as linear movement, which, of course, eventually happens, greatly deepened, sometimes transformed, by the horizontal movement. They stress multiple solutions judged by a variety of different standards, some of which are internal to the game (different things happen when you take different tacks) and some of which are set by the player (who wants to solve the problem on his or her own terms and may play scenes over to solve problems in different ways).

Unless segments of games are timed, and they usually are not (save for special problems or races within certain games or in some aspects of real-time strategy games), how quickly you proceed is not a big value, unless you choose to make it one. (And then you may well miss some of the best stuff in a game.) Finally, while there are certainly better and worse video-game players, and players can and do play competitively with each other via the Internet, games are most certainly playable by a wide variety of people who set their own standards and worry about how well they are doing by those standards, not by who out there in the world is better or worse than they are at defeating Liquid Snake in the fight atop the tank.

Video games challenged a number of other cultural models I held about learning. For one last example, I held a model something like: "When faced with a problem to solve, good learners solve it quickly, the first time they try or soon thereafter. If you have to try over and over again, this is a sign that you are not very good at what you are attempting to learn." All good shooter games have "bosses," particularly strong opponents with far more life than your character. Players regularly spend lots of time and effort trying to kill these bosses. They have to discover new strategies in their various failed attempts and not give up.

When players do succeed at killing the bosses, some (after they have played the game through) set the difficulty level higher, to make getting the bosses even harder. (Many games can be played at a relatively easy, normal, hard, or even harder level; the difficulty level determines things like how many enemies there are and how strong they are.) I once watched a younger lawyer refight a final boss from a PlayStation 2 version of *Baldur's Gate* at the highest level of difficulty. He was a real expert. His character ran up to and away from the boss (a dragon) repeatedly, moving all around a complex dungeon space, hiding here and there, coming out to attack and running away, coaxing the boss into tight corners or close spaces where it could be better attacked. All the while, the player used various potions and healing spells to gain stronger arrows and more health. The battle lasted 20 intense minutes. In the end, with the dragon on its last legs, the lawyer ran out of both magical arrows and healing potions and he died.

Far from being dismayed at his failure (as a school learner might after such a struggle), he responded with some nasty language as he died but also with a big smile on his face. In video games, losing is not losing, and the point is not winning easily or judging yourself a failure. In playing video games, hard is not bad and easy is not good. The six-year-old mentioned earlier was once asked whether easy or hard was better in a video game. Without a pause, he said hard is always good, easy is not. Would that children said such things about learning science in school.

There is a wonderful moment in *Metal Gear Solid*, which is a quite difficult game, where Solid Snake, as he infiltrates the military base, is talking via his built-in communication system to a young Asian woman who is an expert on mapping and radar systems. She and Solid Snake joke with each other, and she usually ends each talk session with him with a Chinese proverb that applies both to his situation in the virtual world of the game and to the player in the real world. At one point she says to Solid Snake something that is not a proverb, of course, but is meant to have much the same effect: "Aren't you glad that you have the time to play a video game? Relax and enjoy yourself."

When players hear this, they might very well realize that they are intensely involved in solving quite hard problems and often failing. Yet they are playing, having fun, enjoying themselves. Wouldn't it be great if we could say to children in school when they were struggling mightily with hard problems in physics: "Aren't you lucky you have the time and opportunity to do science?" and have them smile and nod?

LEARNING PRINCIPLES

A variety of learning principles are built into good video games, yet there is still immense potential for future developments. Certain areas—for example, the ways in which video games allow for the free creation of virtual identities and worlds—cause a great deal of controversy and will undoubtedly cause a great deal more in the future.

Some of the learning principles this chapter has implicated follow. Again, each principle is relevant to both learning in video games and learning in content areas in classrooms. The cultural models about the world principle says that learners should have the opportunity to think reflectively about their cultural models about the world (e.g., the ways in which *Operation Flashpoint* made me rethink my cultural models of warfare). The cultural models about learning principle says that learners should have the opportunity to think reflectively about their cultural models about learning and themselves as learners (e.g., the ways in which *Metal Gear Solid* and a great many other games made me rethink the values of exploration and delaying getting to the major goal). The cultural models about semiotic domains principle says that learners should have the opportunity to think reflectively about their cultural models regarding the nature of semiotic domains they are trying to learn—for instance, about what a given type of video game is or should be like, or what makes something a game in the first place (e.g., Is *Under Ash* a video game or terrorist training? What about *Ethnic Cleansing?*) or what physics is (e.g., A set of facts? A way of thinking about and acting on the world? A set of social practices in which certain sorts of people engage?).

30. **Cultural Models about the World Principle**
     Learning is set up in such a way that learners come to think consciously and reflectively about some of their cultural models regarding the world, without denigration of their identities, abilities, or social affiliations, and juxtapose them to new models that may conflict with or otherwise relate to them in various ways.

31. **Cultural Models about Learning Principle**
     Learning is set up in such a way that learners come to think consciously and reflectively about their cultural models of learning and themselves as learners, without denigration of their identities, abili-

ties, or social affiliations, and juxtapose them to new models of learning and themselves as learners.

32. **Cultural Models about Semiotic Domains Principle**

Learning is set up in such a way that learners come to think consciously and reflectively about their cultural models about a particular semiotic domain they are learning, without denigration of their identities, abilities, or social affiliations, and juxtapose them to new models about this domain.

BIBLIOGRAPHICAL NOTE

Major sources in the literature on cultural models include D'Andrade 1995; D'Andrade & Strauss 1992; Holland, Lachicotte, Skinner, & Cain 1998; Holland & Quinn 1987; Shore 1996; and Strauss & Quinn 1997.

The example from the high school physics class comes from Hammer (1996a). For the relationships between everyday ways of understanding the world and scientific ways, and how to bridge between them, see diSessa 2000; Hammer 1996a,b; and Minstrell 2000.

The review of Operation Flashpoint is dated March 18, 2002 at www.gamezilla.com/reviews/o/ofp.asp.

7

THE SOCIAL MIND:
HOW DO YOU GET YOUR CORPSE
BACK AFTER YOU'VE DIED?

EVERQUEST: LEARNING AS SOCIAL

SO FAR I HAVE TALKED ABOUT VIDEO GAMES IN TERMS OF ONE individual playing the game alone because I wanted to concentrate on learning principles that primarily had to do with the individual mind and body as it confronts the world of experience. Nonetheless, I have shown that learning, even in these individualistic terms, is very much a matter of being situated in a material, social, and cultural world.

When I and my research assistants interview game players (because of our interest in schools, they are mostly young, between the ages of 5 and 19), we find that most play video games not alone but with others in three ways. (Younger players usually do only the first, while teens and above engage in all three modes.)

1. Players can hook multiple controllers into one video-game platform.
2. Players can network a number of computers into a local area network, so that they can play against each other without having to be in the same place.
3. The most popular option is for players to log on to special Internet sites and play certain games with and against sometimes thousands of other players all over the world.

Some games can only be played online, while many others can be played in single-player mode or online. (In fact, reviews tend to criticize games that can only be played in single-player mode.)

When online play first began, players moved through dungeons role-playing as different types of characters, but the universe through which they moved was composed entirely of text. Each player read text that told him or her what was there to be seen or done or what the effects were of various actions the player had taken. There were no pictures, only words. Now players move through fully realized, graphically beautiful, three-dimensional worlds. They can talk to each other by typing in words, though the technology now exists and is spreading where they can speak their words into a headset and be heard on the other people's computers. Players can talk to each other in their roles as fantasy virtual characters (their "avatars") or in terms of their real-world identities or switch between the two.

EverQuest is one of the most popular online games. More than 375,000 players have subscribed to play the game, and servers host more than 90,000 users playing at one time during peak game hours. (A game called *Lineage*, now available in the United States, has more than two million subscribers in South Korea.) *EverQuest* consists of multiple continents and numerous cities in which players carry out, alone or in groups, various quests. They run into other players who can help or, in some circumstances, hurt them (e.g., kill their fantasy virtual character). Sony Corporation now owns *EverQuest*, which was developed and is still run by a company named Verdant. Sony and Verdant put out new expansions (with new continents and cities) to *EverQuest* from time to time.

In the game you can choose to play in an ideal world where the monsters (not real people, but characters controlled by the computer and endowed with artificial intelligence) are the only bad guys and other players cannot kill you (and you can't kill them). Or you can choose to play in a world where you can kill and be killed by other players as well as the creatures that inhabit the countryside. If you make the latter choice, you become a "player-killer" and open yourself up to attack by other player-killers.

When you start playing *EverQuest*, you have to create your character, as in any role-playing game. There are a nearly endless combination of races, classes, skills, and abilities with which to create your character. However, character creation basically breaks down into 14 professions (Bard, Cleric, Druid, Enchanter, Magician, Monk, Necromancer, Paladin, Ranger, Rogue, Shadowknight, Shaman, Warrior, or Wizard) and 12 "races" composed of three human cultures, three cultures of elves, and six others. Each race is limited in which professions it may choose, so, for example, you cannot be an Ogre Monk.

Depending on your race, you are given a number of ability points to distribute among your seven main statistics (strength, stamina, agility, dexterity, wisdom, intelligence, and charisma). Then you name your character, pick your sex, and decide which deity (religion) you wish to follow. Your race, gender, class, and religion will decide how people deal with you in the *EverQuest* world. You can also join a guild, an organization of sometimes hundreds or thousands of (real) people that support each other and cooperate in the game (e.g., to kill particularly powerful gods). Your guild membership also affects how other people react to you in the game.

The *EverQuest* world is a very complex place with its own economic structure based on supply and demand. When a certain item becomes scarce (e.g., a certain piece of armor or certain type of sword), the price goes up. When something is common, the price drops. In some cases, players of games like *EverQuest* and *Diablo 2* have gone online to auction sites such as eBay and bought and sold virtual items in these games (things like gloves that endow the character with special powers or special sorts of swords) for real money. Someone recently bought a virtual item to use in *Diablo 2* for over $2,000.

EverQuest is different from any single-player game in that it never ends. The player cannot "beat" the game. There is no final goal other than the one you set for yourself. *EverQuest* is a persistent world and a game you can, if you like, play forever (as long as you pay the fee). You can log into the game, via the Internet, whenever you like and pick up wherever you left off. In most cases, over 1,000 other people will be playing with you. Indeed, certain places where there are particularly interesting monsters or valuable items to find can get quite crowded.

In games like *EverQuest*, sometimes players "flame" each other (say insulting things to each other) and otherwise do regrettable things. For example, a more powerful player may intrude on a battle between a less powerful one and a monster where the less powerful one is attempting to get the valuable items the monster owns. The powerful player can use a spell to give the monster more life, thereby saving it from the less powerful player's attacks, then kill it him- or herself and take the good stuff, leaving the less powerful player with nothing and having to spend time healing from wounds sustained in the now-wasted battle. Some players try to hack into the program and find a way to "cheat" and give themselves more (virtual) money. At times, this sort of behavior has led to gross inflation in the virtual worlds the players are playing in, rendering money nearly worthless.

When people started games like *EverQuest*, they thought the players would police themselves and create an ideal world of good behavior. However, the players created virtual worlds that contained many of the same flaws our real human worlds do. Game designers have thought up lots of ways to stop players from ruining the experience for others, such as *EverQuest*'s world where you cannot kill or be killed by other players. And, of course, players who behave badly enough can be disallowed from logging on to the game. But the designers barely stay one step ahead of very human characteristics like greed, hunger for power, and the sheer desire to use one's intelligence to outwit other players, the game, and computer systems in general. They also face the fact that many game players get very good at programming, both to design new games themselves (using free software that often comes with games to build expansions or to build new games called mods) and to hack into Internet-based games to transform them in their favor.

As in all role-playing games, in *EverQuest*, the more you play and the more you have accomplished, the higher the level of your character in terms of his or her skills. Higher-level characters can do more and go more places than can lower-level ones.

In *EverQuest*, when your character is killed, your corpse drops to the ground spilling all the valuable objects he or she was carrying (e.g., weapons, money, potions, armor, magical spells, etc.). However, your character, in a weaker form and with worse armor and weapons, also comes back alive, but far away, at the beginning of the area in which you were killed. (Yes, this is odd; you are both dead and alive. Let's just say it's your spirit that has come back.) You (your spirit) must get back to your corpse as quickly as possible, before it decays or other players take your possessions (which, if you are at a fairly high level, are quite valuable).

It's not easy to get back, since you are far away and weaker and have worse weapons, and so you must avoid strong enemies who can kill you again. If you do not get back, you must begin playing again at your lower level (you go down a couple of levels), fighting monsters to return to your former level. There is also another way to get back your corpse. If you have a cleric in your party (remember, players can play in teams with others, each being different characters with different powers) with the power to resurrect corpses, the cleric can resurrect your corpse.

Now, to exemplify the centrally social nature of game play and some key issues in this chapter, let a young man whom I will call Adrian (a pseudonym) tell you a story about playing *EverQuest* and other experiences he has had with video games. Adrian was 15 when the story took place and he had played *EverQuest* a great many hours. After having achieved a quite high level for his character, his character died.

My character was at a very high level: 46 out of a possible 50 levels. We have a clan [a small group that plays together and who are part of a much larger guild] made up of people from across the United States. It takes lots of people to kill the gods, so that's what the guilds are for. I was playing the game with my clan and we actually found a gate to one of the alter planes, the Plane of Fear. To get into the Plane of Fear there is a level requirement; your character has be at least at level 45. We busted into the Plane of Fear and everybody killed a God of Fear. We killed all these godly characters, and, then, this hunchback gorilla—the Plane of Fear is like a giant jungle—this giant gorilla came up behind me and swatted me like a fly and killed me with two hits. My friends didn't see it, so they couldn't protect me.

So I was killed. Whenever you die, you can come back to life, but you lose experience. I came back to life at level 44—so I lost two levels. It had taken me about 12 hours of playing the game to gain those two levels. It would take me 12 more to get them back. I was very upset. I was mad because I couldn't go back to the Plane of Fear, since I was now level 44 and you needed to be at least level 45 to get in.

There are clerics in the game, and when you play with clerics, they can actually resurrect you. When they resurrect you, you get back all your experience—so I'd be level 46 when I came back. I was talking [via the Internet] to people [who were clerics in my guild] and I gave them my home phone number. I'm like "When you guys finally find my corpse, resurrect it." But the game has a timer—if you're on the computer for three hours, it will wait for three hours and then it will say that your body is too old to get resurrected. I said to my father, "Dad, get the hell off the phone." [In other words: There are only three hours in which his corpse can be resurrected. It will take the clerics time to fight their way to the corpse. Adrian needs to know the moment the clerics resurrect it, so he can immediately get back online and retrieve his character and possessions before the three hours are up. Thus, he is waiting for the crucial phone call, hoping it comes in time.]

There was a limited window of time in which I could be resurrected. And, if I didn't get resurrected, then I'd be level 44 and I'd never get my equipment back. So, I was like "Oh, my god, no." And then I logged off and I was like pacing around the room, and I said, "I'm gonna die. I'm gonna die."

I mean, I'd invested like tons of time in the character. "I'm gonna die, I'm gonna die, I'm gonna die." And then one of my partners—a guy in his 30s—in my guild called me long distance from Indiana. He called me at like 11:45 P.M. from Indiana, and he told me that they got my corpse. He resurrected me and then I was back level 46, and then I spent—I think I played until like four in the morning killing things in the Plane of Fear, and then I went to sleep. When I woke up, it was like three in the afternoon the next day.

I still talk to the guy from Indiana sometimes. All of us have websites and message boards to talk on, to keep in contact with each other. Even with all like the Internet security stuff, we try not to give out our personal information, but after you get to know the person for a while, it becomes like second nature. I mean, with my character in *EverQuest* whenever I have gotten on I would say, "Hey, everyone." And, then there would be like a stream of like 40 people saying "Hi" to me, using my login name.

I actually have a website that tells you how to exploit game tips. My site and sites like it have interesting stuff on them about hackers trying to create a world where people don't have to pay to play the game. Not as a way to avoid paying, but for the challenge. The people who make the game don't really like these people at all. But what these people are trying to do is they're trying to take *EverQuest* and manipulate the game, even though much of has been heavily encrypted. They try to decrypt the files. They try to take the graphics, and try to take the game engine itself, manipulate it, and then put all that stuff on their own server, so people can play without pay.

What they're trying to do is trying to take the game and trying to make it so everyday people can play it for free. What I try to do on my website is I try to take people who play on the Internet, and if they don't like spending—I told you to get from level 44 to 46 it takes you like 12 hours of work, and no one has that amount of time—I tell them how they can take shortcuts in the game to get higher levels, so they can play at the level that other people play it at. And the game company doesn't like it, because they want you to play a lot. They want you to play a lot, and they want your money.

My little brother plays *EverQuest* now. He spends more time playing the game, I spend more time trying to crack the game open. To see what makes it work using hex editors. You can download these off the Internet. What a hex editor does is it basically breaks up computer code into pretty much binary code, and on the left side it gives you a bunch of zeros and ones and, then, on the right side it tells you what the code actually does. And, so, if you go and look on the right side, you can actually edit it. You don't learn this stuff by taking a class on it. It's just like here and there you pick stuff up.

You may not be able to learn it all from one place, there's many sources [e.g., other people, chat rooms, websites, texts, etc.].

Actually, the very first time I edited a game was when I was playing *Civilization*. I played *Civilization*. I beat *Civilization*. I was reading down the credits and I'm like "Okay, that's pretty cool." Then, I was like "Okay, that's kind of cool, now let's see—it'd be kinda cool if I was like to experiment. I wanna see what makes it tick."

So I went inside and found this like little data file that's like called *credits.dat*. I'm like "Okay, what does this do?" I double-click on it—and it asks what program I want to use to open it up with. And I click use Picture View [i.e., tells the computer to try to open the file *credits.dat* with the program named Picture View] and it came up with this jumble of stuff. I'm like "Okay, so I'm going to close that." I double-clicked on *credits.dat* again, and it asks again what program I want to use to open it with. And I try Internet Explorer this time, and it showed a bunch of jumbled code again. I'm like "Hmm. All-right."

And I try it again and then it's like, all right, "I'll use Notepad this time." And, I open it up in Notepad and right in front of me there are the credits for the game. And I was like "Hey that's kind of cool." It says "*Civilization* by Sid Meier." Okay, and I backspace, I typed in my name—"by Adrian Name" [his first and last name]. And then I saved the file, I beat the game again, and when the credits rolled, it said that I had created the game. I thought, "That's kinda cool."

I spend more time now tinkering with games and making games myself than I do actually playing them. Right now me and my friends aren't really playing. We're playing like *Diablo II* every now and then, we're just wasting time until *WarCraft III* comes out, and, then all of us are going to get it and we're gonna kill each other. When me and my friend talk about the games, we tell each other like what we think of new games that we've got. Essentially we tell each other what the strategy guides tell you.

When Adrian, who is an excellent student, is asked how he likes school, he has this to say: "School is fine. I don't live and breathe school, but it's fine."

Adrian's remarks exemplify several themes we have found with a number of the players we have interviewed. First, play for him is inherently social, in several different ways. He plays in a team with others. His team is part of a much larger group to which he belongs. He communicates with these people both inside the game and outside of it: about the game, about games in general, and about a wide variety of other issues. Players have told us that the people they play with range in age from the early teens to their 30s. One U.S. 15-year-old regularly plays *StarCraft* with, among others, two mid-30s Canadian college professors, and man and wife. The 15-year-old regularly chats with these professors, while playing, both in terms of their in-game fantasy roles and their real-world identities.

Second, the knowledge and skills Adrian has in regard to playing *EverQuest* is "distributed." It exists in his own head and body. But some of it exists in other people on whom he can call for help. The clerics who came to his rescue not only had powers in the game that Adrian's character did not have (they were clerics), they were also older and more advanced players who knew how to handle the situation. (I have left out of the story the fact that the three-hour limit actually ran out and Adrian and his friends together worked out a cheat to forestall the clock.)

Third, Adrian's knowledge and skills are not only distributed across himself and other people; some actually reside in various tools and technologies, like the hex editors he can use to manipulate the code of a game. The knowledge built into the hex editor counts as Adrian's knowledge because he knows how to leverage this tool. The real thinking and acting unit become "Adrian plus tool."

Fourth, Adrian's attitude toward games and the computer is itself game-like and highly metareflective. He looks at the game, whether *Civilization* or *EverQuest*, as a space that can be explored and "played with." He brings to this metalevel process the same exploratory and reflective attitudes that are required to play the game well in the first place. As part of this process, he greatly extends his knowledge and social connections. He sets up a web page to help others get to higher levels more quickly in *EverQuest*. He connects with a group of hackers who seek to understand the underlying program of *EverQuest* so thoroughly that they can actually transfer the game to another site where people can play the game free. He learns so much about computers and game design that, a few years later, when he is on his way to major in computer science and game design in college, he has already mastered most of the material in many of the courses he will need to take.

When we asked Adrian why he was interested in how hackers could "undermine" the Verdant company's hold over *EverQuest*, his reply was that, as he inspected their programming for the game, especially how they fixed various bugs that arose from time to time, he found their programming "inelegant." They took shortcuts and built programs that worked but weren't, as far as Adrian was concerned, optimal, especially at an aesthetic level. (Chapter 4 discussed the importance of developing appreciative systems.) Companies like Verdant don't know whether to arrest or hire young people like Adrian. And, indeed, company staff members regularly "lurk" on websites and chat rooms devoted to *EverQuest* and designed by players to learn new things and use them themselves.

So learning here is social, distributed, and part and parcel of a network composed of people, tools, technologies, and companies all interconnected together. Adrian is a node in such a network. and much of his knowledge and skill flows from his being such a richly interconnected node. Yet schools still isolate children from such powerful networks—for example, a network built around some branch of science—and test and assess them as isolated individuals, apart from other people and apart from tools and technologies that they could leverage to powerful ends.

Adrian's story also reflects a view of the mind current in some important work in cognitive psychology—a view that we might label "the social mind" perspective. This is not necessarily the mainstream view, but it is a viewpoint that, in one guise or another, plays a central role in helping people to think about learning in our modern, high-tech world—learning in businesses, communities, and in cutting-edge schools though, sadly, not in many mainstream schools. I turn to this viewpoint in the next section.

THE SOCIAL MIND

In chapter 4, I argued that human beings think and reason in terms of patterns they have picked up from their experiences in the world and used the example of how we recognize something as "simple" as a bedroom. Having seen and been in lots of bedrooms, when you think of a bedroom, something like an image of a typical bedroom comes to your mind.

Of course, what comes to your mind is not actually a picture. Rather, systems of neural elements in your brain stand for concepts like beds, carpets, lamps, and all the other things you associate with bedrooms. These things are the conceptual elements out of which your larger concept of a bedroom is composed. These neural systems and, thus, the concepts they encode are associated with each other through stronger or weaker links in terms of which each system (e.g., the one standing for beds) more or less strongly activates the others (e.g., the systems standing for chests of drawers, night tables, lamps, etc.).

Thus we can think of a pattern in the mind (e.g., the bedroom pattern) as a set of nodes (the bed node, the table node, the carpet node, the lamp node, etc.) linked to each other through stronger or weaker links. When two items are relatively strongly linked, thinking of one makes a person quite readily think of the other. For example, if you think of a bed, you probably can also quite readily bring to mind things like sheets, pillows, and blankets, because these are strongly linked to or associated with beds for many people. If two items are less strongly linked, then the one less readily brings to mind the other. For example, you probably associate books less strongly with beds than you do sheets, pillows, and blankets, though for some us who read before we go to bed, there is still some link or association.

So your concept of a bedroom is just all the elements of a typical bedroom that come to mind when you think of bedrooms and the ways in which they are more or less strongly linked or associated with each other. However, this pattern of linked elements (nodes in your mind/brain) is not static. It can change quickly. As I pointed out in chapter 4, if you have called to mind a pretty typical middle-class bedroom and I now tell you the bedroom I'm talking about has a hot plate in it, then you change the elements and their links in your mind, adding a hot plate and, perhaps, think of all the elements (and the stronger and weaker links among them) of a typical college student's bedroom or perhaps that of a person with minimal financial resources.

So we humans often think in terms of patterns. Pattern thinking is very powerful. It allows us to do two very important things. For one thing it allows us to think and reason by using the experiences we have had in life. We form our images (patterns) about bedrooms from our experiences in the world (and virtual experiences in reading and viewing media) with bedrooms and their elements. We don't just think in terms of abstract generalizations untied to our embodied experiences in the world. This is why it is often a bad thing to denigrate people's reasoning, in or out of school, since when we denigrate their reasoning, we are very often also denigrating their experiences in life (which are, of course, tied to their social groups and cultures).

Pattern thinking also allows us to make guesses (predictions) about the world that go beyond our actual experiences. For example, let's say I have experienced lots of cases where the following elements are strongly associated: being a professor, with tenure, in the field of physics, in a prestigious college, being male, being white. If I hear about someone who is a male tenured professor of physics in a prestigious college, I may add in the prediction that he is white, thanks to the fact that all these other things are, in my experience, strongly associated with being white.

Or let's say I hear about a female tenured professor of physics in a prestigious college. I may still assume she is white, since the other elements in the pattern (professor, of physics, with tenure, prestigious college) are strongly linked to being white in my experience. Even though these four elements are weakly or even negatively linked to being female and strongly linked to being male, the fact that the four things are still strongly associated with being white may swamp this negative link to being female and suggest the hypothesis to me that the person we are talking about is nonetheless white. I may never have experienced a female physicist, but I can reason about her based on my actual experiences, predicting that she will be white.

These examples bring out clearly both the power and the problems of thinking in terms of patterns. On one hand, we could not survive and function if we did not engage in such pattern thinking. People who know that massive brown bears (like grizzly bears) are dangerous but quibble over whether the medium-size black bear running toward them, a bear of a type they have not seen before, is or is not dangerous, and wait to find out, are dead or badly wounded. Best to fill out the pattern and assume that the link between bear and dangerous holds even in the absence of the elements brown and massive, at least when the bear is chasing you.

On the other hand, such pattern thinking can lead not only to good predictions in many cases but to prejudices or stereotypes in other situations. For example, the pattern in regard to physicists could lead one to assume that African Americans cannot do physics, a hurtful and false assumption. This, indeed, is the problem with restricting things like physics to white males—it leads to pattern thinking that, in this case, is wrong precisely because our experiences in the world have been artificially restricted, here by the workings of racism and patriarchy. (Consider: It used to be assumed African Americans couldn't play tennis and golf well, until Arthur Ash and Tiger Woods changed those patterns.)

BIRDS

Why am I discussing concepts and the mind? Because I want to claim that such a discussion leads us to an important paradox: If the human mind is a powerful pattern recognizer—and the evidence very much suggests it is—then what it most important about thinking is not that it is "mental," something happening inside our heads, but rather that it is *social*, something attuned to and normed by the social groups to which we belong or seek to belong. Since this statement so violates our commonsense notions of psychology, let me hasten to explain.

Let's, for a moment, consider a birdwatching club. Birdwatchers are good at seeing some elements (features) of birds and quickly extending the pattern to name a particular type of bird. Thus they may see a flash of gray-brown and a splash of white under the body as a small bird flits in and out of tall grass in an open grassland. They will, at least in much of the United States, conclude they have seen a bobolink, even if they have not seen all the bird's other salient features. If they see a flash of brown-brown and a splash of white under the body of a slightly larger bird flitting among the trees of a forest, they will conclude they have seen a flicker, a type of woodpecker, even if they have not seen the bird's distinctive purple spots and yellow shaft.

The first thing a birdwatching club needs to do is ensure that all its members have had the right experiences in the world to have formed such patterns and engaged in such ways of filling them out in the field. People can wander around on their own and experience—and pay attention to—all sorts of things to do with birds, many of them interesting, but not all that helpful if you want to be a contributing member of the birdwatching club. Perhaps every time you have hiked you have never seen birds in open grassland (easy to happen, unless you are out early in the morning or at dusk, when the birds are active and often sitting atop a grass stalk or small plant, since otherwise the birds are on the ground hidden below the tall grass). You conclude that there are no bird species that live in open grassland. You have formed a (wrong) pattern in which open grassland is negatively associated with birds. The bird club will see to it that you get out to some open grassland at the right time of day so you can see the bobolinks and meadowlarks. Why? Because they want you to have similar enough experiences as the other club members so that you can share knowledge with them.

The first thing the bird club does is see to it that new members come to share a lot of experiences of the world of birds and birding with the other members, so that they will share some common patterns and ways of completing them when they have seen only some features in a pattern. Then the members can make lists of all the birds around in the winter in a given part of the country or find out that birds that live in open grasslands are much more endangered than the forest songbirds that have received almost all the publicity concerning their supposed decline. Now they also can engage in competition as to who are the best birdwatchers in the sense of being able to identify the most different species of birds in a given place during a certain set amount of time, since they are now all adept at the basic practice and norms of the "game."

But there is a second thing the bird club must do. Say Mary Smith, a member in good standing, all of a sudden comes to the club one day and says, given what she has seen out in the field, that she is pretty sure that what she saw was a dodo, an extinct species of bird. Perhaps, more realistically, Mary Smith keeps claiming to have seen ivory-billed woodpeckers (which are probably extinct, but we're not sure) rather than pileated woodpeckers (which certainly exist, though they are not horribly common), based on a flicker of some distinctive features. (She never seems to get a full view of the bird before it flies off.) Both birds look similar, though ivory-billed woodpeckers are bigger and have a somewhat different bill. Given how unlikely it is that anyone will see an ivory-billed woodpecker (though, if they are not extinct, it is possible), the club will insist that any member who claims to have seen one has seen it well and very carefully checked the identification. (If you see a big black woodpecker with a red crest that looks a lot like Woody Woodpecker, it's almost certainly a pileated woodpecker.)

If, in either case, dodo or ivory-billed woodpecker, Mary Smith persists, what happens? At first, the club refuses to publish her lists in its newsletter. Eventually, if she persists further, the club kicks her out. What's going on here? The club is norming (yes, policing, if you like) its members' patterns and ways of filling them out. If a member deviates too far from the patterns and ways of filling them out in the field that the club, as a social group, considers normative, then the club "punishes" the member in order to bring him or her back in line. It's not that, if ivory-billed woodpeckers still exist, no member could see one and get it published in the club's newsletter. But seeing an ivory-billed woodpecker, like seeing any bird in the context of birdwatching as a social practice, is not just a mental event, it's also a social event. There are social rules or norms about what counts as having seen an ivory-billed woodpecker, and, in this case, they are strict.

The point of this diversion about birdwatching is this: The patterns and ways of filling them out that count are not really the ones inside the heads of the members (though they are there, of course). All the members, as individual human beings, have a myriad of patterns about birds, and ways of filling them out in the field, in their heads. But the club, as a social group, has a set of norms and values that determines certain sorts of patterns and ways of filling them out in the field as "ideal" (central). This ideal might actually not be what is in anyone's head. The ideal is an "attractor," an ideal toward which individuals in the club gravitate and toward which the social practices (the "policing") of the club pushes them when they get too far away from it.

If someone questions what constitutes the "right" pattern in regard to seeing an ivory billed woodpecker or, more realistically, what are the right patterns in terms of which one can identify the many types of (similar-looking) sparrows or seagulls, people in the club don't open up anyone's head. They engage in dialogue (negotiation and contestation) with each other, inspect their practices, read their texts, and, yes, ask certain people what they think, probably the old-timers or "insiders" and not the newcomers or marginal members. In the end, if thinking is a matter of pattern reorganization and filling our patterns, then thinking is at least as much social as it is mental and individual. Actually, it is more social than mental and individual. Of course, this idea violates traditional ways of thinking about psychology. So be it.

Even if you are not into birds, you surely have seen many sparrows and you have formed patterns in your mind in regard to them. You probably associate being little and brown with being a type of sparrow very strongly. You may well associate being in a city or in the yard of a suburban house with being a sparrow. You may, in terms of the patterns in your mind, recognize a few different types of sparrows (perhaps you have noticed that some in your yard have a little yellow cap on their head and some don't), or maybe you don't and see them all as basically the same type of bird. You have a set of elements associated with sparrows in your head, and you associate them more or less strongly with each other and with being a sparrow.

These sparrow patterns you have in your head, which are perfectly normal for "everyday" people, will not work for being a "birder." From the standpoint of a birdwatching club, they are the wrong patterns, and the club, should you seek to join it, would help to give you other experiences that would shift the patterns in your head more toward its ideal. For people who have been normed by other birdwatchers and their practices and texts, their heads contain patterns in terms of which there are a great many different types of sparrows, many of which look quite a bit a like. They associate a great many of these with nonurban and nonsuburban settings, and, in fact, they associate the common house sparrow with finches and not New World sparrows at all.

Since the world is replete with features and people are powerful pattern recognizers, anyone can form almost any sort of interesting pattern in his or her head—forming all sorts of concepts and subconcepts. None of this is "right" or "wrong" until we ask which social group helps to norm (or police) patterns (concepts) in this or that domain that we wish to be part of. If you want to join a birdwatching club, you have to admit that the patterns in your head about sparrows are wrong; if you don't want to join the club, then the patterns may very well be just fine from the point of view of some other group, if only your own culture, community, or family. Again, the patterns are in our heads, but they become meaningful ("right" or "wrong") only from the perspective of the workings of social groups that "enforce" certain patterns as ideal norms toward which everyone in that group should orient (even if the patterns in their heads never resemble the ideal perfectly). Of course, for some purposes, though perhaps not for others, some groups' practices work better than do those of other groups.

What I have said about our birdwatching club is true of any group. We humans belong to a myriad of social and cultural groups. Some of these groups are families and communities of various sizes. Some are cultural groups defined in various ways. Some are what I have called in previous chapters "affinity groups." (The birdwatching club would be an affinity group.) Affinity groups are groups wherein people primarily orient toward a common set of endeavors and social practices in terms of which they attempt to realize these endeavors. In such groups people orient less towards shared gender, race, culture, or face-to-face relationships, although all of these can play a secondary role. People can be in affinity groups where they rarely see many of the members face-to-face (e.g., the group may communicate in part at a distance via media, whether it's print, the Internet, or what have you). Adrian was part of several different overlapping affinity groups in his work and play with video games.

Could a person think and reason outside the scope of any group, that is, with no group serving to norm his or her patterns and ways of filling them out? As Wittgenstein pointed out long ago, in a different context, such people would have no way to accurately test whether their patterns were veridical. Of course, the world would speak back when they tried to operate in and on it in terms of their patterns. But this would just be more experience of the world in terms of which their patterns were formed in the first place. Only when others have normed our patterns and ways of filling them out, so that we can be fairly confident that we are not "fooling" ourselves because of our own self-interest, desires, or idiosyncratic ways, can we trust our patterns in a particular domain.

Does this mean that no one can think an "original" thought? Of course not. But all the scientists, for example, who have thought original thoughts that their fellow scientists have never (eventually) come to see as close to the ideal patterns in their domain have thought thoughts that, at least of yet, no one knows about. As of yet, at least, their thoughts don't "count" as part of their domain and are not "published" (spread in speech or writing).

And, of course, what counts to a group as an ideal pattern and way of filling it out in new experiences changes with time. I have already pointed out that the norms and values of groups are contested and negotiated. They are no more stable than is our concept of a bedroom (which we can shift when I link a hot plate to the room), and for the same reason. When the group confronts a new experience (in the world or in ideas), this experience can change the links (associations) among all the elements in the patterns the group considers ideal or normative, though this change happens through dialogue in speech and writing, not just via private thoughts.

DISTRIBUTED KNOWLEDGE

So, thinking and reasoning are inherently *social*. But they are also inherently *distributed*, and more and more so in our modern technological world. By this I mean that each of us lets other people and various tools and technologies do some of our thinking for us. Even in my own field of linguistics, I certainly do not need to know everything. I can always ask other linguists about things I am unsure of. I can consult articles and books. This much is obvious, though not in school. In school we test people apart from their thinking tools, which include other people as well as texts and various sorts of tools and technologies. We want to know what they can do all by themselves. But in the modern world—and this is certainly true of many modern high-tech workplaces—it is equally or more important to know what people can think and do with others and with various tools and technologies.

But this is still too individualistic a way to look at the matter of distributed thinking and doing. The power of distribution—of storing knowledge in other people, texts, tools, and technologies—is really in the way in which all these things are networked together. The really important knowledge is in the network—that is, in the people, their texts, tools, and technologies and, crucially, the ways in which they are interconnected—not in any one "node" (person, text, tool, or technology), but in the network as a whole. Does the network store lots of powerful knowledge? Does it ensure that this knowledge moves quickly and well to the parts of the system that need it now? Does it adapt to changed conditions by learning new things quickly and well? These are the most crucial knowledge questions we can ask in the modern world. They are hardly reflected at all in how we organize schooling and assessment in schooling.

Let me give you a very simple example of a very powerful system working to distribute knowledge in such a way that a person like myself is made much smarter than I could ever be by myself. *Half-Life* is one of the most renowned first-person shooter games of all time. One online review had this to say about people who have never heard of the game: "If you haven't heard of *Half-Life* by now, you've either been stuck in a closet or on some alien planet for the past year."

In *Half-Life*, you play a scientist named Gordon Freeman who works at a massive top-secret underground facility named Black Mesa. When you show up to work one day, you realize not all is right. Some of your fellow scientists are worried about various odd happenings, and the occasional blown electrical panel around the facility gives you some worries of your own. Your fellow scientists look quite harried when they usher you into the hazardous materials testing chamber (while they monitor the situation from the outside) to work on a new sample, giving you assurances that sound anything but reassuring.

In one of the great scenes in any video game, a catastrophic explosion occurs, the air turns green, flashes of light erupt everywhere, and intermittently aliens of various sorts appear and disappear. Everything starts collapsing around you, and your fellow scientists, from outside the chamber, tell you to run for your life as they, quite unsuccessfully for the most part, run for theirs.

You, as Gordon Freeman, are left to figure out what has happened and to try to undo the damage that, once again (it's a regular occurrence in video games), science has wrought. At the outset it certainly doesn't appear you can do much. Most of your fellow scientists and the security guards at the plant are

dead. The others are terrified and stunned, though they will open various se-
cured doors for you. As you seek to escape the sprawling underground complex,
you see destruction everywhere and run into aliens, including your fellow scientists turned into zombies by alien head-crabs having fallen on them, trying to
kill you. In the beginning you have no weapon, save a crowbar you have found.

Things get worse. Not long after your problems begin, you discover that
the military is coming into the Black Mesa to contain the situation and rescue
any survivors. When they show up, you quickly realize that they are not there
to rescue anyone but to kill them, thereby eliminating any witnesses to the
catastrophe. This sets you to wondering, as you now seek to avoid both soldiers and aliens, why the U.S. government is so intent on covering up a supposed "accident." Intriguingly, a mysterious man in a suit carrying a briefcase
shows up here and there, one step ahead of you. Who is he?

You (as Gordon) are miles beneath the New Mexico desert. To begin to
solve your problems, you need to make it to the surface and seek help. Eventually, after a great many problems and many many hours of play, you cross
into the alien dimension and must kill the alien big boss behind all the other
aliens. This is an epic battle, but leads you back to earth to confront the U.S.
government's nefarious role in the events. One of the Internet reviews captures the feel of the game well: "Alarms are sounding, slimy monsters are
drooling, blue-collar security guards are fighting to protect the scientists, and
army goons are mowing down anything that moves. What we need is a hero,
someone to sort out this three-way slug-fest with extra helpings of pump-ac-
tion justice. Unfortunately, it's going to have to be someone else because you
just ran out of ammo and bent your crowbar on some toothy monster's skull.
You'll be lucky to get out of this alive."

When I played *Half-Life*, I felt a great sense of accomplishment when I
got to the end of the game and up to the final battle with the alien big boss. I
had played for many hours, quite regularly tearing out what little hair I have
left as I faced a myriad of tough fights and problems. In the final battle, I
found myself in a giant cavern. Mysterious bulging circles on the ground
propelled me up into the air when I jumped on them, sometimes allowing me
to land on high-up ledges. It was good that these bulging circles were there,
because floating high above me, at the cavern's ceiling, was the alien boss, a
massive head that looked like an alien baby.

The boss sent out waves of light that could kill me in seconds. Further,
he was surrounded by smaller flying aliens that shot destructive rays at me.

The boss seemed to be able to make ever more of these flying aliens as I killed them. To keep safe and even have a chance of killing the boss I ran madly around, hiding behind rock and crystal formations. I madly bounced in the air using the bulging circles, attempting to get to a high enough ledge to have a good sighting on the floating alien boss. To kill him, the player has to soften him up enough with fire from a particularly powerful weapon and then, when he opens up his head, shoot directly into his brain.

Alas, after much effort and dying many times (and starting again from a saved game from the beginning of the battle), I realized that I had come into the cavern without enough ammunition to do the job. And there was no going back. I sat atop a high ledge, a good spot, but eventually with no ammunition and a very angry boss. I knew I could get more ammunition, but only by jumping to the ground and then climbing far down a large tunnellike hole. At the bottom of this hole was more ammunition, but then I had to jump from ledge to ledge back up the hole (it had low gravity) even to get back to the ground floor of the cavern and renew the fight. Worse, as I tried to jump back up the hole, from ledge to ledge, a long long way up, the boss's flying alien support staff kept firing at me from above.

Now, I am a very bad jumper in video games. I was yet worse, of course, with the flying aliens shooting at me and forcing me to try to shoot at them as I attempted to move up the hole jumping from ledge to ledge. Time and again, just as I made some progress up the walls of the hole, I fell midjump back to the bottom. Time and again the flying aliens eventually killed me. I had devoted a great many hours to this game. Due to my own ineptness at jumping, I could not finish it and find out the end of the story. (Who *is* that man in the suit?)

But video-game players can be part of a powerful network, if they so desire and know how. Their own ineptness need not stop them. There is knowledge they can use, if they know how to leverage it, stored in other people and in various tools and technologies. I got on the Internet, looked up several game sites, and found a cheat code that allowed me to input commands to the game that made me invisible to the flying aliens. This allowed me to jump without being distracted by their firing at me. When I got back to the cavern's floor, I turned off the cheat code and continued the battle. I had enough ammunition and, though with great effort, finished off the alien boss. Now I know who the man in the suit is.

A cheat is a fairly simple procedure that encodes a great deal of knowledge about designing and programming video games that I don't personally have. For example, here is a cheat code for gaining infinite life (you can't die) in the game *Star Wars Jedi Knight II: Jedi Outcast:* When the game is running, press the Shift key and the tilde ("~") key together. A screen will come up with a cursor (and some lines of program). Now type "devmapall" and press the Enter key. Then type "god" and press the Enter key. Finally, press the Shift key and the tilde key together again. Now you can't die. Each game has different sorts of cheat codes, usually designed to be used by people testing the games when they are in production.

Of course, it is not much fun playing *Jedi Outcast* without being able to die. It was, however, quite functional for me to use a cheat code in playing *Half-Life*. In using the cheat codes, I could have given myself an infinite amount of ammunition or life, but I wanted to use a code that would simply remedy my ineptness at jumping and allow me to finish the rest of the game on my own skills.

The little cheat code, which contains a good deal of programming knowledge in a user-friendly format, supplemented me in just the right way, allowing me to be more powerful, while fulfilling my goals of finishing the game on my own as much as possible. Ironically, my individual achievement of finishing *Half-Life*, of which I was proud, was nonetheless still a social achievement. I had tapped into a large network of interconnected chat rooms and game sites that offer other people's knowledge and many tools with which to supplement myself.

I had used this network before. Along with being a bad jumper, I have a completely miserable sense of direction and location in space. This is not a good thing when playing a video game, since many games contain mazes of various sorts. Early on in playing games, I was deeply frustrated by these mazes. However, one day, when I was reading comments on a chat room devoted to some game or another, a player (of who knows what age, race, or gender, since he or she used an alias) said that the way to get out of a maze was always to turn left whenever you could. The player was answering a query from someone else. I have no idea why this works—or even if it does in all cases—but it has always worked for me. (I suppose always turning right works, too, though I haven't tried it.)

Of course, at least initially, I got far more out of my connection to the network than any other people in it got from me. One day, however, I was gratified to find out that a number of players on one site could not figure out how to get a certain cheat code to work. It turned out that the code required one to get into DOS (the operating system that PCs used before Windows), find the right directory, and type in DOS commands. These particular play-ers were probably all young—too young to remember DOS or to have ever done much with it. I, of course, am old enough to have used DOS a great deal. Ironically, I was able to tell them—young people whom I am sure knew a great deal more about games, computers, and programming than do I—how to operate the cheat code. So here we see that even a weak link in a net-work can make the network more powerful in the right circumstances.

These, of course, are ludicrously simple examples. I am purposely trying to use very simple examples to make the point clearly. In such a network, the other players and various tools like cheat codes are *part of what I know* (and I am part of what the other players know), even though neither the players nor (at least, initially) the cheat codes are in my mind. My knowledge is not only social, it is distributed outside my body. If you were to assess just my skills playing video games alone in my own home, you would underestimate me. You need to assess me as a node in a network and see how I function as such a node. The knowledge I gain playing games, limited as it is for an old baby-boomer, is but a part of my functioning as such a node, and it is knowledge that can spread into the network as well. In turn, knowledge flows to me, making me better than your original estimate would have assumed.

If we want to know how good students are in science—or how good em-ployees are in a modern knowledge-centered workplace—we should ask all of the following (and not just the first): What is in their heads? How well can they leverage knowledge in other people and in various tools and technologies (in-cluding their environment)? How are they positioned within a network that connects them in rich ways to other people and various tools and technologies? Schools tend to care only about what is inside students' heads as their heads and bodies are isolated from others, from tools and technologies, and from rich environments that help make them powerful nodes in networks. Adrian would-n't play a game in these circumstances, nor would most of the other players whom we have interviewed. Good workplaces in our science- and technology-driven "new capitalism" don't play this game. Schools that do are, in my view, DOA in our current world—and kids who play video games know it.

SCIENCE IN THE CLASSROOM

Jean Lave, a leading theorist of socially situated cognition, has developed a view of learning that fits well with all I have said here. She argues that learning is not best judged by a change in minds (the traditional school measure), but by "changing participation in changing practices." Most important, learning is a change not just in practice, but in *identity*—for Lave, "crafting identities in practice becomes the fundamental project. Rather than particular tools and techniques for learning as such, there are ways of becoming a participant, ways of participating, and ways in which participants and practices change. In any event, the learning of specific ways of participating differs in particular situated practices. The term 'learning mechanism' diminishes in importance, in fact it may fall out altogether, as 'mechanisms' disappear into practice. Mainly, people are becoming kinds of persons."

Lave's perspective fits perfectly with the team- and project-based focus of many modern workplaces. It fits, too, with the idea that in the modern world of the "new capitalism" (a capitalism based more on knowledge than on industrial assembly lines) we must more and more come to see ourselves not in terms of a linear progression up a "career ladder" in one single job but as a "portfolio" composed of the rearrangable skills and identities we have acquired in our trajectory through diverse projects inside and outside of "workplaces" as we move from job to job, project to project, and career to career in a fast-changing world. It fits, also, with the new capitalist stress on leveraging the tacit knowledge workers acquire "online" as they adapt to constant changes in practice. And, finally, it fits well with how players learn as they play video games as members of clans and guilds with their own web sites and chat rooms.

In education, Lave's views on learning are well exemplified in the classrooms (called "communities of learners") designed by Ann Brown and Joseph Campione, two leading educational cognitive scientists. Unfortunately, Brown died not long ago, leaving the area of learning theory (and practice) much impoverished. Brown and Campione's classrooms use a wide variety of devices to ensure that knowledge and understanding are public, collaborative, dispersed, and distributed. Two of these methods are reciprocal teaching and the jigsaw method.

In reciprocal teaching, the teacher and a group of students take turns leading a discussion about a reading passage. The leader begins by *asking a question*. The group rereads the passage and discusses possible problems of interpretation when necessary. Attempts to *clarify* any comprehension problems occur opportunistically. At the end of the discussion, the leader *summarizes* the gist of what has been read. The leader also asks for *predictions* about future content. In this way the core components of successful reading comprehension (usually thought of as the preserve of "private minds") are rendered public, overt, and distributable. Much like "quality circles" in the new capitalism, people are asked to publicly display and share their knowledge for the benefit of the group (and the system as a whole).

In the *jigsaw method* of cooperative learning, students are assigned a subpart of a classroom topic to learn and subsequently teach to others via reciprocal teaching. In Brown and Campione's extrapolation of this method, the setting is a science classroom. Students do collaborative research in research groups each devoted to a different sub-topic of a larger theme or overall topic such as animal defense mechanisms, changing populations, or food chains. Then they redistribute themselves into learning groups where each student takes a turn teaching (using the reciprocal teaching method) the subtopic he or she has mastered in the previous research group.

In the jigsaw method, each module (team) is initially expert on only one part of the whole topic, no team is expert on the whole. But each team distributes its knowledge to the whole. There is no single "leader" (teacher); each member plays the role of researcher, student, and teacher in different configurations and contexts. There is no "center," only a flexible network of distributed roles and responsibilities.

There are still other important features of Brown and Campione's classrooms, including a pervasive use of modern computer, telecommunications, and network technologies. Students, for example, engage in e-mail conversations with outside experts and search the web for relevant information. These are both ways to network the classroom, and the children in it, into a larger knowledge system.

Students in these classrooms also each "major" in some area. A given child may choose to be the expert on a given piece of software, a specific technology, or some specific area of concern. This child—who is, of course, still fully involved as a group member in the whole project of his or her group—helps or coaches other children in his or her specialist area.

All aspects of Brown and Campione's classrooms are put in place to subserve learning within a "zone" of joint activity, another feature these classrooms share with modern knowledge- and technology-centered workplaces. Brown and Campione borrow from the Russian psychologist Lev Vygotsky the concept of a "zone of proximal development." They define this zone as "the distance between [an individual's] current levels of comprehension and levels that can be accomplished in collaboration with people or powerful artifacts."

The core idea is that novices, largely unconsciously, "internalize" or accommodate to the goals, values, and understandings of those more expert than themselves through scaffolded joint activity with those others and their associated tools and technologies. The beauty of Brown and Campione's classrooms is that the other students, the various technologies in the classroom, and the very structure of the activities themselves take on the role of the scaffolding, structuring expert, not just the traditional classroom teacher.

Brown and Campione's classrooms and many modern workplaces constitute what some have called communities of practice and what I have called affinity groups. I am not using the term community of practice, both because it has been given various meanings and because I wish to avoid the romantic notions that seem to accompany the word "community"; affinity groups can be good, evil, or anything inbetween.) Video-game players like Adrian are prime examples of members of an affinity group. For me, an affinity group, whether in a workplace, school, or community, often has the following features:

1. Members of an affinity group bond to each other primarily through a *common endeavor* and only secondarily through affective ties, which are, in turn, leveraged to further the common endeavor. Implication: Affective ties and sociocultural diversity can be dangerous, because they divide people if they transcend the endeavor, good otherwise.

2. The common endeavor is organized around a *whole process* (involving multiple but integrated functions), not single, discrete, or decontextualized tasks. Implication: No rigid departments, borders, or boundaries.

3. Members of the affinity group have *extensive* knowledge, not just intensive knowledge. By "extensive" I mean that members must be involved with many or all stages of the endeavor; able to carry out multiple, partly overlapping, functions; and able to reflect on the endeavor as a whole system, not just their part in it. Implication: No narrow specialists, no rigid roles.

4. In addition to extensive knowledge, members each have *intensive* knowledge—deep and specialist knowledge in one or more areas. Members may well also bring special intensive knowledge gained from their outside experiences and various sociocultural affiliations (e.g., their ethnic affiliations) to the affinity group's endeavors. Implication: Non-narrow specialists are good.

5. Much of the knowledge in an affinity group is *tacit* (embodied in members' mental, social, and physical coordinations with other members and with various tools, and technologies), and *distributed* (spread across various members, their shared sociotechnical practices, and their tools and technologies), and *dispersed* (not all on site, but networked across different sites and institutions). Implication: Knowledge is not first and foremost in heads, discrete individuals, or books but in networks of relationships.

6. The role of leaders in affinity groups is to *design* the groups, to continually *resource* them, and to help members turn their tacit knowledge into *explicit knowledge*, while realizing that much knowledge will always remain tacit and situated in practice. Implications: Leaders are not "bosses," and only knowledge that is made explicit can be spread and used outside the original affinity group.

In such affinity groups, people are committed through their immersion in practice, since it is the practice itself that gives them their identity and not some "occupation," fixed set of skills, or culture apart from the practice. Diverse individual skills and cultures are recruited as resources for the group, not as identities that transcend the affinity group itself.

Of course, there are many variations on classrooms like those designed by Brown and Campione. Ironically, however, when the U.S. economy was doing poorly in comparison to the Japanese economy and other Asian economies, classrooms like these were popular and spreading. They were what policymakers wanted. However, when the U.S. economy rose and the Asian ones fell, many policymakers decried such classrooms and called for a return to skill and drill and a renewed focus on the learner as a social isolate (isolated both from other people and from knowledge tools).

What happened, in my view, is that policymakers began to see that the "new capitalism" was not going to make of every worker a "knowledge worker," as had previously been thought. Rather, the new global high-tech economy called for lots of service workers in addition to lots of knowledge workers. The service workers needed good communication skills and a willingness to be cooperative and pliant but often did not need much sophisticated technical or specialist knowledge. Thus some schools—the more advantaged ones with more economically advantaged learners—would prepare future knowledge workers via thinking curricula, while others—the less advantaged ones with the less economically advantaged learners—would prepare service workers and the remaining industrial and manual workers in the new capitalism via skill and drill on the "basics."

Perhaps my view is too cynical. But, in any case, and for whatever reason, young people who play video games often experience a more intense affinity group, leverage more knowledge from other people and from various tools and technologies, and are more powerfully networked with each other than they ever are in school.

LEARNERS AS INSIDERS AND PRODUCERS

Video games incorporate a powerful learning principle that fits well with inquiry-based classrooms and with workplaces that encourage workers to think proactively and critically to build new knowledge in practice for the business but poorly with traditionalist, passive, skill-and-drill school-based learning. Many good video games come with free software, on the disk that contains the game, that allows players to build new extensions ("mods" or fan modifications) to the game or even new games altogether.

For example, a player who plays a shooter game on the Internet with other players can make a new "map" (a new environment in which the players can battle with each other). In fact, game companies actively encourage players to make such maps, and make them available to other players via the Internet, to supplement the ones the company has already made, thereby getting new design work done for free. Often, too, players can, when they finish a game in single-player mode, design a whole new level to the game and continue playing. And some have even made up whole new games (mods that are also called total conversions), using the software connected to a specific game to design a different game altogether, and sold them via the Internet. (*Half-Life* has given rise to a very vibrant mod community that has developed such games as *Counter-Strike*, *Day of Defeat*, and *Action Half-Life*.)

Good video games allow players not just to be passive consumers but also active producers who can customize their own learning experience. The game designer is not an insider and the player an outsider, as, in school, in so many instances, the teacher is the insider and the learners are outsiders who must take what they are given as mere consumers. Rather, game designers and game players are both insiders and producers—if players so choose—and there need be no outsiders.

While using software to design new extensions or new games is a dramatic example of learner/player as producer, good video games build in this principle at many different levels. In almost all games, the player can choose among various difficulty levels. In some games, the player can switch the difficulty level even in the middle of the game when things get too hard or too easy (and switch it back again thereafter). In addition, as I pointed out in an earlier chapter, good video games allow players to choose different styles of play (e.g., stealth or overt aggression) and to solve problems in multiple ways (e.g., logic, systematic trial and error, free exploration, getting or not getting hints, etc.), thereby allowing them to customize the experience to their favored style of learning or to try out new styles.

Some total conversions made by groups of players (who often work together over the Internet and never see each other face-to-face), using free software from the game companies themselves, constitute games that are as good, or better, than commercially available games. Players of these total conversions often must own the original game, because the mods still use files from the original. Thus, game companies are happy to help make the mods available, via the Internet, to other players. *Day of Defeat* is a total conversion of the game *Half-Life*. While *Half-Life* is about scientists and aliens, *Day of Defeat* is a realistic military game about World II. *Day of Defeat* is now made available (for a small access fee) by the company that made *Half-Life* and is more popular than many commercially made military games. The same company had already bought another total conversion outright (*Counter-Strike*) and sold it as a commercial game.

Here is what the online magazine *Salon.com* had to say in April 2002 about the phenomenon of game players becoming game designers: "Many of the best game companies now count on modders to show them the way creatively and to ensure their own survival in a savagely competitive market. This stands in marked contrast to the music and film industry, which vindictively discourages fans from tinkering with their content and clings to an outdated interpretation of copyright. By fostering the creativity of their fans, their more agile peers in the game industry have not only survived but prospered."

Let's listen a moment to a 12-year-old boy, whom I will call Max (a pseudonym), talk about playing and designing new maps for the very popular skateboard game series, *Tony Hawk's Pro Skater* (*Tony Hawk's Pro Skater 4* is the most recent game to appear in the series). In this game, players can choose to skate with the skills of Tony Hawk, a legendary (but real) skateboard professional, or as one of a number of other professional skaters. Players skate through many different urban and nonurban environments, filled with other people and various obstacles, engaging in wild leaps and tricks. Max is explaining how he makes new maps for *Tony Hawk's Pro Skater* (new environments or skate parks within which players can skate and solve problems). As he talks, he is showing the interviewer some of his maps. As in all face-to-face talk, by reading a transcript, you will not understand every detail, but the point will be clear enough:

> It's pretty simple. What you do is first you pick a starting spot and then you put out a block, to move this you use the mouse, that's the starting block, you don't see the arrows, but that's where you start. Um, this is a quarter pipe and that's like a ramp that you go up, so you can set that, too, and this piece, it rotates, so that was kind of obvious.
>
> I've made about 20 maps or so. The first map was pretty random. It was pretty bad, it was cluttered. You'd bump into things and that's not very fun. My first map had a lot of variety, but it was cluttered, no space between, 'cause I just put EVERYTHING in—that's why it was bad. I tried to put everything in—just to try it out. I could get through it, but it wasn't fun.
>
> So I started over again and, then, I started a theme. It just came to my head to make a park, like where there's trees and things. There's trees and I kinda made a lot of that and you can ride on that. It looks pretty, too. And I had stairs and railings, like the arboretum and stuff like that. That one was a very good map.
>
> Another one I did was "Find the Secret Room," and I tried to make this really boring place outside and put walls, and this little small unnoticed room [you had to discover]. I let my friends play on my maps—they come here to play—and I'll say "Hey, try this out." They were able to find the secret room. It was not very good. It was fun, but the room wasn't well hidden. I started making maps when I first got the game, like probably the second day I played.

Max is only 12. Nonetheless, this is producer talk. It's designer talk. Max is developing a rich appreciative system in terms of which to evaluate his design decisions (and he does not spare himself criticism). Max, as a learner, is also a producer and insider by the second day he has owned the game—and this is the first game for which he has made maps. Do 12-year-olds engage in this sort of producer, designer talk, connected to a growing appreciative system in their science classrooms? If not—and chances are great in today's test and drill-and-skill schools that they do not in many cases—then they are experiencing a much more powerful view of learning when they are playing video games, an enterprise that many in our culture think is a "waste of time," than they are in school.

LEARNING PRINCIPLES

As in previous chapters next I list learning principles implicated in our discussion in this chapter that are built into good video games. Again, each principle is relevant both to learning in video games and to learning in content areas in classrooms. Again, too, there is no order to the principles; they are each important.

33. **Distributed Principle**

    Meaning/knowledge is distributed across the learner, objects, tools, symbols, technologies, and the environment.

34. **Dispersed Principle**

    Meaning/knowledge is dispersed in the sense that the learner shares it with others outside the domain/game, some of whom the learner may rarely or never see face-to-face.

35. **Affinity Group Principle**

    Learners constitute an "affinity group," that is, a group that is bonded primarily through shared endeavors, goals, and practices and not shared race, gender, nation, ethnicity, or culture.

36. **Insider Principle**

    The learner is an "insider," "teacher," and "producer" (not just a "consumer") able to customize the learning experience and domain/game from the beginning and throughout the experience.

BIBLIOGRAPHICAL NOTE

The literature on sociocultural approaches to learning is immense; for a sampling of a variety of different perspectives, see: Bereiter 1994; Brown 1994; Cobb, Yackel, & McClain 2000; Delpit 1995; Engestrom, Miettinen, & Punamaki 1999; Kirshner & Whitson 1997; Lave & Wenger 1991; Lee & Smagorinsky 1999; Moll 1992; Wenger 1998; Wertsch 1998; and Wertsch, Del Rio, & Alvarez 1995.

For work on views of mind that stress pattern recognition within embodied experience, see the references to connectionist views in chapter 4's bibliographical note. See also Gee 1992. On the notion of distributed knowledge (or distributed cognition), see Brown 1994; Brown, Collins, and Dugid 1989; Hutchins 1995; and Latour 1999. For Lave's work, see Lave 1988, 1996 (pp. 161, 157); and Lave & Wenger 1991. For

Brown and Campione's classrooms, see Brown 1994; Brown & Campione 1994; and Brown, Ash, Rutherford, Nakagawa, Gordon, & Campione 1993 (p. 191). On reciprocal teaching, see Brown & Palincsar 1989. On the jigsaw method, see Aronson 1978. On the zone of proximal development, see Vygotsky 1978.

My notion of an affinity groups is inspired by putting together Beck 1992, 1994; Rifkin 2000; Wenger 1998 as well as work on modern workplaces; see Gee, Hull, & Lankshear 1996. Learners as insiders is a common principle in modern business, where there is a trend to make the consumer an insider and producer; see, for example, Kelly 1998 and Rifkin 2000. More generally on the new capitalism, see these sources Gee, Hull, & Lankshear 1996; and Greider 1997.

The excerpts from two reviews of *Half-Life* are from reviews by Emil Pagliarulo, December 4, 1998 at www.avault.com/reviews/review and *Shaffer Buttars*, January 12, 1999 at www.gamezilla.com/reviews, respectively. The quote from *Salon.com* is from Wagner James Au, "Triumph of the Mod," *Salon.com*, April 16, 2002, p.2.

8

CONCLUSION:
DUPED OR NOT?

THE ARGUMENT IN THIS BOOK IS NOT THAT WHAT PEOPLE ARE learning when they are playing video games is always good. Rather, what they are doing when they are playing good video games is often good learning. We can learn evil things as easily as we can learn moral ones. That's precisely why an organization like the neo-Nazi National Alliance wants to make a game like *Ethnic Cleansing*, a game in which the player kills African Americans, Latinos, and Jewish people, playing as a member of the Klu Klux Klan or a skinhead. However horrible its views, this organization realizes that video games are powerful learning devices for shaping identities. It realizes that they are even powerful learning devices for learning the *content* of the National Alliance's white power perspective on reality, ironically, given the grandfather's remark in chapter 2 that video games are a waste of time because children don't learn any content while playing them.

The power of video games, for good or ill, resides in the ways in which they meld learning and identity, a matter discussed throughout this book. If a player takes on what I called in chapter 3 a projective identity vis-à-vis the virtual character he or she is playing in a game, this constitutes a form of identification with the virtual character's world, story, and perspectives that become a strong learning device at a number of different levels. This is so because, in taking on a projective identity, the player projects his or her own hopes, values, and fears onto the virtual character that he or she is co-creating with the video game's designers. Doing this allows the player to imagine a new identity born at the intersection of the player's real-world identities and the virtual identity of the character he or she is playing in the game. In turn, this projective identity helps speak to, and possibly transform, the player's hopes, values, and fears.

However, people are not dupes. They do not necessarily take from a video game, any more than they do from a book or movie, any one predictable message predetermined by the design of the game, movie, or text. It is quite possible that some people could play *Ethnic Cleansing* and form a projective identity that both lets them understand the sort of hate organizations like the National Alliance harbor and want to redouble their efforts to work for a world of peace, diversity, and tolerance. And, note, both these things are important: We cannot work for a world of peace, diversity, and tolerance while disdaining to understand those who resist, hate, and feel disenfranchised in such a world.

This certainly doesn't mean you should play *Ethnic Cleansing*. It does not mean you shouldn't despise neo-Nazi viewpoints. It doesn't mean you shouldn't protect yourself from neo-Nazis. It does mean that if you have no idea why people who would create or be drawn to such a game are so angry and filled with hate, then you are very unlikely to do anything more than recruit more members for organizations like the National Alliance by claiming your own moral superiority. However, to understand their rage means to understand the workings of history, economics, and culture. That is, it means gaining, in or out of school, an education, one that certainly goes far beyond what anyone can currently learn from video games. Sadly, this is not the sort of education usually offered in U.S. schools, least of all those driven back to passive learning and skill-and-drill by the current standardized-testing regime.

I am not here advocating any sort of "postmodernist" view that "anything goes" and all perspectives are simply sociocultural "constructions" and "culturally relative" (a very poor characterization of good work in postmodernism). Things can be "constructed" and still be true or false, solid or shabby. I certainly believe that we all need to defend ourselves from those who would disdain and even physically harm us. I don't advocate face-to-face dialogue with people pointing a gun at your head, either. What I do advocate is understanding the "play" of identities and perspectives as they work for and against each other in the world, now and throughout history. This is even a form of self-defense.

The left and right wings of the political spectrum have seriously misled us about how people learn from the cultural resources around us. For example, both sides tend to agree that canonical literature (the so-called Great Books) is indoctrinating. The right wing applauds the work the canon can do to align people with what it sees as mainstream and universal values, values that it also sees as already its own. The left wing decries this same thing, claiming that the values embedded in the canon are, far from being universal, just a historically and culturally specific instantiation of the values of certain sorts of western, "middle-class" white people, people who wish to use the canon to enshrine their values and perspectives as higher and better than those of other people and other cultures.

Both views show a woeful ignorance of—and even a certain disdain for—how many people—especially many poor people, people who rarely get invited into academic debates about the canon, in any case—actually read and used, in the past, canonical works like those of Homer, Shakespeare, Milton, Carlyle, Arnold, Austen, Emerson, and a great many others. Of course, schools and churches have tried through the centuries, up to and including our own new century, to get people to read such literature—and the Bible—in *their* way, so as to enforce their values, values that, in many cases (certainly not all), stressed the subordination of women, nonwhites, and the poor. However, many a woman, nonwhite, or poor person actually read canonical works as empowering works that made them challenge the class hierarchy of their societies and the ways in which schools, churches, and rich people upheld this hierarchy in their own favor.

Jonathan Rose's massive tome, The *Intellectual Life of the British Working Classes*, is chock full of stories from the eighteenth century through the twentieth of women, poor people, and nonwhite people who read canonical literature as representing their own values and aspirations and not those of the wealthy and powerful. For example, Mary Smith (b. 1822) was a shoemaker's daughter who had this to say: "For long years Englishwomen's souls were almost as sorely crippled and cramped by the devices of the school room, as the Chinese women's feet by their shoes." Here's what Smith had to say about reading Shakespeare, Dryden, and Goldsmith: "These authors wrote from their hearts for humanity, and I could follow them fully and with delight, though but a child. They awakened my young nature, and I found for the first time that my pondering heart was akin to that of the whole human race. . . . Carlyle's gospel of Work and exposure of Shams, and his universal onslaught on the nothings and appearances of society, gave strength and life to my vague but true enthusiasm."

Of course, the left wing will say that Mary Smith was a hegemonic dupe moving to the dictates of the elites in her society without knowing it and mistakenly taking their values to be her own. But the only people who were duped by the canon were the right wing who thought it uncritically represented their viewpoints and the left wing who agreed with them. Mary Smith read what for us is "high literature" but what for her was "popular" enough, to say that even the daughter of a shoemaker was the equal, in intelligence and humanity, of any rich person.

So why did she read canonical works as empowering her humanity and rights to equality in a hierarchical society? It's because she identified *herself* with the characters and viewpoints in these books. She projected herself into them. She didn't distance herself from the hero because he was a male and a king in a Shakespeare play, however much she might have wanted and certainly deserved female heroes.

Rather, she saw herself as projected into that powerful monarch. Perhaps sometimes when she read Shakespeare, she was a king and other times a queen, just as, in playing *Arcanum,* I can make my female hero as strong as any male at melee fighting. Perhaps sometimes when she read Shakespeare, she was not a traditional monarch at all but a monarch shoemaker with the dignity and the human worth of a monarch. Perhaps sometimes she was all these and more at once. Remember, she was not just taking on the life of a virtual character in the book or play. She was also projecting herself into that character, creating something that both she and Shakespeare made, neither one of them alone.

Neither the right nor the left wing wrote the scripts for the plays in Mary Smith's mind, no matter how influenced she, like all of us, was by the political and cultural factors of her time. Shakespeare was deeply influenced by his own times, but he wrote original scripts nonetheless. So did Mary Smith. She read books that today's students find boring, with the excitement that today's students find in video games, because, perhaps, she read them at least in part much like those students sometimes play video games—actively, critically, and projectively.

What Smith learned as she became these virtual characters in a projective way was the values and perspectives of the various personae behind canonical literature. She did not see these values and perspectives as the preserve of only rich elites. They represented, in the form she gave them, her own values and aspirations. They made her see her equality to wealthy elites.

She saw that, like all people, she had just as much capacity for greatness, truth, and morality as any hero, king, or rich person. And, of course, canonical works are full of people who are not males or kings, people acting out their true human worth in hierarchical worlds that hurt and disdain them. In the end, Mary Smith and many more like her believed that canonical literature, far from representing the values of wealthy elites, undermined their values and showed them for the hypocrites they were.

Right wingers and left wingers who argue over the canon tend to act as if people like Mary Smith will read books realizing and accepting their "inferior station" and either want to emulate their "betters" (the right-wing perspective) or passively accept their inferiority as dupes of the elites in the society (the left-wing view). The Mary Smiths of the world need do no such thing. They already know that they are thinking, worthy beings. They sometimes see in canonical literature examples of who and what they could be, if others in society ceased to disdain them. And, again, these examples are mutual creations they build with the authors of the book when they project themselves into the virtual creations of these authors.

Does all this mean I think there is some definitive list of "Great Books"? No, by no means. For me, the canon is and was never a closed list. For me, any book is canonical if it lends itself to the powerful projective work in which Mary Smith engaged and leads people to desire not more hierarchy of the sort elites so often celebrate but more opportunities for the display of human worth and the greater development of human capacities for all people. Of course, that last statement is a value-laden one. A work is canonical, for me, if it gives people, in Kenneth Burke's phrase, new and better "equipment for living" in a harsh and unfair world. It is canonical if it allows them to imagine, and seek, in however small a way, to implement newer and better selves and social worlds.

In this sense, works like Ralph Ellison's *Invisible Man* and Gloria Naylor's *Mama Day* are canonical for me and many other people. And, of course, there are a good many books written by women, nonwhite people, and poor people that never got on the "official" canon as a list due to the workings of racism and patriarchy but are most certainly, in my terms, canonical.

Traditional canonical works, like those of Homer, Shakespeare, Milton, and Dryden, function today quite differently than they did in Mary Smith's day. Smith's society denied her any sort of schooling that gave her access to these books. In fact, her society felt it inappropriate for a shoemaker's daughter to be reading such books (which hardly comports well with the left's view that elites thought canonical literature would make people like Mary Smith quiescently accept their status). She picked them up anyway with defiance, and saw in them resonances with herself that just further proved her own intelligence and worth.

But schools have, by and large, tamed the canon. They have made it into the stuff of tests, multiple-choice answers, and standardized responses. Everyone now, finally, has access to the canon at a time when schools have rendered it toothless and the left applauds ignoring it as a historical vestige of old, dead, western, aristocratic elites.

Furthermore, young people today have access to far more texts, images, and diverse media, of far more kinds, than even the rich of Mary's Smith time had. Milton's *Paradise Lost* played a very different role in the textual ecology of Smith's world than it does for a young person today. For her it was a precious book, hard won through a great deal of physical labor (to buy it, if she didn't borrow it) and mental labor (to read it seriously). For a young person today, it is cheap to buy and the school tells them how to read it in the "right" way (or get a poor grade).

This is no plea for reading Milton, though I am sure many people still get a great deal out of traditional canonical literature when they read it of their own choosing, usually outside of school. There is plenty of evidence that people still read and watch many things that serve some of the same purposes that canonical literature did for Mary Smith.

I am not pleading for the "canon" here, least of all as a list. Nor am I claiming that every poor person read like Mary Smith. I am claiming that elites can use anything—canonical literature, the Bible, biology, or any other sort of text—to attempt to dupe people by trying to force them to read it in the elite's way. I am claiming, as well, that there are plenty of Mary Smiths who are more than capable of saying "No, thank you" and reading it both *their way* and intelligently.

Video games are a new form of art. They will not replace books; they will sit beside them, interact with them, and change them and their role in society in various ways, as, indeed, they are already doing strongly with movies. (Today many movies are based on video games and many more are influenced by them.) We have no idea yet how people "read" video games, what meanings they make from them. Still less do we know how they will "read" them in the future. It won't do to start this investigation by assuming they are dupes of capitalist marketers—though, of course, some of them very likely are. But there will always be Mary Smiths out there who use cultural products, whether "high" or "low," for good purposes.

Video games are at the very beginning of their potential—"we ain't seen nothin' yet." They will get deeper and richer. Eventually some form of conversation between real people and computer-created characters will occur alongside the conversations among people in their virtual and real identities that already take place in Internet gaming. There are and will be vile games, and eventually there will be some "canonical" games, games that lend themselves powerfully to elevating the aspirations and imaginings of all people for better and more just worlds. These may be new aspirations and imaginings or ones that fill old visions with new meanings and hope.

But for now, video games are what they are, an immensely entertaining and attractive interactive technology built around identities. I have made but one claim for them here. They operate with—that is, they build into their designs and encourage—good principles of learning, principles that are better than those in many of our skill-and-drill, back-to-basics, test-them-until-they-drop schools. It is not surprising that many politicians, policymakers, and their academic fellow travelers who think poor children should be content with schooling for service jobs don't like video games. They say they don't like them because they are violent. But, in reality, video games do violence to these people's notions of what makes learning powerful and schools good and fair.

BIBLIOGRAPHICAL NOTE

The quotes from Jonathan Rose's book can both be found on p. 45.

APPENDIX

THE 36 LEARNING PRINCIPLES

1. Active, Critical Learning Principle

All aspects of the learning environment (including the ways in which the semiotic domain is designed and presented) are set up to encourage active and critical, not passive, learning.

2. Design Principle

Learning about and coming to appreciate design and design principles is core to the learning experience.

3. Semiotic Principle

Learning about and coming to appreciate interrelations within and across multiple sign systems (images, words, actions, symbols, artifacts, etc.) as a complex system is core to the learning experience.

4. Semiotic Domains Principle

Learning involves mastering, at some level, semiotic domains, and being able to participate, at some level, in the affinity group or groups connected to them.

5. Metalevel Thinking about Semiotic Domains Principle

Learning involves active and critical thinking about the relationships of the semiotic domain being learned to other semiotic domains.

6. "Psychosocial Moratorium" Principle

Learners can take risks in a space where real-world consequences are lowered.

7. Committed Learning Principle

Learners participate in an extended engagement (lots of effort and practice) as extensions of their real-world identities in relation to a virtual identity to which they feel some commitment and a virtual world that they find compelling.

8. Identity Principle

Learning involves taking on and playing with identities in such a way that the learner has real choices (in developing the virtual identity) and ample opportunity to meditate on the relationship between new identities and old ones. There is a tripartite play of identities as learners relate, and reflect on, their multiple real-world identities, a virtual identity, and a projective identity.

9. Self-Knowledge Principle

The virtual world is constructed in such a way that learners learn not only about the domain but about themselves and their current and potential capacities.

10. Amplification of Input Principle

For a little input, learners get a lot of output.

11. Achievement Principle

For learners of all levels of skill there are intrinsic rewards from the beginning, customized to each learner's level, effort, and growing mastery and signaling the learner's ongoing achievements.

12. Practice Principle

Learners get lots and lots of practice in a context where the practice is not boring (i.e., in a virtual world that is compelling to learners on their own terms and where the learners experience ongoing success). They spend lots of time on task.

13. Ongoing Learning Principle

The distinction between learner and master is vague, since learners, thanks to the operation of the "regime of competence" principle listed next, must, at higher and higher levels, undo their routinized mastery to adapt to new or changed conditions. There are cycles of new learning, automatization, undoing automatization, and new reorganized automatization.

14. "Regime of Competence" Principle

The learner gets ample opportunity to operate within, but at the outer edge of, his or her resources, so that at those points things are felt as challenging but not "undoable."

15. Probing Principle

Learning is a cycle of probing the world (doing something); reflecting in and on this action and, on this basis, forming a hypothesis; reprobing the world to test this hypothesis; and then accepting or rethinking the hypothesis.

16. Multiple Routes Principle

There are multiple ways to make progress or move ahead. This allows learners to make choices, rely on their own strengths and styles of learning and problem solving, while also exploring alternative styles.

17. Situated Meaning Principle

The meanings of signs (words, actions, objects, artifacts, symbols, texts, etc.) are situated in embodied experience. Meanings are not general or decontextulized. Whatever generality meanings come to have is discovered bottom up via embodied experiences.

18. Text Principle

Texts are not understood purely verbally (i.e., only in terms of the definitions of the words in the text and their text-internal relationships to each other) but are understood in terms of embodied experiences. Learners move back and forth between texts and embodied experiences. More purely verbal understanding (reading texts apart from embodied action) comes only when learners have had enough embodied experience in the domain and ample experiences with similar texts.

19. Intertextual Principle

The learner understands texts as a family ("genre") of related texts and understands any one such text in relation to others in the family, but only after having achieved embodied understandings of some texts. Understanding a group of texts as a family (genre) of texts is a large part of what helps the learner make sense of such texts.

20. Multimodal Principle
Meaning and knowledge are built up through various modalities (images, texts, symbols, interactions, abstract design, sound, etc.), not just words.

21. "Material Intelligence" Principle
Thinking, problem solving, and knowledge are "stored" in material objects and the environment. This frees learners to engage their minds with other things while combining the results of their own thinking with the knowledge stored in material objects and the environment to achieve yet more powerful effects.

22. Intuitive Knowledge Principle
Intuitive or tacit knowledge built up in repeated practice and experience, often in association with an affinity group, counts a great deal and is honored. Not just verbal and conscious knowledge is rewarded.

23. Subset Principle
Learning even at its start takes place in a (simplified) subset of the real domain.

24. Incremental Principle
Learning situations are ordered in the early stages so that earlier cases lead to generalizations that are fruitful for later cases. When learners face more complex cases later, the learning space (the number and type of guesses the learner can make) is constrained by the sorts of fruitful patterns or generalizations the learner has found earlier.

25. Concentrated Sample Principle
The learner sees, especially early on, many more instances of fundamental signs and actions than would be the case in a less controlled sample. Fundamental signs and actions are concentrated in the early stages so that learners get to practice them often and learn them well.

26. Bottom-up Basic Skills Principle
Basic skills are not learned in isolation or out of context; rather, what counts as a basic skill is discovered bottom up by engaging in more and more of the game/domain or game/domains like it. Basic skills are genre elements of a given type of game/domain.

27. Explicit Information On-Demand and Just-in-Time Principle

The learner is given explicit information both on-demand and just-in-time, when the learner needs it or just at the point where the information can best be understood and used in practice.

28. Discovery Principle

Overt telling is kept to a well-thought-out minimum, allowing ample opportunity for the learner to experiment and make discoveries.

29. Transfer Principle

Learners are given ample opportunity to practice, and support for, transferring what they have learned earlier to later problems, including problems that require adapting and transforming that earlier learning.

30. Cultural Models about the World Principle

Learning is set up in such a way that learners come to think consciously and reflectively about some of their cultural models regarding the world, without denigration of their identities, abilities, or social affiliations, and juxtapose them to new models that may conflict with or otherwise relate to them in various ways.

31. Cultural Models about Learning Principle

Learning is set up in such a way that learners come to think consciously and reflectively about their cultural models of learning and themselves as learners, without denigration of their identities, abilities, or social affiliations, and juxtapose them to new models of learning and themselves as learners.

32. Cultural Models about Semiotic Domains Principle

Learning is set up in such a way that learners come to think consciously and reflectively about their cultural models about a particular semiotic domain they are learning, without denigration of their identities, abilities, or social affiliations, and juxtapose them to new models about this domain.

33. Distributed Principle

Meaning/knowledge is distributed across the learner, objects, tools, symbols, technologies, and the environment.

34. Dispersed Principle

Meaning/knowledge is dispersed in the sense that the learner shares it with others outside the domain/game, some of whom the learner may rarely or never see face-to-face.

35. Affinity Group Principle

Learners constitute an "affinity group," that is, a group that is bonded primarily through shared endeavors, goals, and practices and not shared race, gender, nation, ethnicity, or culture.

36. Insider Principle

The learner is an "insider," "teacher," and "producer" (not just a "consumer") able to customize the learning experience and domain/game from the beginning and throughout the experience.

REFERENCES

Adams, M. J. (1990). *Learning to read: Thinking and learning about print.* Cambridge, Mass.: MIT Press.

Alvermann, D. E., Moon, J. S., & Hagood, M. C. (1999). *Popular culture in the classroom: Teaching and researching critical media literacy.* Newark, DE: International Reading Association and National Reading Conference.

Aronson, E. (1978). *The jigsaw classroom.* Beverly Hills, Calif.: Sage.

Bakhtin, M. M. (1986). *Speech genres and other late essays.* Austin: University of Texas Press.

Barsalou, L. W. (1999a). Language comprehension: Archival memory or preparation for situated action. *Discourse Processes* 28: 61–80.

Barsalou, L. W. (1999b). Perceptual symbol systems. *Behavioral and Brain Sciences* 22: 577–660.

Barton, D. (1994). *Literacy: An introduction to the ecology of written language.* Oxford: Blackwell.

Bates, B. (2002). *Game design: The art & business of creating games.* Roseville, Calif.: Prima Publishing.

Bauman, Z. (2000). *Individualized society.* Cambridge: Polity Press.

Beach, K. (1999). Consequential transitions: A sociocultural expedition beyond transfer in education. *Review of Research in Education* 24: 101–139.

Beck, U. (1992). *Risk society.* London: Sage.

Beck, U. (1994). *Ecological politics in the age of risk.* Cambridge: Polity.

Beck, U., Giddens, A., & Lash, S. (1994). *Reflexive modernization: Politics, traditions and aesthetics in the modern social order.* Stanford, Calif.: Stanford University Press.

Bereiter, C. (1994). Constructivism, socioculturalism, and Popper's World 3. *Educational Researcher* 23: 21–23.

Bereiter, C, & Scardamalia (1989). *Surpassing ourselves: An inquiry into the nature and implications of expertise.* Chicago: Open Court.

Beaufort, A. (1999). *Writing in the real world: Making the transition from school to work.* New York: Teachers College Press.

Bransford, J. D., Brown, A. L., & Cocking, R. R., Eds. (1999). *How people learn: Brain, mind, experience, and school.* Washington, D.C.: National Academy Press.

Bransford, J. D., & Schwartz, D. L. (1999). Rethinking transfer: A simple proposal with multiple implications. *Review of Research in Education* 24: 61–100.

Brooks, R. A. (2002). *Flesh and machines: How robots will change us.* New York: Pantheon Books.

Brown, A. L. (1994). The advancement of learning. *Educational Researcher* 23: 4–12.

Brown, A. L., Ash, D., Rutherford, M., Nakagawa, K., Gordon, A., & Campione, J. (1993). Distributed expertise in the classroom. In G. Salomon, Ed., *Distributed cognitions: Psychological and educational considerations*. New York: Cambridge University Press, pp. 188–228.

Brown, A. L., & Campione, J. C. (1994). Guided discovery in a community of learners. In K. McGilly, Ed., *Classroom lessons: Integrating cognitive theory and classroom practice*. Cambridge, Mass.: MIT Press, pp. 229–270.

Brown, A. L., Collins, A., & Dugid (1989). Situated cognition and the culture of learning. *Educational Researcher* 18: 32–42.

Brown, A. L., & Palincsar, A. S. (1989). Guided, cooperative learning and individual knowledge acquisition. In L. B. Resnick, Ed., *Knowing, learning, and instruction: Essays in honor of Robert Glaser*. Hillsdale, N.J.: Lawrence Erlbaum, pp. 393–451

Bruer, J. T. (1993). *Schools for thought: A science of learning in the classroom*. Cambridge, Mass.: MIT Press.

Castells, M. (1996). *The information age: Economy, society, and culture, volume 1: The rise of the network society*. Oxford: Blackwell.

Chall, J. S. (1967). *Learning to read: The great debate*. New York: McGraw-Hill.

Chi, M. T. H., Feltovich, P. J., & Glaser, R. (1981). Categorization and representation of physics problems by experts and novices. *Cognitive Science* 13: 145–182.

Churchland, P. M. (1989). *A neurocomputational perspective: The nature of mind and the structure of science*. Cambridge, Mass.: MIT Press.

Churchland, P. S. (1986). *Neurophilosophy: Toward a unified science of the mind/brain*. Cambridge, Mass.: MIT Press.

Churchland, P. S., & Sejnowski, T. J. (1992). *The computational brain*. Cambridge, Mass.: Bradford/MIT Press.

Clancey, W. (1997). *Situated cognition: On human knowledge and computer representations*. Cambridge: Cambridge University Press.

Clark, A. (1989). *Microcognition: Philosophy, cognitive science, and parallel distributed processing*. Cambridge, Mass.: MIT Press.

Clark, A. (1993). *Associative engines: Connectionism, concepts, and representational change*. Cambridge: Cambridge University Press.

Clark, A. (1997). *Being there: Putting brain, body, and world together again*. Cambridge, Mass.: MIT Press.

Cobb, P., Yackel, E., & McClain, K., Eds. (2000). *Symbolizing and communicating in mathematics classrooms: Perspectives on discourse, tools, and instructional design*. Mahwah, N.J.: Lawrence Erlbaum.

Coe, R. M., Lingard, L., & Teslenko, Eds. (2001). *The rhetoric and ideology of genre: Strategies for stability and change*. Cresskill, N.J.: Hampton Press.

Coles, G. (1998). *Reading lessons: The debate over literacy*. New York: Hill and Wang.

Cope, B., & Kalantzis, M., Eds. (2000). *Multiliteracies: Literacy learning and the design of social futures*. London: Routledge.

Cognition and Technology Group at Vanderbilt (1997). *The Jasper Project: Lessons in curriculum, instruction, assessment, and professional development*. Mahwah, N.J.: Lawrence Erlbaum.

D'Andrade, R. (1995). *The development of cognitive anthropology*. Cambridge: Cambridge University Press.

D'Andrade, R., & Strauss, C., Eds. (1992). *Human motives and cultural models*. Cambridge: Cambridge University Press.

Delpit, L. (1995). *Other people's children: Cultural conflict in the classroom.* New York: The New Press.

Dias, P., Freedman, A., Medway, P., & Pare, A., Eds. (1999). *Worlds apart: Acting and writing in academic and workplace contexts.* Mahwah, N.J.: Lawrence Erlbaum.

Dias, P., Pare, A., & Farr, M., Eds. (2000). *Transitions: Writing in academic and workplace settings.* Cresskill, N.J. : Hampton Press.

diSessa, A. A. (2000). *Changing minds: Computers, learning, and literacy.* Cambridge, Mass.: MIT Press.

Edwards, D., & Mercer, N. (1987). *Common knowledge: The development of understanding in the classroom.* London: Methuen.

Elman, J. (1991a). Distributed representations, simple recurrent networks and grammatical structure. *Machine Learning* 7: 195–225.

Elman, J. (1991b). *Incremental learning, or the importance of starting small.* Technical Report 9101, Center for Research in Language, University of California at San Diego.

Engestrom, Y., Miettinen, R., & Punamaki, R. L., Eds. (1999). *Perspectives on activity theory.* Cambridge: Cambridge University Press.

Erikson, E. (1968). *Identity, youth and crisis.* New York: Norton.

Finn, P. J. (1999). *Literacy with an attitude: Educating working-class children in their own self-interest.* Albany, N.Y.: State University of New York Press.

Fleck, L. (1979, org. 1935). *The genesis and development of a scientific fact.* Chicago: University of Chicago Press.

Foucault, M. (1980). *Power/knowledge: Selected interviews and other writings 1972–1977.* Ed. by C. Gordon, L. Marshall, J. Meplam, and K. Soper. Brighton, Sussex: The Harvester Press.

Freire, P. (1995). *The pedagogy of the oppressed.* New York: Continuum.

Gardner, H. (1991). *The unschooled mind: How children think and how schools should teach.* New York: Basic Books

Gee, J. P. (1992). *The social mind: Language, ideology, and social practice.* New York: Bergin & Garvey.

Gee, J. P. (1994). First language acquisition as a guide for theories of learning and pedagogy. *Linguistics and Education* 6: 331–354.

Gee, J. P. (1996). *Social linguistics and literacies: Ideology in Discourses,* 2nd ed. London: Taylor & Francis.

Gee, J. P. (1997). Thinking, learning, and reading: The situated sociocultural mind. In D. Kirshner and J. A. Whitson, Eds., *Situated cognition: Social, semiotic, and psychological perspectives.* Norwood, N.J.: Lawrence Erlbaum, pp. 235–259.

Gee, J. P. (1999a). Reading and the New Literacy Studies: Reframing the National Academy of Sciences' Report on Reading. *Journal of Literacy Research* 31: 355–374.

Gee, J. P. (1999b). *An introduction to discourse analysis: Theory and method.* London: Routledge.

Gee, J. P. (2000–2001). Identity as an analytic lens for research in education. *Review of Research in Education* 25: 99–125.

Gee, J. P. (2001). Progressivism, critique, and socially situated minds. In C. Dudley-Marling & C. Edelsky, Eds., *The fate of progressive language policies and practices.* Urbana, Ill.: National Council of Teachers of English, pp. 31–58.

Gee, J. P., Hull, G., & Lankshear, C. (1996). *The new work order: Behind the language of the new capitalism.* Boulder, Colo.: Westview Press.

Giddens, A. (1991). *Modernity and self-identity.* Cambridge: Polity Press.

Giddens, A. (1992). *The transformation of intimacy*. Cambridge: Polity Press.

Glenberg, A. M. (1997). What is memory for? *Behavioral and Brain Sciences* 20: 1–55.

Glenberg, A. M., & Robertson, D. A. (1999). Indexical understanding of instructions. *Discourse Processes* 28: 1–26.

Greenfield, P. (1984). *Media and the mind of the child: From print to television, video games and computers*. Cambridge, Mass.: Harvard University Press.

Greider, W. (1997). *One world, ready or not: The manic logic of global capitalism*. New York: Simon & Schuster.

Habermas, J. (1984). *Theory of communicative action, vol. 1*. London: Heinemann.

Hacking, I. (1995). *Rewriting the soul: Multiple personality and the sciences of memory*. Princeton, N.J.: Princeton University Press.

Hacking, I. (1998). *Mad travelers: Reflections on the reality of transient mental illnesses*. Charlottesville: University of Virginia Press.

Hammer, D. (1996a). More than misconceptions: Multiple perspectives on student knowledge and reasoning, and an appropriate role for education research. *American Journal of Physics* 64: 1316–1325.

Hammer, D. (1996b). Misconceptions or p-prims: How may alternative perspectives of cognitive structure influence instructional perceptions and intentions? *Journal of the Learning Sciences* 5: 97–127.

Heath, S. B. (1983). *Ways with words: Language, life and work in communities and classrooms*. Cambridge: Cambridge University Press.

Herz, J. C. (1996). *Joystick nation*. Boston: Little, Brown and Company.

Hill, C., & Larsen, E. (2000). *Children and reading tests*. Stamford, Conn.: Ablex.

Holland, D., Lachicotte, W., Skinner, D., & Cain, C. (1998). *Identity and agency in cultural worlds*. Cambridge, Mass.: Harvard University Press.

Holland, D., & Quinn, N. Eds. (1987). *Cultural models in language and thought*. Cambridge: Cambridge University Press.

Hutchins, E. (1995). *Cognition in the wild*. Cambridge, Mass.: MIT Press.

Karmiloff-Smith, A. (1992). *Beyond modularity: A developmental perspective on cognitive science*. Cambridge, Mass.: MIT Press.

Kelly, K. (1998). *New rules for the new economy: Ten radical strategies for a connected world*. New York: Viking.

Kent, S. L. (2001). *The ultimate history of video games: The story behind the craze that touched our lives and changed the world*. Roseville, Calif.: Prima.

King, L., Ed. (2002). *Game on: The history and culture of videogames*. New York: Universe Publishing.

Kirshner, D., & Whitson, J. A., Eds. (1997). *Situated cognition: Social, semiotic, and psychological perspectives*. Mahwah, N.J.: Lawrence Erlbaum.

Kloesel, C., & Houser, N., Eds. (1992). *The essential Peirce: Selected philosophical writings (1867–1893)*. Bloomington: Indiana University Press.

Kress, G. (1985). *Linguistic processes in sociocultural practice*. Oxford: Oxford University Press.

Kress, G. (1996). *Before writing: Rethinking paths into literacy*. London: Routledge.

Kress, G., Jewitt, C., Ogborn, J., & Tsatsarelis, C. (2001). *Multimodal teaching and learning: The rhetorics of the science classroom*. London: Continuum.

Kress, G., & van Leeuwen, T. (1996). *Reading images: The grammar of visual design*. London: Routledge.

Kress, G., & van Leeuwen, T. (2001). *Multimodal discourse: The modes and media of contemporary communication*. London: Edward Arnold.

Lakoff, G. (1987). *Women, fire, and dangerous things: What categories reveal about the mind*. Chicago: University of Chicago Press.

Lakoff, G., & Johnson, M. (1980). *Metaphors we live by*. Chicago: University of Chicago Press.

Latour, B. (1999). *Pandora's hope: Essays on the reality of science studies*. Cambridge, Mass.: Harvard University Press.

Lave, J. (1988). *Cognition in practice*. Cambridge: Cambridge University Press.

Lave, J. (1996). Teaching, as learning, in practice. *Mind, Culture, and Activity* 3: 149–164.

Lave, J., & Wenger, E. (1991). *Situated learning: Legitimate peripheral participation*. Cambridge: Cambridge University Press.

Lee, C. D., & Smagorinsky, P., Eds. (1999). *Vygotskian perspectives on literacy research: Constructing meaning through collaborative inquiry*. Cambridge: Cambridge University Press.

Lemke, J. (1990). *Talking science: Language, learning, and values*. Norwood, N.J.: Ablex.

Loftus, G. R., & Loftus, E. F. (1983). *Mind at play: The psychology of video games*. New York: Basic Books.

Margolis, H. (1987). *Patterns, thinking, and cognition: A theory of judgment*. Chicago: University of Chicago Press.

Margolis, H. (1993). *Paradigms and barriers: How habits of mind govern scientific beliefs*. Chicago: University of Chicago Press.

Martin, E. (1995). *Flexible bodies: Tracking immunity in American culture: From the days of polio to the age of AIDS*. New York: Beacon.

Martin, J. R. (1990). Literacy in science: Learning to handle text as technology. In Francis Christe, Ed., *Literacy for a changing world*. Melbourne: Australian Council for Educational Research, pp. 79–117.

Mayer, R. E. (1992). *Thinking, problem-solving, cognition*, 2nd ed. New York: Freeman.

McGilvray, J. (1999). *Chomsky: Language, mind, and politics*. Cambridge: Polity Press.

Medlin, D. L., Lynch, E. B., & Coley, J. D. (1997). Categorization and reasoning among tree experts: Do all roads lead to Rome? *Cognitive Psychology* 32: 49–96.

Miller, L. S. (1995). *An American imperative: Accelerating minority educational advancement*. New Haven, Conn.: Yale University Press.

Minstrell, J. (2000). Student thinking and related assessment: Creating a facet-based learning environment. In N. S. Raju, J. W. Pelligrino, M. W. Bertenthal, K. J. Mitchell, & L. R. Jones, Eds., *Grading the nation's report card: Research from the evaluation of NAEP*. Washington, D.C.: National Academy Press, pp. 44–73.

Mishler, E. (2000). *Storylines: Craftartists' narratives of identity*. Cambridge, Mass.: Harvard University Press.

Moll, L., Ed. (1992). *Vygotsky and education: Instructional implications and applications of sociohistorical psychology*. Cambridge: Cambridge University Press.

New London Group (1996). A pedagogy of multiliteracies: Designing social futures. *Harvard Educational Review* 66: 60–92.

Nolan, R. (1994). *Cognitive practices: Human language and human knowledge*. Oxford: Blackwell.

Ogborn, J., Kress, G., Martins, I., & McGillicuddy, K. (1996). *Explaining science in the classroom*. Buckingham, U. K.: Open University Press.

Pearson, P. D. (1999). A historically based review of *Preventing Reading Difficulties in Young Children. Reading Research Quarterly* 34: 231–246.

Pelligrino, J. W., Chudowsky, N., & Glaser, R. (2001). *Knowing what students know: The science and design of educational assessment.* Washington, D.C.: National Academy Press.

Pinker, S. (1999). *How the mind works.* New York: Norton.

Poole, S. (2000). *Trigger happy: Videogames and the entertainment revolution.* New York: Arcade.

Rifkin, J. (2000). *The age of access: The new culture of hypercapitalism where all of life is a paid-for experience.* New York: Jermey P. Tarcher/Putnam.

Rogoff, B. (1990). *Apprenticeship in thinking: Cognitive development in social context.* New York: Oxford University Press.

Rose, J. (2001). *The intellectual life of the British working classes.* New Haven, Conn.: Yale University Press.

Rouse, R. (2001). *Game design: Theory & practice.* Plano, Texas: Wordware Publishing.

Rumelhart, D. E., McClelland, J. L., & the PDP Research Group (1986). *Parallel distributed processing: Explorations in the microstructure of cognition, vol. 1: Foundations.* Cambridge, Mass.: MIT Press.

Schon, D. A. (1987).*Educating the reflective practitioner.* San Francisco, Calif.: Jossey-Bass.

Scollon, R., & Scollon, S. B. K. (1981). *Narrative, literacy, and face in interethnic communication.* Norwood, N.J.: Ablex.

Scribner, S., & Cole, M. (1981). *The psychology of literacy.* Cambridge, Mass.: Harvard University Press.

Shore, B. (1996). *Culture in mind: Cognition, culture, and the problem of meaning.* New York: Oxford University Press.

Snow, C. E., Burns, M. S., & Griffin, P., Eds. (1998). *Preventing reading difficulties in young children.* Washington, D.C.: National Academy Press.

Sternberg, R., & Grigorenko, E. L. (1999). *Our labeled children: What every parent and teacher needs to know about learning disabilities.* New York: Perseus.

Strauss, C., & Quinn, N. (1997). *A cognitive theory of cultural meaning.* Cambridge: Cambridge University Press.

Street, B. (1984). *Literacy in theory and practice.* Cambridge: Cambridge University Press.

Street, B. (1995). *Social literacies: Critical approaches to literacy in development, ethnography and education.* London: Longman.

Taylor, C. (1989). *Sources of the self: The making of the modern identity.* Cambridge, Mass.: Harvard University Press.

Taylor, C. (1992). *The ethics of authenticity.* Cambridge, Mass.: Harvard University Press.

Taylor, C. (1994). The politics of recognition. In C. Taylor, K. A. Appiah, S. C. Rockefeller, M. Waltzer, & S. Wolf (1994), *Multiculturalism: Examining the politics of recognition.* Ed. by A. Gutman. Princeton, N.J.: Princeton University Press, pp. 25–73.

Tomasello, M. (1999). *The cultural origins of human cognition.* Cambridge, Mass.: Harvard University Press.

Varenne, H., & McDermott, R. (1999). *Successful failure: The school America builds.* Boulder, Colo.: Westview Press.

Vygotsky, L. S. (1978). *Mind in society: The development of higher psychological processes.* Cambridge, Mass.: Harvard University Press.

Wenger, E. (1998). *Communities of practice: Learning, meaning, and identity.* Cambridge: Cambridge University Press.

Wertsch, J. V. (1998). *Mind as action.* Oxford: Oxford University Press.

Wertsch, J. V., Del Rio, P., & Alvarez, A., Eds. (1995). *Sociocultural studies of mind.* Cambridge: Cambridge University Press.

INDEX